Modern Automotive Technology
MLR Shop Manual

Maintenance and Light Repair Job Sheets for Performance-Based Learning

by

Chris Johanson
ASE Certified Master Technician

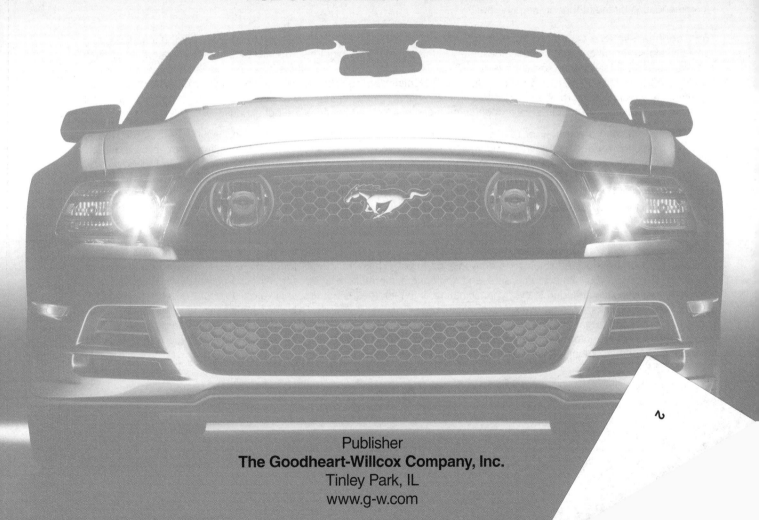

Publisher
The Goodheart-Willcox Company, Inc.
Tinley Park, IL
www.g-w.com

Introduction

The National Automotive Technicians Education Foundation, or NATEF, is an independent, nonprofit organization dedicated to improving the quality of automobile technician training programs. One of NATEF's duties is to evaluate technician training programs according to an established set of standards. As part of its program standards, NATEF has developed a task list that includes tasks from each of the eight ASE automotive certification areas. All tasks on the list are assigned a priority number: P-1, P-2, or P-3.

Hands-on performance of the NATEF tasks, as well as knowledge of the theory behind each task, provides crucial training for employment in the automotive service field and tells potential employers that the new technician is both knowledgeable and skilled.

Using the Manual

This manual contains thorough coverage of all tasks listed in the Maintenance and Light Repair NATEF Task List. Each job in this manual is a hands-on activity that corresponds to one or more of the NATEF tasks. The jobs have been carefully organized and developed to increase the student's chances of passing the ASE Auto Maintenance and Light Repair Certification Test by having the student apply what has been learned in the classroom.

The jobs are not correlated to specific textbook chapters, but will be assigned when the instructor determines that the student has sufficient knowledge to complete them. This manual steps the student through all essential NATEF tasks including inspecting, testing, and diagnosing vehicle systems and removing and replacing self-contained components.

When performing the jobs, the student should:

- Follow the instructions carefully and proceed through the steps in the order that they are presented.
- Carefully read all notes, cautions, and warnings before proceeding.
- Record specifications and the results of diagnostic procedures in the spaces provided.
- Consult the instructor when directed by the text and when unsure of how to proceed.
- Never attempt a step if unsure of how to perform it correctly.

Features of the Manual

This manual is divided into nine areas corresponding to the eight areas covered under the Maintenance and Light Repair NATEF Task List, as well as *Safety and General Shop Practices*. The jobs in this manual are designed to be accomplished in one or two lab sessions. Check boxes are provided in the left-hand column of the job so the student can mark off tasks as they are performed. Blanks are provided for recording service-related information.

Three types of special notices appear throughout the jobs in this manual. These notices point out special information or safety considerations for the task being performed. They are color coded according to the type of information being provided:

Note

 Note features provide additional information, special considerations, or professional advice about the task being performed. Note features are blue.

Caution

 Caution features appear near critical steps in a service procedure. These features warn the reader that failure to properly perform the task can lead to equipment of vehicle damage. Caution features are yellow.

Warning

 Warning features also appear near certain critical steps in the service procedure. These features warn the reader that failure to properly perform the task could result in personal injury. Warning features are red.

If properly implemented, this manual will help the student to do well in his or her courses, pass the Auto Maintenance and Light Repair NATEF Certification Test, and find a job in the automotive industry.

Chris Johanson

Table of Contents

Suspension and Steering

Brakes

Electrical/Electronic Systems

Heating and Air Conditioning

Engine Performance and Driveability

Job

Perform Safety and Environmental Inspections

1

After completing this job, you will be able to locate the shop's fire extinguishers, fire exits, and eye wash stations. You will be able to locate and properly use safety glasses and other shop safety equipment. You will also learn the general safety rules of an auto shop. You will learn the methods of preventing environmental damage through environmentally friendly work procedures.

Procedures

> **Warning**
>
> Before performing this job, review all pertinent safety information in the text and discuss safety procedures with your instructor.

Personal Protective Equipment

☐ 1. Eye protection (safety glasses or goggles) should be worn during any operation that could injure your eyes. See **Figure 1-1**. This includes, for example, hammering, drilling, grinding, sandblasting, using compressed air, carrying a battery, or working around a spinning engine fan.

List five common tasks that require the use of safety goggles:_____

_____

_____

Where are the safety glasses and goggles kept in your shop? _____

_____

_____

Figure 1-1. Eye protection should be worn while working in the shop. A—Safety glasses. B—Safety goggles. C—Face shield.

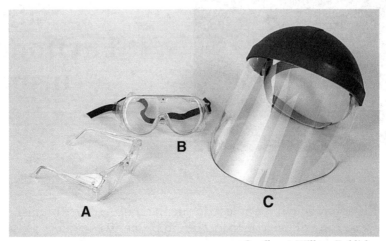

Goodheart-Willcox Publisher

☐ 2. Hearing protection (earplugs or protective earmuffs) should be worn during any loud activities. These include tasks like hammering, operating pneumatic tools, and grinding.

List five common tasks that require the use of hearing protection: _____

_____

_____

Where are the earplugs and protective earmuffs kept in the shop? _____

_____

_____

☐ 3. Dust masks and respirators may be required performing certain tasks or working with certain chemicals.

Where are respirators and dust masks kept in the shop?_____

_____

Material Safety Data Sheets

☐ 1. Walk through the shop and familiarize yourself with the chemicals stored there.

☐ 2. Find the material safety data sheets for the chemicals in the shop. Look up information about the chemicals stored in the shop.

Were any chemicals improperly stored according to the material safety data sheets? Yes ___ No ___

If Yes, describe the chemicals and inform your instructor: _____

_____

Were material safety data sheets missing for any of the chemicals in the shop? Yes ___ No ___

If Yes, describe the chemicals and inform your instructor: _____

_____

☐ 3. Obtain an MSDS from your instructor.

Job 1—Perform Safety and Environmental Inspections (continued)

☐ 4. List the following information from the MSDS.

General class of material covered by the MSDS (if applicable): _____

Trade (manufacturer's) name for the material:_____

Chemical or generic name of the material: _____

Known breathing hazards of the material:_____

_____

Known fire hazards of the material:_____

_____

Known skin damage hazards of the material: _____

_____

Proper storage and disposal methods: _____

_____

Emergency response to spills of the material:_____

_____

Fire and Shop Safety

☐ 1. Walk around the shop and locate all of the fire extinguishers, the fire exit, and fire alarms. Such information is crucial in the event of an emergency.

How many fire extinguishers and alarms are there in your shop?_____

_____

Where are the fire extinguishers located?_____

_____

What types of fire extinguishers are available in the shop?_____

_____

Where are the fire alarms? _____

_____

How do you leave the shop in case of a fire? _____

_____

☐ 2. To help prevent an emergency, memorize these important fire prevention tips:

- Always take actions to prevent a fire.
- Store gasoline-soaked and oily rags in safety cans, **Figure 1-2**.
- Wipe up spilled gasoline and oil immediately.
- Hold a rag around the fitting when removing a car's fuel line, **Figure 1-3**.

Figure 1-2. Special safety cans should be used to store oily rags.

Goodheart-Willcox Publisher

3. Identify the location of safety equipment and special hazard areas within the shop.

Where are the eye wash stations located? _____

_____

_____

Where are first aid stations located?_____

_____

_____

What other special hazard areas exist within the shop? _____

_____

_____

How are the special hazard areas identified? _____

_____

_____

Electrical Safety

1. Check the shop for unsafe electrical conditions, such as damaged electrical cords and overloaded outlets.

   Were any unsafe electrical conditions found? Yes ___ No ___

   If Yes, describe them in as much detail as possible: _____

   _____

   _____

2. Make sure that all electrically operated tools and equipment with three-prong electrical plugs have their grounding prongs intact, **Figure 1-4**.

   Do any tools or equipment have the grounding prong removed? Yes ___ No ___

   If Yes, list the items: _____

   _____

Job 1—Perform Safety and Environmental Inspections (continued)

Figure 1-3. This technician is using a shop rag to prevent fuel from leaking as he disconnects a fuel line.

Goodheart-Willcox Publisher

> **Warning**
>
> Do *not* use tools or equipment on which the grounding prong has been removed.

☐ 3. Obtain the use of a vehicle.

☐ 4. Check the following:
   • Battery and battery terminal condition.
   • Battery bracket and tray corrosion.
   • Ignition secondary wiring condition.
   • Condition of all visible wiring.
   • Condition of hybrid vehicle high-voltage system wiring.

Figure 1-4. The grounding prong has been broken off the electrical plug on the right. Do not use a piece of equipment if the grounding prong has been removed.

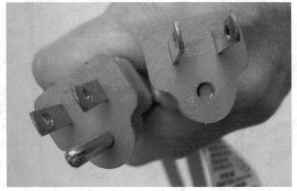

Goodheart-Willcox Publisher

> **Warning**
>
> Hybrid high-voltage wires are orange, **Figure 1-5**. Follow all safety precautions when inspecting the insulation and connectors. Remember that these wires carry several hundred volts, and can deliver a lethal shock!

Were any defects found? Yes ___ No ___

If Yes, describe:_____

_____

5. Describe the dangers posed by the following:

Damaged high-voltage wiring insulation: _____

_____

_____

Loose or corroded connections: _____

_____

_____

Battery gases: _____

_____

_____

Short-circuited wiring: _____

_____

_____

Careless handling of hybrid high-voltage system wiring: _____

_____

_____

Figure 1-5. Be extremely careful when working around the orange high-voltage wires found on hybrid vehicles.

Goodheart-Willcox Publisher

Job 1—Perform Safety and Environmental Inspections (continued)

Compressed Air Safety

☐ 1. Locate the shop's compressed air supply.

What is the air pressure setting on the shop compressor? _____

Describe the dangers posed by compressed air: _____

_____

_____

_____

Shop Cleanliness

☐ 1. Check the shop floor for unsafe conditions, including spills and trip hazards.

List any unsafe conditions: _____

_____

_____

☐ 2. Check the shop tools for cleanliness and organization.

List any ways that tool storage can be improved:_____

_____

_____

Clothing Safety

☐ 1. Different types of gloves are required for different service procedures.

List tasks that require leather gloves:_____

_____

List tasks that require nitrile gloves: _____

_____

List tasks that require electrically insulated rubber (electric lineman's) gloves: ____

_____

List tasks for which mechanic's gloves would be appropriate: _____

_____

_____

☐ 2. Examine your clothing from a safety standpoint.

List and explain any changes that would make your clothing safer or better-suited in the shop: _____

_____

_____

Carbon Monoxide

☐ 1. Locate the exhaust hoses in the shop.

Where are they located? _____

_____

☐ 2. Locate the controls to operate the shop's exhaust fans.

Where are they located? _____

_____

Grinder and Drill Press Safety

☐ 1. Go to the electric grinder and inspect it closely. Locate the power switch. Observe the position of the tool rest and face shield. Also, check the condition of the grinding wheel.

Is the electric grinder in the shop safe? Yes ___ No ___

If No, explain:_____

_____

☐ 2. Locate and inspect the operation of the shop's drill press. Find the on/off button, feed lever, chuck, and other components.

List the safety precautions associated with operating a drill press: _____

_____

Floor Jack and Jack Stand Safety

☐ 1. Check out a floor jack and a set of jack stands.

☐ 2. Without lifting a vehicle, practice operating a floor jack. Close the valve on the jack handle. Pump the handle up and down to raise the jack. Then, lower the jack slowly. It is important that you know how to control the lowering action of the jack.

In what direction must you turn the jack handle valve to raise the jack? _____

To lower the jack? _____

> **Warning**
>
> ⚠ Ask your instructor for permission before beginning the next step. Your instructor may need to demonstrate the procedures to the class.

☐ 3. After getting your instructor's approval, place the jack under a proper lift point on the vehicle (frame, rear axle housing, suspension arm, or reinforced section of the unibody), **Figure 1-6**. If in doubt about where to position the jack, refer to a service manual for the particular vehicle. Instructions will usually be given in one of the front sections of the service information.

Where did you position the floor jack?_____

_____

Job 1—Perform Safety and Environmental Inspections (continued)

Figure 1-6. One manufacturer's recommended lift points are shown here. Consult the proper service literature to determine the lift points for the specific vehicle you are working on.

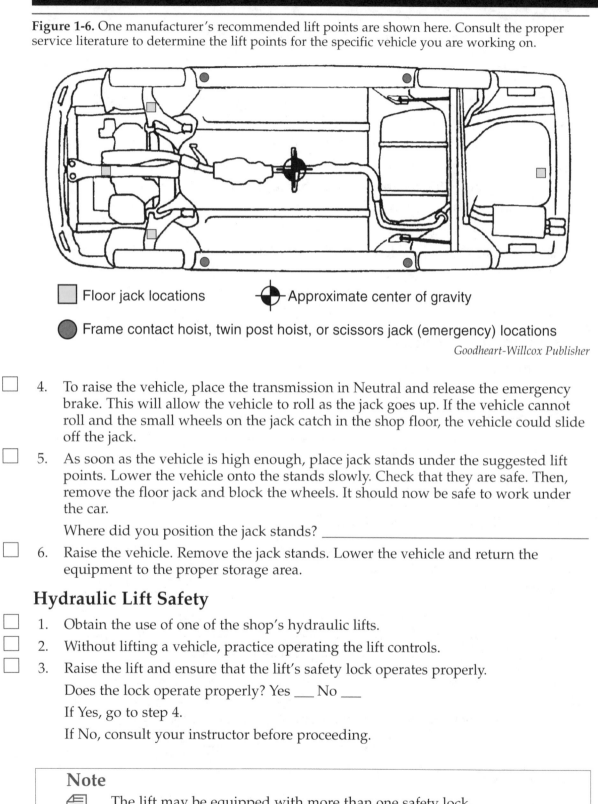

■ Floor jack locations   ✛ Approximate center of gravity

● Frame contact hoist, twin post hoist, or scissors jack (emergency) locations

Goodheart-Willcox Publisher

☐ 4. To raise the vehicle, place the transmission in Neutral and release the emergency brake. This will allow the vehicle to roll as the jack goes up. If the vehicle cannot roll and the small wheels on the jack catch in the shop floor, the vehicle could slide off the jack.

☐ 5. As soon as the vehicle is high enough, place jack stands under the suggested lift points. Lower the vehicle onto the stands slowly. Check that they are safe. Then, remove the floor jack and block the wheels. It should now be safe to work under the car.

Where did you position the jack stands? _____

☐ 6. Raise the vehicle. Remove the jack stands. Lower the vehicle and return the equipment to the proper storage area.

Hydraulic Lift Safety

☐ 1. Obtain the use of one of the shop's hydraulic lifts.

☐ 2. Without lifting a vehicle, practice operating the lift controls.

☐ 3. Raise the lift and ensure that the lift's safety lock operates properly.

Does the lock operate properly? Yes ___ No ___

If Yes, go to step 4.

If No, consult your instructor before proceeding.

> **Note**
> The lift may be equipped with more than one safety lock.

☐ 4. After getting your instructor's approval, drive a vehicle onto the lift.

> **Note**
>
> If the rack is a drive-on type, skip steps 5 through 9.

☐ 5. Consult service information to determine the proper lift points for the vehicle.

☐ 6. Position the pads under the vehicle's lift points.

☐ 7. Raise the vehicle so that the pads lightly contact the vehicle's lift points.

☐ 8. Recheck the lift points to ensure that the pads are contacting them properly.

Are the pads contacting the frame at the proper points? Yes ___ No ___

If Yes, go to step 9.

If No, lower the rack and repeat steps 6 and 7.

☐ 9. Raise the vehicle until the safety lock is engaged. It should now be safe to work under the vehicle.

☐ 10. Make sure all personnel are out from under the lift. Release the safety lock.

☐ 11. Lower the lift.

Environmental Protection

☐ 1. Carefully observe all areas of the shop to see how wastes are produced and stored.

☐ 2. Locate and list the types of solid waste produced.

_____

_____

How are solid wastes disposed of?_____

_____

_____

☐ 3. Locate and list the types of liquid waste produced.

_____

_____

How are liquid wastes disposed of?_____

_____

_____

☐ 4. Locate and list types of gases or airborne particles produced.

_____

_____

How are these contaminates prevented from entering the atmosphere? _____

_____

_____

Job 1—Perform Safety and Environmental Inspections (continued)

☐ 5. From the previous lists, identify the types of solid and liquid waste that could be recycled:

_____

_____

Identify the materials that could be returned for a core deposit:_____

_____

_____

Do any Environmental Protection Agency (EPA) regulations apply to the wastes generated in the shop? Yes ___ No ___

If Yes, briefly summarize them: _____

_____

Do any local and state regulations apply to the wastes generated by the shop? Yes ___ No ___

If Yes, briefly summarize them: _____

_____

List any of the shop's waste disposal practices that require improvement:_____

_____

Explain what improvements could be made: _____

_____

_____

Job Wrap Up

☐ 1. Return all tools and equipment to storage.

☐ 2. Clean the work area.

☐ 3. Did you encounter any problems during this procedure? Yes ___ No ___

If Yes, describe the problems: _____

_____

_____

What did you do to correct the problems?_____

_____

_____

☐ 4. Have your instructor check your work and sign this job sheet.

Performance Evaluation—Instructor Use Only

Did the student complete the job in the time allotted? Yes ___ No ___

If No, which steps were not completed?_____

How would you rate this student's overall performance on this job?_____

5–Excellent, 4–Good, 3–Satisfactory, 2–Unsatisfactory, 1–Poor

Comments: _____

_____

_____

INSTRUCTOR'S SIGNATURE _____

Job

Identify High-Voltage Circuits and Take Special Safety Precautions before Servicing a Hybrid Vehicle

After completing this job, you will be able to identify hybrid vehicle high-voltage circuits, disconnect high-voltage circuits before performing other service, and work safely around high-voltage circuits and parts.

Instructions

As you read the job instructions, answer the questions and perform the tasks. Print your answers neatly and use complete sentences. Consult the proper service literature and ask your instructor for help as needed.

> **Warning**
>
> Before performing this job, review all pertinent safety information in the text and discuss safety procedures with your instructor.

Procedures

☐ 1. Obtain a vehicle to be used in this job. Your instructor may direct you to perform this job on a shop vehicle.

☐ 2. Gather the tools needed to perform the following job.

> **Warning**
>
> Do not assume that a dead high-voltage battery is safe. A high-voltage battery that will no longer operate the vehicle may still produce several hundred volts.

☐ 3. Check manufacturer's service information to identify the following:
- Vehicle high- and low-voltage circuits.

In your own words, identify the main high-voltage circuits: _____

_____

_____

In your own words, identify the main low-voltage circuits _____

_____

- Battery disconnect device.

Location: _____

- Other safety procedures.

List: _____

_____

☐ 4. Put on insulated rubber gloves.

☐ 5. Locate the high-voltage components and cables on the vehicle.

List the major components: _____

_____

Note

Many high-voltage cables on most hybrid vehicles are covered with orange insulation for easy identification.

☐ 6. Check the vehicle service literature to determine whether the vehicle has a heated coolant storage tank. Yes ___ No ___

If Yes, explain in your own words the precautions that should be taken before performing any service involving the engine cooling system: _____

_____

_____

_____

Note

Steps 7 through 13 are optional. Check with your instructor before proceeding.

☐ 7. Look up the manufacturer's procedure for disabling the vehicle's high-voltage system.

Describe the procedure in your own words: _____

_____

_____

_____

Job 2—Identify High-Voltage Circuits and Take Special Safety Precautions before Servicing a Hybrid Vehicle (continued)

☐ 8. Review the procedure with your instructor and, if approved, perform the procedure.

☐ 9. Wait at least five minutes to allow the full discharge of the high-voltage components.

☐ 10. With a voltmeter or multimeter, test the high-voltage cables for low or zero voltage. Less than 12 volts is considered safe.

☐ 11. Follow instructions to remove the high-voltage battery disconnect device.

In your own words, describe the method used:_____

_____

_____

☐ 12. Perform other service operations as needed.

Describe these operations, if applicable:_____

_____

_____

☐ 13. After repairs are completed, reinstall the applicable device to restore high-voltage to the vehicle.

Questions

Regenerative Braking Systems

_____ 1. Conventional braking systems turn vehicle movement into _____.

_____ 2. Regenerative braking systems turn vehicle movement into _____.

_____ 3. In regenerative braking, what part of the vehicle drive system turns into a generator?
A. Internal combustion engine.
B. Planetary transmission.
C. Differential.
D. Drive motor.

_____ 4. The regenerative braking control system changes to charging mode when the _____ pedal is pressed.

_____ 5. True or False? A vehicle with regenerative braking does not have a friction brake system.

Job Wrap Up

☐ 1. Return all tools and equipment to storage.

☐ 2. Clean the work area.

☐ 3. Did you encounter any problems during this procedure? Yes ___ No ___

If Yes, describe the problems: _____

_____

_____

What did you do to correct the problems?_____

_____

_____

☐ 4. Have your instructor check your work and sign this job sheet.

Performance Evaluation—Instructor Use Only

Did the student complete the job in the time allotted? Yes ___ No ___

If No, which steps were not completed?_____

How would you rate this student's overall performance on this job?_____

5–Excellent, 4–Good, 3–Satisfactory, 2–Unsatisfactory, 1–Poor

Comments: _____

_____

_____

INSTRUCTOR'S SIGNATURE _____

Job

Use Precision Measuring Tools

3

Many vehicle components are made or assembled to tolerances of one thousandths of an inch (.001 inch, or .0254 mm). Measuring size and clearance may seem unimportant compared to other jobs, but is often necessary to do the job right. Inaccurate measurement can result in improper repairs or vehicle damage. Upon completion of this job, you will be able to use precision measuring tools.

Instructions

As you read the job instructions, answer the questions and perform the tasks. Print your answers neatly and use complete sentences. Consult the proper service literature and ask your instructor for help as needed.

> **Warning**
>
> Before performing this job, review all pertinent safety information in the text and discuss safety procedures with your instructor.

> **Note**
>
> Precision tools should regularly be checked for accuracy. Check them against another tool of known accuracy, or by using special gauges. If a precision tool is dropped or struck, immediately check it for accuracy. Many measuring tools can be adjusted to compensate for wear or damage. Follow the manufacturer's adjusting instructions.

Procedures

Use a Feeler Gauge

☐ 1. Determine the correct gap of the assembly to be checked and/or adjusted.

☐ 2. Obtain a set of feeler gauges and select the proper thickness feeler gauge for the job.

☐ 3. Slide the feeler gauge between the surfaces of the device to be adjusted.

4. Using different size feeler gauges, determine the size of the gap between the surfaces. This can be determined by the presence of a slight drag when the feeler gauge is moved between the surfaces.

5. If the gap can be adjusted, increase or reduce the gap until a slight drag is felt when sliding the feeler gauge through the gap.

6. If necessary, tighten the gap adjuster mechanism and recheck the gap after tightening.

7. Record the final size as measured with the feeler gauge.

   Reading: _____ mm or inch (circle one).

Use an Outside Micrometer

1. Clean the part to be measured

2. Select the proper size micrometer and ensure that the anvil and spindle are clean.

3. Open the micrometer enough so that the part to be measured can fit between the anvil and spindle. See **Figure 3-1**.

4. Grasp the micrometer in one hand and insert the part between the anvil and spindle.

> **Note**
>
> If measuring larger parts, place the part on a work bench and use both hands to grasp the micrometer.

5. While holding the part against the anvil, turn the thimble with your thumb and forefinger until the spindle touches the part. Use only enough pressure on the thimble to cause the part to just fit between the anvil and spindle.

> **Caution**
>
> Do not clamp the micrometer tightly. Over tightening may damage both the micrometer and part.

Figure 3-1. A micrometer with a range of 0 to 1 inch. The end ratchet is used to ensure that the same pressure is applied for each measurement.

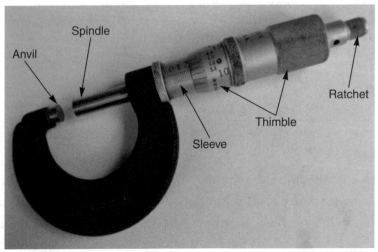

Goodheart-Willcox Publisher

Job 3—Use Precision Measuring Tools (continued)

☐ 6. Slip the part in and out of the micrometer while giving the thimble a final adjustment. The part must slip through the micrometer with a very light force.

> **Note**
>
> Placing the proper force on the micrometer is often called *feel*. Practice using a micrometer whenever possible. Some micrometers have a ratcheting tension knob on the end of the thimble. It allows the user to bring the spindle down against the part with the same amount of tension each time.

☐ 7. When satisfied your adjustment is correct, read the micrometer setting as explained in the *Read a Metric Micrometer* or *Read an Inch Micrometer* sections of this job. Be careful not to move the thimble while making the reading.

Use an Inside Micrometer

☐ 1. Clean the bore to be measured

☐ 2. Select the proper size micrometer and ensure that the end points are clean.

☐ 3. Enlarge the micrometer enough to touch the sides of the bore.

☐ 4. Insert the micrometer in the bore.

☐ 5. While keeping the anvil firmly against one side of the bore, rock the free end from side-to-side and up-and-down. This ensures that the micrometer is at right angles to the bore.

☐ 6. Continue enlarging the micrometer while rocking and tipping it until it cannot be moved with light pressure.

> **Caution**
>
> Do not over tighten the inside micrometer as this may damage both the micrometer and bore.

☐ 7. When satisfied your adjustment is correct, read the micrometer setting as explained in the *Read a Metric Micrometer* or *Read an Inch Micrometer* sections that follow. Be careful not to move the thimble while making the reading.

Read a Metric Micrometer

☐ 1. Read the highest numbered line showing on the sleeve and record it in the appropriate space in step 5. This reading represents whole millimeters.

☐ 2. Count the number of lines showing on the sleeve past the highest numbered line recorded in the last step and record it in the appropriate space in step 5. Each line represents 1/2 of a millimeter.

☐ 3. Read the numbered line on the thimble that aligns with the long horizontal line on the sleeve and record it in the appropriate space in step 5. Each line represents 1/100th of a millimeter.

☐ 4. Add the numbers to obtain the measurement and record it in the spaces in step 5.

☐ 5. Add this reading to the starting size of the micrometer being used and record it below.

Step 1 reading: _____ mm.

Step 2 reading: _____ mm.

Step 3 reading: _____ mm.

Step 4 total readings: _____ mm.

Step 5 total readings plus starting size: _____ mm.

Read an Inch Micrometer

☐ 1. Read the highest numbered line on the sleeve and record it in the appropriate space in step 5. This number represents tenths of an inch.

☐ 2. Count the number of full sleeve marks past the number given in the last step and record it in the appropriate space in step 5. Each line represents 0.025″.

☐ 3. Look at the line on the thimble that aligns with the long horizontal line on the sleeve. Each line on the thimble equals 0.001″. Record the number in the appropriate space in step 5.

Note

If the thimble marks are not quite aligned with the sleeve long line, estimate the fraction of a mark.

☐ 4. Add the readings in the last three steps and record it in the appropriate space in step 5.

☐ 5. Add the sum from step 4 to the starting size of the micrometer being used. For example, if the micrometer range was 2–3 inches, add two inches to the total reading and record the total below.

Step 1 reading: _____ inch

Step 2 reading: _____ inch.

Step 3 reading: _____ inch

Step 4 total readings: _____ inch.

Step 5 total readings plus starting size: _____ inch.

Reading a Dial Indicator

Caution

Be careful when using a dial indicator, as it can be easily damaged. Return the dial indicator to its case when you are done using it.

☐ 1. Obtain a dial indicator with sufficient range to make the measurement.

☐ 2. Install the dial indicator using clamps or a magnetic base as applicable. See **Figure 3-2**.

Job 3—Use Precision Measuring Tools (continued)

Figure 3-2. This dial indicator, shown without the base, has a pointer located below the dial face.

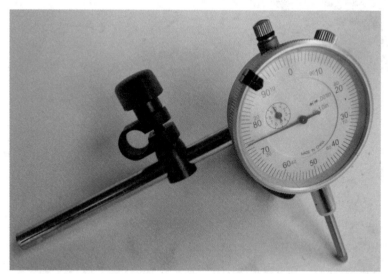

Goodheart-Willcox Publisher

> **Caution**
>
> Be sure that the indicator is firmly mounted and the plunger is parallel to the direction of movement to be measured. Installing the plunger at an angle to the movement will result in an inaccurate measurement.

☐ 1. Place the contact point against the work to be measured.

☐ 2. Force the indicator toward the work so the indicator needle travels far enough around the dial that movement in either direction can be measured.

☐ 3. Securely tighten the dial indicator fixture.

☐ 4. Push the work to be measured away from the dial indicator to remove all play.

☐ 5. Turn the dial face to align the pointer with the 0 mark.

☐ 6. Push the work to be measured toward the dial indicator.

☐ 7. Read the play as shown on the indicator.

Reading: _____ mm or inch (circle one).

Reading a Dial Caliper

☐ 1. Clean the part to be measured.

☐ 2. Select the proper size dial caliper and ensure that the jaws are clean.

☐ 3. Close the jaws lightly and zero the caliper dial.

☐ 4. Open the dial caliper enough to pass between the caliper jaws.

☐ 5. Lightly clamp the jaws around the part. See **Figure 3-3**.

☐ 6. Read the size on the caliper dial.

Reading: _____ mm or inch (circle one).

Figure 3-3. A typical dial caliper. The caliper face can be rotated to zero the caliper before the reading is made.

Central Tools

Job Wrap Up

☐   1.   Return all tools and equipment to storage.

☐   2.   Clean the work area.

☐   3.   Did you encounter any problems during this procedure? Yes ___ No ___

        If Yes, describe the problems: _____

        _____

        _____

        What did you do to correct the problems?_____

        _____

        _____

☐   4.   Have your instructor check your work and sign this job sheet.

Performance Evaluation—Instructor Use Only

Did the student complete the job in the time allotted? Yes ___ No ___

If No, which steps were not completed?_____

How would you rate this student's overall performance on this job?_____

5–Excellent, 4–Good, 3–Satisfactory, 2–Unsatisfactory, 1–Poor

Comments: _____

_____

_____

INSTRUCTOR'S SIGNATURE _____

Job

Identify, Use, Maintain, and Store Tools Safely

4

After completing this job, you will be able to perform various basic tool related tasks, including selecting the proper hand tools for a particular job, safely using tools, cleaning and storing tools, and maintaining tools.

Instructions

As you read the job instructions, answer the questions and perform the tasks. Print your answers neatly and use complete sentences. Consult the proper service literature and ask your instructor for help as needed.

> **Warning**
>
> Before performing this job, review all pertinent safety information in the text and discuss safety procedures with your instructor.

Questions

Hand Tools

_____ 1. True or False? Always buying a quality tool is a waste of money.

_____ 2. To prevent rusting, tools should be _____ occasionally.
   A. oiled
   B. washed
   C. heated
   D. magnetized

_____ 3. The hammer shown below is called a(n) _____ hammer.

Goodheart-Willcox Publisher

_____ 4. True or False? The hammer shown in question 3 is the most commonly used automotive repair hammer.

5. When would the hammer shown below be used?

_____

_____

_____

Goodheart-Willcox Publisher

_____ 6. True or False? Hammer heads are so hard that a chip cannot break off no matter how the hammer is misused.

_____ 7. To punch out rivets use a(n) _____ punch.

_____ 8. To align two holes in mating parts, use an alignment _____.

_____ 9. To keep a drill bit from skidding when starting to drill a hole, use a(n) _____ punch to make a small depression in the metal to be drilled.

Job 4—Identify, Use, Maintain, and Store Tools Safely (continued)

_____ 10. When using any kind of chisel or punch with a hammer, it is especially important to protect your _____.

_____ 11. To keep chips from flying during punch and chisel use, grind away any _____ tops.

_____ 12. The image below shows a(n) _____ screwdriver.

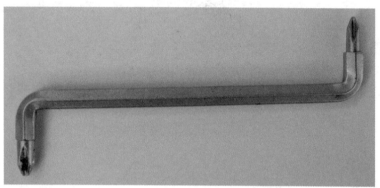

Goodheart-Willcox Publisher

_____ 13. The tools shown below are used to remove and install fasteners with _____ heads.

Goodheart-Willcox Publisher

_____ 14. A flat bladed screwdriver with a rounded tip should be _____.
A. used only for electrical work
B. used as a chisel only
C. discarded
D. None of the above.

_____ 15. The hand wrench shown below is a combination of a(n) ____ wrench and an open-end wrench.

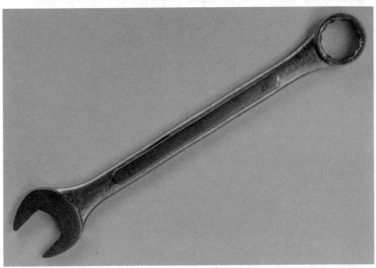

Goodheart-Willcox Publisher

_____ 16. The ____ wrench shown below is used to remove and install tubing fittings.

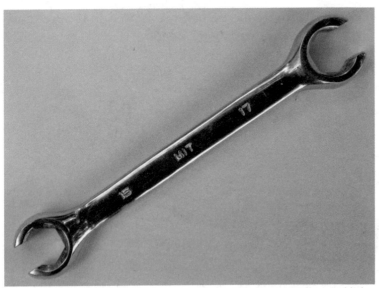

Goodheart-Willcox Publisher

_____ 17. The numbers 15 and 17 stamped on the wrench shown in question 16 indicate the sizes of the wrench ends in ____.

18. In your own words, why should hand wrenches be cleaned and dried before being used?

_____

_____

Job 4—Identify, Use, Maintain, and Store Tools Safely (continued)

For questions 19–23, match the figure with the tool name.

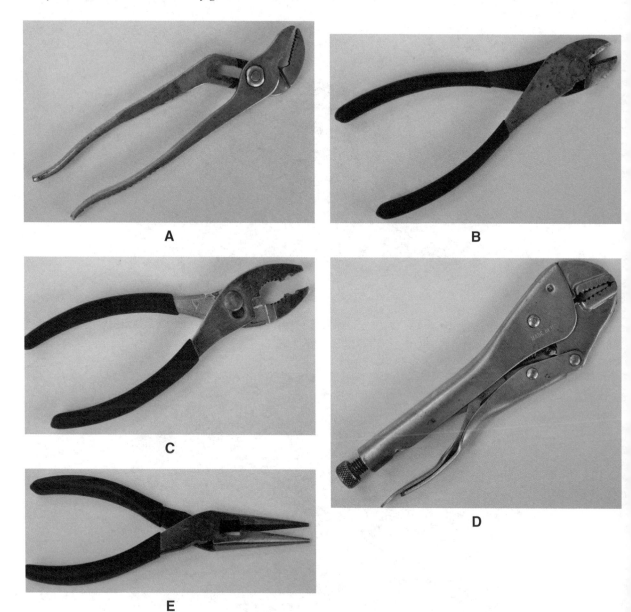

Goodheart-Willcox Publisher

_____ 19. Standard slip-joint pliers.

_____ 20. Locking pliers.

_____ 21. Slip-joint, tongue-and-groove pliers.

_____ 22. Needle nose pliers.

_____ 23. Diagonal cutters.

24. In your own words, why should you *not* use a pair of pliers to loosen a nut or bolt?

_____

_____

_____ 25. The wrenches shown below are called _____ wrenches.

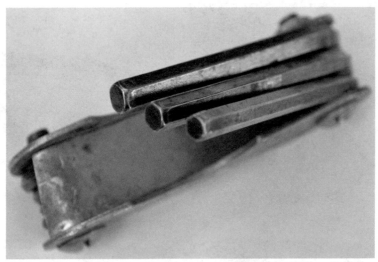

Goodheart-Willcox Publisher

_____ 26. The type of socket wrench shown below is usually called a(n) _____.

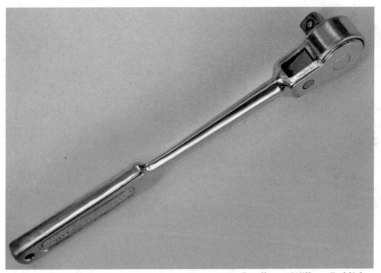

Goodheart-Willcox Publisher

Job 4—Identify, Use, Maintain, and Store Tools Safely (continued)

27. What is the *advantage* of the wrench shown below?

_____

_____

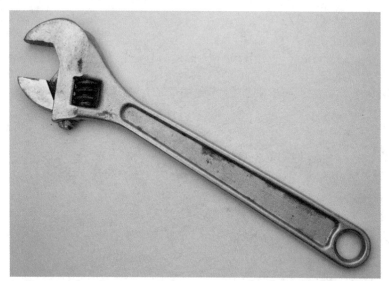

Goodheart-Willcox Publisher

28. What is the *disadvantage* of the wrench shown with question 27?

_____

_____

_____ 29. The wrench shown below is a called a(n) _____ wrench.

Goodheart-Willcox Publisher

_____ 30. The wrench shown with question 29 is often handy when loosening or repositioning parts of the _____ system.

_____ 31. True or False? A 12-point socket is stronger and less likely to round off a bolt head than a 6-point socket.

_____ 32. All of the following are commonly used socket drive for automotive repair, *except*:
   A. 1/4"
   B. 3/8"
   C. 1/2"
   D. 3/4"

_____ 33. The _____ shown below is used with socket drive extensions.

Goodheart-Willcox Publisher

_____ 34. The puller shown below has three _____.

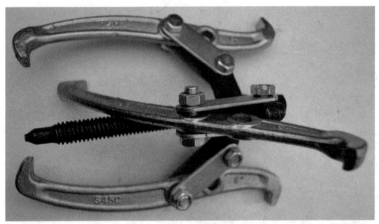

Goodheart-Willcox Publisher

_____ 35. What task would a puller like the one shown in question 34 likely be used for?
   A. Removing a gear or pulley from a shaft.
   B. Removing a camshaft from the block.
   C. Removing a seal from a housing.
   D. All of the above.

Job 4—Identify, Use, Maintain, and Store Tools Safely (continued)

_____ 36. The tool shown below is used to _____ tubing.

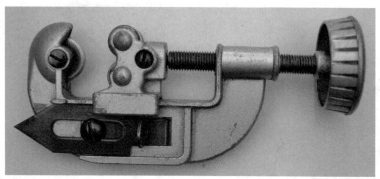

Goodheart-Willcox Publisher

_____ 37. The tool shown below is used to _____ tubing.

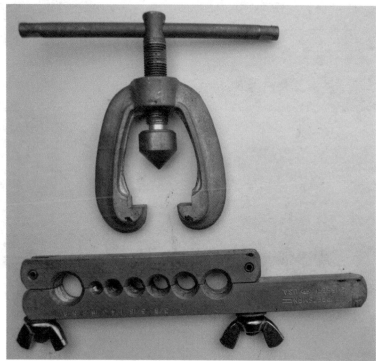

Goodheart-Willcox Publisher

For questions 38–42, match the figure with the tool name.

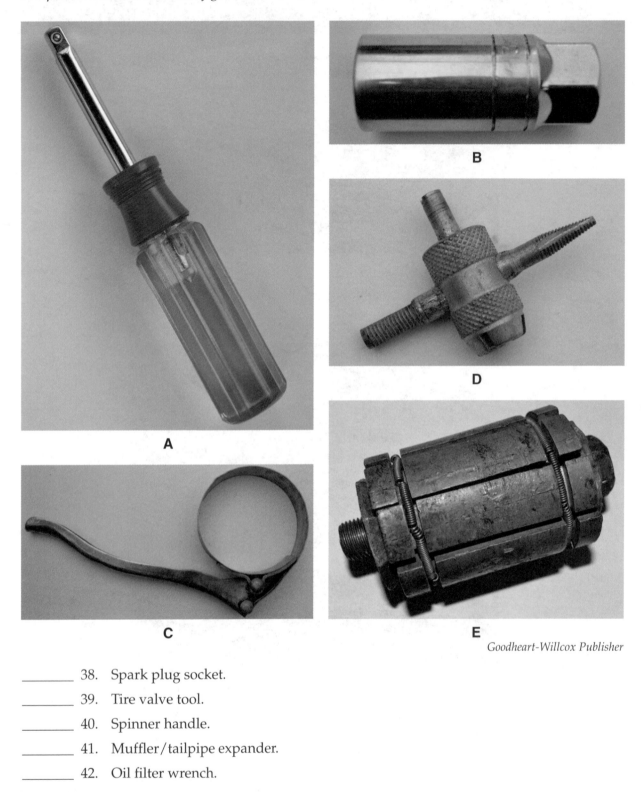

Goodheart-Willcox Publisher

_____ 38. Spark plug socket.

_____ 39. Tire valve tool.

_____ 40. Spinner handle.

_____ 41. Muffler/tailpipe expander.

_____ 42. Oil filter wrench.

Job 4—Identify, Use, Maintain, and Store Tools Safely (continued)

_____ 43. Which of the following is commonly turned by an electric motor?
   A. Tap.
   B. Die.
   C. Drill bit.
   D. All of the above.

_____ 44. To cut thin sheet metal, which of the following hacksaw blades would be best?
   A. 32 teeth per inch.
   B. 24 teeth per inch.
   C. 18 teeth per inch.
   D. 14 teeth per inch

_____ 45. Hacksaw blades are held in a device called a(n) _____.

Power Tools

_____ 46. Most air ratchets are made to accept sockets with a(n) _____" drive size?

_____ 47. True or False? The air supply to air-operated tools should always contain some moisture for lubrication and heat removal.

_____ 48. The piece of shop equipment shown below is called a(n) _____.

Goodheart-Willcox Publisher

_____ 49. True or False? An air drill can be used for long periods without overheating.

_____ 50. An air-powered _____ is often used to prepare a vehicle body for painting.

_____ 51. Which of the following should *never* be cleaned with an air pressure nozzle?
    A. Engine bearings and crankshaft.
    B. Transmission/transaxle oil pan.
    C. Drum brake assembly.
    D. Power steering internal components.

_____ 52. An air chisel is often used to remove suspension system or _____ system parts.

_____ 53. An electric drill can be operated by shop power or a self-contained _____.

_____ 54. Before drilling a part with a drill press, what should the technician do to the work to be drilled?
    A. Clamp it to the drill press work surface.
    B. Hold it very tightly using gloves.
    C. Have a helper hold it very tightly using gloves.
    D. Any of the above.

_____ 55. To hold parts firmly when drilling, tapping or loosening fasteners, tightly clamp the work in a(n) _____.

Job Wrap Up

☐ 1. Did you encounter any problems answering these questions? Yes ___ No ___

If Yes, describe the problems: _____

_____

_____

☐ 2. Have your instructor check your work and sign this job sheet.

Performance Evaluation—Instructor Use Only

Did the student complete the job in the time allotted? Yes ___ No ___
If No, which steps were not completed?_____
How would you rate this student's overall performance on this job?_____
5–Excellent, 4–Good, 3–Satisfactory, 2–Unsatisfactory, 1–Poor
Comments: _____

_____

_____

INSTRUCTOR'S SIGNATURE _____

Job

Preparing a Vehicle for Service

5

After completing this job, you will be able to locate, identify, and use diagnosis and repair information for a specific vehicle from a variety of sources and complete a work order to include customer information, vehicle identifying information, customer concern, related service history, cause, and correction.

Instructions

As you read the job instructions, answer the questions and perform the tasks. Print your answers neatly and use complete sentences. Consult the proper service literature and ask your instructor for help as needed.

> **Warning**
> Before performing this job, review all pertinent safety information in the text and discuss safety procedures with your instructor.

Procedures

☐ 1. Ask your instructor to assign a vehicle with a problem to diagnose or a service procedure to perform.

Describe the problem or procedure assigned:_____

_____

_____

☐ 2. Obtain the following information from the vehicle to be serviced:

Vehicle Identification Number (VIN): _____

Engine displacement (from underhood emissions label): _____ L, or
_____ ci

Spark plug gap (from underhood emissions label): _____

Date of manufacture (from vehicle certification label): _____

Type of refrigerant (from underhood certification label, if applicable):_____

Use Printed Service Literature

☐ 1. Consult your instructor and obtain service literature relating to the assigned task. The service literature can be a service manual, diagnostic manual, troubleshooting chart, or any other source of printed service information.

Title of printed literature: _____

☐ 2. Review the formats of the service literature you have and complete the following sections by placing a check mark next to each type of literature you have:

Type of Literature

☐ Manufacturer's service manual.

☐ Manufacturer's diagnostic manual.

☐ Manufacturer's troubleshooting chart.

☐ Aftermarket supplier's manual.

☐ Technical service bulletin.

☐ Other (describe): _____

Format

☐ Chapters.

☐ Sections.

☐ Subsections.

☐ Other (describe):_____

Page Numbering

☐ By chapter and section.

☐ From first page.

☐ Other (describe):_____

Index

☐ By job topic.

☐ By vehicle subassembly.

☐ Other (describe):_____

☐ 3. Using the table of contents or the index, locate the chapter or section relating to the task assigned by your instructor.

Describe where this information is located:_____

_____

On what page does the information begin?_____

☐ 4. Read the service information and then describe it in your own words in the spaces provided.

_____

_____

_____

_____

Use Technical Service Bulletins (TSBs)

☐ 1. Access a database or other source of technical service bulletins (TSBs). TSBs are usually grouped by manufacturer, with drive train and chassis subgroupings.

Job 5—Preparing a Vehicle for Service (continued)

☐ 2. Note whether any TSBs reference the vehicle and drive train that are to be serviced. Determine the focus of the TSB information:

Does the TSB address a specific vehicle or vehicle system? Yes ___ No ___

Does the TSB address a specific vehicle problem? Yes ___ No ___

Explain:_____

_____

TSB number: _____

TSB title: _____

☐ 3. Diagnose the problem according to TSB instructions.

☐ 4. Correct the problem according to TSB instructions.

☐ 5. Recheck vehicle for problem.

Was the problem corrected? Yes ___ No ___

If No, explain:_____

_____

_____

Use a Computer, CDs, and the Internet to Obtain Service Information

☐ 1. Ask your instructor to assign a vehicle problem.

Describe the type of problem assigned: _____

_____

☐ 2. Make arrangements to use the shop computer or another school computer as determined by your instructor. Then, answer the following questions:

Who manufactures the computer? _____

What is the computer speed (if known)? _____

What drives does the computer have? Check all that apply:

☐ Hard drive(s).

☐ Flash (thumbnail) drive.

☐ CD drive.

☐ DVD drive.

☐ 3.5" floppy drive.

☐ Other (list):_____

> **Note**
> If the computer is running, skip the following step.

☐ 3. Start the computer and ensure that it boots up properly.

In your own words, describe how you can tell that the computer has started correctly:_____

_____

☐ 4. Use the computer to access the required program.

Software program to be used:_____

Software program maker:_____

Note

If the program is installed on the computer's hard drive, ignore the references to CDs in steps 5 through 8.

☐ 5. Obtain the needed CDs, as determined by your instructor.

☐ 6. Insert the first CD into the computer. In many cases, this will be the menu or master disc.

☐ 7. Using the computer keyboard and/or mouse, perform the following tasks:

- Locate the needed files on the CD(s).
- Locate service information related to the assigned task.

If asked to do so by your instructor, print out the selected information and attach it to this activity sheet or summarize the information in the space provided.

_____

_____

_____

_____

☐ 8. Exit the program and remove the CD from the drive.

☐ 9. Follow your instructor's directions to access the Internet.

☐ 10. Obtain the needed website address from your instructor.

☐ 11. Call up the website. If you do not know how to access the World Wide Web, ask your instructor for directions.

☐ 12. Locate the required information on the website. If asked to do so by your instructor, print out the selected information and attach it to this activity sheet or summarize the information in the space provided.

_____

_____

_____

_____

☐ 13. Exit the website, close your web browser, and follow your instructor's directions to terminate the Internet connection, if necessary.

☐ 14. If you are instructed to shut down the computer, follow your instructor's directions closely to ensure that you shut it down properly.

Job 5—Preparing a Vehicle for Service (continued)

Obtain Vehicle Service History

☐ 1. Obtain a vehicle service history from your instructor. This may consist of:
  - Receipts for previous service.
  - Computer service records at the repair facility.
  - A journal of maintenance and repairs performed.
  - Another type of service record.

  Type of service history: _____

  _____

☐ 2. Read the vehicle service history and answer the following questions.

  Was the vehicle properly maintained? Yes ___ No ___

  How can you tell? _____

  _____

  Does anything in the vehicle service history indicate a developing problem?
  Yes___ No___

  If Yes, what is the problem?_____

  _____

☐ 3. Return any printed information, CDs, or flash drives to storage.

Complete a Work Order

> **Note**
>
> If your instructor directs, this job may be done as part of another service operation.

☐ 1. Obtain a shop work order from your instructor.

☐ 2. Enter today's date in the proper space on the work order.

☐ 3. Enter the customer name and address in the proper work order spaces. If the vehicle is a shop unit, enter the name and address of your school.

☐ 4. Record phone number(s) where the customer can be reached. If the vehicle is a shop unit, use the school phone number or create a number.

☐ 5. In the proper work order spaces, enter the following info about the vehicle:

  Make:_____

  Model: _____

  Year: _____

  Mileage: _____

☐ 6. Enter the VIN where indicated on the work order.

☐ 7. In the proper work order spaces, record the customer complaint(s) or other relevant customer remarks. Be brief but record all necessary information.

> **Note**
>
> Many repair/work orders use the *three Cs* format. The three Cs are concern, cause, and correction.
>
> - *Concern* is what brings the vehicle owner into the shop. This includes any vehicle complaint that requires diagnosis and repair. It does not include normal maintenance procedures. Carefully listen to and record all relevant customer remarks.
> - *Cause* is the reason for the owners concern. This is where diagnosis is required. The cause may be obvious, or may require considerable diagnosis effort to locate. Diagnosis may require test driving the vehicle, and performing various diagnostic tests. If possible review previous service records to determine what has been done to correct the problem in the past. List all diagnostic procedures, the time involved to performing these procedures.
> - *Correction* consists of the actions performed to repair the vehicle. List all repair procedures, the time involved to performing these procedures, and any parts or supplies used.

- [ ] 8. Before entering a vehicle:
  - Place a paper floor mat over the drivers' side carpet.
  - Install a steering wheel cover over the steering wheel.
  - Place a protective cover on the driver's seat.
- [ ] 9. Make repairs as necessary. If the repairs require underhood service, install a fender cover:
  - Make sure that the underside of the fender cover is free of grease or dirt.
  - Place fender cover downward over the fender of the vehicle.
- [ ] 10. When repairs are complete, list the following in the appropriate work order spaces:
  - Cause of the vehicle problem.
  - Corrections made (Repairs or adjustments performed).
  - Parts installed and their price.
- [ ] 11. Add the parts prices and write the total in the parts total space on the work order.
- [ ] 12. Determine the total labor time of the above operations and write it in the appropriate space on the work order.
- [ ] 13. Multiply the total labor time by the labor rate for your area and write the total in the labor price space on the work order. Your instructor may furnish a labor rate to use.
- [ ] 14. If necessary, add the cost of shop supplies such as lubricants and shop towels in the appropriate space on the work order.
- [ ] 15. Add the parts, labor, and shop supply totals and write this amount in the proper space.
- [ ] 16. Calculate the sales tax:
  - Determine the sales tax rate for your area.
  - Multiply the parts, labor, and shop supply by this rate (total from step 15 × tax rate).
  - Write the sales tax amount in the proper space.
- [ ] 17. Make a grand total of all charges.

Job 5—Preparing a Vehicle for Service (continued)

☐ 18. Make other remarks on the work order as necessary. Examples of other remarks are the need for additional work or fasteners that must be retorqued after several use cycles.

☐ 19. If necessary, remove the fender cover by lifting it from the body. Do not slide it off.

☐ 20. Check that all parts are reinstalled, paying particular attention to any trim parts that could easily be overlooked, such as wheel covers.

☐ 21. Remove steering wheel covers, paper floor mats, upholstery covers, and any other vehicle protection items.

☐ 22. If the carpet, upholstery, or steering wheel has been soiled, remove the material with a non-damaging cleaning solution.

☐ 23. Recheck your work and submit the completed work order to your instructor.

Job Wrap Up

☐ 1. Return all tools and equipment to storage.

☐ 2. Clean the work area.

☐ 3. Did you encounter any problems during this procedure? Yes ___ No ___

If Yes, describe the problems: _____

_____

What did you do to correct the problems?_____

_____

_____

☐ 4. Have your instructor check your work and sign this job sheet.

Performance Evaluation—Instructor Use Only

Did the student complete the job in the time allotted? Yes ___ No ___

If No, which steps were not completed?_____

How would you rate this student's overall performance on this job?_____

5–Excellent, 4–Good, 3–Satisfactory, 2–Unsatisfactory, 1–Poor

Comments: _____

_____

INSTRUCTOR'S SIGNATURE _____

Notes

Job
Verify Warning Indicator Operation and Retrieve Trouble Codes

6

After completing this job, you will be able to check warning indicator operation and use a scan tool to retrieve diagnostic trouble codes.

Instructions

As you read the job instructions, answer the questions and perform the tasks. Print your answers neatly and use complete sentences. Consult the proper service literature and ask your instructor for help as needed.

> **Warning**
>
> ⚠ Before performing this job, review all pertinent safety information in the text and discuss safety procedures with your instructor.

Procedures

☐ 1. Obtain a vehicle to be used in this job. Your instructor may direct you to perform this job on a shop vehicle.

☐ 2. Gather the tools needed to perform the following job.

> **Note**
>
> Although the charging system light and ammeter do not monitor engine condition, they are included in the checking procedures below because they are commonly associated with the oil and temperature lights, and because a defective charging system will eventually keep the engine from cranking.

Check the Operation of Engine Warning Lights

> **Note**
>
> Some newer vehicles may monitor an engine condition with both a light and a gauge in the instrument panel. If both warning systems are used, each should be checked.

Oil Pressure Lights

☐ 1. Turn the ignition switch to the *On* position but do not start the engine.
Is the oil pressure light on? Yes ___ No ___

☐ 2. Start the engine.
With the engine running, does the oil pressure light go out? Yes ___ No ___

Engine Temperature Light

☐ 1. Turn the ignition switch to the *Start* position.
Does the temperature light come on? Yes ___ No ___

☐ 2. Release the ignition switch. Does the temperature light go off? Yes ___ No ___

Coolant Level Light

☐ 1. Turn the ignition switch to the *On* position but do not start the engine.
Is the coolant level light on? Yes ___ No ___

> **Note**
>
> The coolant level light may be on or off with the ignition switch in the *On* position. The light is working properly if it moves from one state to the other (*On* to *Off* or *Off* to *On*) when the engine is cranked.

☐ 2. Turn the ignition switch to the *Start* position.
Is the coolant level light on? Yes ___ No ___

Charging System Light

☐ 1. Turn the ignition switch to the *On* position but do not start the engine.
Is the charging system light on? Yes ___ No ___

☐ 2. Start the engine.
With the engine running, does the charging system light go out? Yes ___ No ___

☐ 3. If any of the lights do not operate as expected, check with your instructor to determine what further diagnosis and service steps to perform.

Check the Operation of Engine Gauges

Oil Pressure Gauge

☐ 1. Turn the ignition switch to the *On* position but do not start the engine.
Does the oil pressure gauge read zero oil pressure? Yes ___ No ___

☐ 2. Start the engine.
With the engine running, does the oil pressure gauge begin to rise? Yes ___ No ___

Engine Temperature Gauge

☐ 1. Ensure that the vehicle engine has not been operated in the last 4 to 6 hours.

☐ 2. Start the engine.
Does the temperature gauge read approximately ambient (surrounding air) temperature? Yes ___ No ___

☐ 3. Allow the engine to warm up. Does the temperature gauge begin to rise after a few minutes of operation? Yes ___ No ___

Job 6—Verify Warning Indicator Operation and Retrieve Trouble Codes (continued)

Charging System Ammeter

☐ 1. Turn the ignition switch to the *On* position but do not start the engine.

   Does the ammeter show a value at or below battery voltage? Yes ___ No ___

☐ 2. Start the engine. With the engine running does the ammeter show a value above battery voltage? Yes ___ No ___

☐ 3. If any of the gauges do not operate as indicated, check with your instructor to determine what further diagnosis and service steps to perform.

Retrieve Diagnostic Trouble Codes with a Scan Tool

> **Note**
>
> There are many kinds of scan tools. The following procedure is a general guide to scan tool use. Always obtain the service instructions for the scan tool that you are using. If the scan tool literature calls for a different procedure or series of steps from those in this procedure, always perform procedures according to the scan tool literature.

☐ 1. Obtain a scan tool and related service literature for the vehicle selected.

   Type of scan tool:_____

☐ 2. If necessary, attach the proper test connector cable and power lead to the scan tool.

☐ 3. Ensure that the ignition switch is in the *Off* position.

☐ 4. Locate the correct diagnostic connector.

   Describe the location of the diagnostic connector: _____

   _____

☐ 5. Attach the scan tool test connector cable to the diagnostic connector. If necessary, use the proper adapter to connect the scan tool.

> **Note**
>
> The connector should be accessible from the driver's seat. If you cannot locate the diagnostic connector, refer to the vehicle's service literature.

☐ 6. Attach the scan tool's power lead to the cigarette lighter or battery terminals as necessary.

> **Note**
>
> OBDII scan tools are powered from terminal 16 of the diagnostic connector, and no other power connections are needed.

☐ 7. Observe the scan tool's screen to ensure that the scan tool is working properly. Most scan tools will complete an internal self-check and notify the technician if there is a software or communication problem.

☐ 8. Enter vehicle information as needed to program the scan tool:

- Most OBDII scan tools automatically read the vehicle identification number (VIN) when the ignition switch is turned to the on position. This gives the scan tool the information needed to check for codes and perform other operations.

- Older scan tools are programmed with the proper vehicle information by entering the vehicle year, engine type, and other information. This information is usually contained in certain numbers and letters in the VIN.

☐ 9. Turn the ignition key to the *On* position.

☐ 10. Observe the scan tool to determine whether any trouble codes are present.

Are any trouble codes present? Yes ___ No ___

If Yes, go to step 13.

If No, consult your instructor. Your instructor may wish to produce a code for this job by temporarily disconnecting a sensor or output device.

☐ 11. List all trouble codes in the space provided:

Trouble codes:_____

_____

☐ 12. Use the scan tool literature or factory service manual to determine the meaning of the codes.

Code	Defect
_____	_____
_____	_____
_____	_____
_____	_____
_____	_____

☐ 13. Using the trouble code information in step 14, write a brief description of what you think might be wrong with the vehicle.

_____

_____

_____

☐ 14. If your instructor directs you to do so, perform the following actions:

- Make further checks to isolate the problem(s) revealed by the trouble codes.
- Correct the problem(s) as necessary. Refer to other jobs as directed.
- Use the scan tool to confirm that the codes do not reset.

☐ 15. When the test is completed, turn the ignition switch to the *Off* position.

☐ 16. Remove the scan tool test connector cable from the diagnostic connector.

☐ 17. Detach the scan tool power lead from the cigarette lighter or battery terminals, if applicable.

Job 6—Verify Warning Indicator Operation and Retrieve Trouble Codes (continued)

Job Wrap Up

☐ 1. Return all tools and equipment to storage.

☐ 2. Clean the work area.

☐ 3. Did you encounter any problems during this procedure? Yes ___ No ___

If Yes, describe the problems: _____

_____

_____

What did you do to correct the problems?_____

_____

_____

☐ 4. Have your instructor check your work and sign this job sheet.

Performance Evaluation—Instructor Use Only

Did the student complete the job in the time allotted? Yes ___ No ___

If No, which steps were not completed?_____

How would you rate this student's overall performance on this job?_____

5–Excellent, 4–Good, 3–Satisfactory, 2–Unsatisfactory, 1–Poor

Comments: _____

_____

_____

INSTRUCTOR'S SIGNATURE _____

Notes

_____

_____

_____

_____

_____

_____

_____

_____

_____

_____

_____

_____

_____

_____

_____

_____

_____

_____

_____

_____

_____

_____

_____

_____

_____

_____

_____

_____

_____

_____

_____

_____

_____

_____

_____

_____

_____

_____

_____

_____

_____

_____

Job

Inspect an Engine for Leaks

7

After completing this job, you will be able to check an engine for leaks.

Instructions

As you read the job instructions, answer the questions and perform the tasks. Print your answers neatly and use complete sentences. Consult the proper service literature and ask your instructor for help as needed.

> **Warning**
>
> Before performing this job, review all pertinent safety information in the text and discuss safety procedures with your instructor.

Procedures

☐ 1. Obtain a vehicle to be used in this job. Your instructor may direct you to perform this job on a shop vehicle or engine.

☐ 2. Gather the tools needed to perform the following job.

Visual Inspection

☐ 1. Inspect the top of the engine for leaks. Such leaks will usually be visible at the point of leakage.

- Common upper-engine oil leak points are valve covers, timing covers, and the oil filler cap.

Were any oil leaks found? Yes ___ No ___

If Yes, list the locations of the oil leaks:_____

_____

- Common upper-engine fuel leak points are fuel fittings, hose clamps, and pressure regulators.

Were any fuel leaks found? Yes ___ No ___

If Yes, list the locations of the fuel leaks: _____

_____

- Common upper-engine coolant leak points are hoses, hose fittings, radiator seams, and the radiator cap.

  Were any coolant leaks found? Yes ___ No ___

  If Yes, list the locations of the coolant leaks: _____

> **Note**
>
> Pressure testing the cooling system is covered in Job 13.

☐ 2. Obtain a drop light or other source of illumination.

☐ 3. Examine the underside of the vehicle for evidence of oil or grease. Slight seepage is normal.

  Was excessive oil or grease observed? Yes ___ No ___

  If Yes, where does the oil/grease appear to be coming from? _____

> **Note**
>
> Airflow under the vehicle will blow leaking oil backwards. The leak may be some distance forward from where the oil appears.

Powder Method

☐ 1. Thoroughly clean the area around the suspected leak.

☐ 2. Apply talcum powder to the clean area.

☐ 3. Lower the vehicle from the lift and drive it several miles or carefully run it on the lift for 10–15 minutes.

☐ 4. Raise the vehicle (if necessary) and check the area around the suspected leak.

> **Warning**
>
> The vehicle must be raised and supported in a safe manner. Always use approved lifts or jacks and jack stands.

  Does the powder show streaks of oil, fuel, or coolant? Yes ___ No ___

  If Yes, what type of fluid is leaking and where does it appear to be coming from?

Black Light Method

☐ 1. Ensure that the engine has enough oil or coolant. Add oil or coolant as needed.

☐ 2. Add fluorescent dye to the unit through the filler plug, being careful not to spill dye on the outside of the engine.

Job 7—Inspect an Engine for Leaks (continued)

☐ 3. Lower the vehicle from the lift and drive it several miles, or carefully run it on the lift for 10–15 minutes.

☐ 4. Raise the vehicle, if necessary.

> **Warning**
>
> ⚠ The vehicle must be raised and supported in a safe manner. Always use approved lifts or jacks and jack stands.

☐ 5. Turn on the black light and direct it toward the area around the suspected leak. See **Figure 7-1**.

Does the black light show the presence of dye? Yes ___ No ___

If Yes, where does the dye appear to be coming from?_____

_____

_____

Figure 7-1. A black light can be used to locate leaks when necessary.

Tracer Products Division of Spectronics Corporation

☐ 6. Consult your instructor about the steps to take to correct the leak. Steps may include one or more of the following:

- Tightening fasteners.
- Replacing gaskets or seals.
- Replacing a cracked, broken, or punctured part.

Steps to be taken:_____

_____

_____

☐ 7. Make the necessary repairs.

Job Wrap Up

☐ 1. Return all tools and equipment to storage.

☐ 2. Clean the work area.

☐ 3. Did you encounter any problems during this procedure? Yes ___ No ___

If Yes, describe the problems: _____

_____

_____

What did you do to correct the problems?_____

_____

_____

☐ 4. Have your instructor check your work and sign this job sheet.

Performance Evaluation—Instructor Use Only

Did the student complete the job in the time allotted? Yes ___ No ___

If No, which steps were not completed?_____

How would you rate this student's overall performance on this job?_____

5–Excellent, 4–Good, 3–Satisfactory, 2–Unsatisfactory, 1–Poor

Comments: _____

_____

_____

INSTRUCTOR'S SIGNATURE _____

Job

Replace a Gasket

8

After completing this job, you will be able to remove and install a gasket on an automotive part. You will also learn how to use RTV to form a gasket.

Instructions

As you read the job instructions, answer the questions and perform the tasks. Print your answers neatly and use complete sentences. Consult the proper service literature and ask your instructor for help as needed.

> ### Warning
> ⚠ Before performing this job, review all pertinent safety information in the text and discuss safety procedures with your instructor.

Procedures

☐ 1. Obtain a vehicle to be used in this job. Your instructor may direct you to perform this job on a shop vehicle or engine.

☐ 2. Gather the tools needed to perform the following job.

Replace a Gasket

☐ 1. Make sure all lubricant has been drained from the unit containing the part and gasket to be removed.

> ### Note
> Skip the preceding step if the lubricant does not cover the part to be removed when the vehicle is not running. Care should be taken that the lubricant is not contaminated with gasket material or other foreign material during this task.

☐ 2. Remove the part covering the gasket.

☐ 3. Scrape all old gasket material from both sealing surfaces.

☐ 4. Thoroughly clean the removed part and remove any gasket material or other debris on the related components in the vehicle.

☐ 5. Inspect the removed part and the sealing surface in the vehicle for gouges, cracks, dents and warped areas.

Describe the condition of the removed part and the sealing surface in the vehicle.

_____

_____

☐ 6. Repair or replace the parts if defects are found.

☐ 7. Obtain a replacement gasket and compare it with the part's sealing surface. See **Figure 8-1**. Make sure that the following conditions are met:

   • The replacement gasket is the correct size and shape.

   • The gasket material is correct for this application.

☐ 8. Place a light coat of sealer or adhesive, as applicable, on the removed part to hold the gasket in place during reinstallation.

> **Note**
>
> Skip the preceding step if the gasket is being installed inside an automatic transmission or transaxle. Sealer also may not be needed on other applications.

☐ 9. Place the gasket in place on the part.

☐ 10. Reinstall the part, being careful not to damage or misalign the gasket.

☐ 11. Install the fasteners. Do not tighten any fastener until all fasteners are started.

Figure 8-1. Compare the new gasket to the part-sealing surface to ensure that it is correct.

Goodheart-Willcox Publisher

Job 8—Replace a Gasket (continued)

☐ 12. Tighten all fasteners to the correct torque. Follow these rules to avoid gasket damage and leaks:

- Tighten the fasteners in the manufacturer's sequence. If a sequence is not available, follow the sequence shown in **Figure 8-2**. If the part is irregularly shaped, start from the inner fasteners and work outward.
- Tighten each fastener slightly, then move to the next fastener. Repeat the sequence until final torque is reached.
- Be especially careful not to overtighten fasteners holding sheet metal components.
- Rubber gaskets, sometimes called "spaghetti gaskets," require very low torque values. **Figure 8-3** is a typical spaghetti gasket. Be extremely careful not to overtighten these types of gaskets.

☐ 13. Reinstall the correct type and amount of fresh lubricant into the unit as needed.

>
> **Note**
> If there is any possibility that the lubricant was contaminated during the gasket replacement process, it should be replaced.

☐ 14. Operate the vehicle and check for leaks.

Figure 8-2. A—When tightening a square or rectangular pan or cover, always start from the center and work outward. This allows the gasket to spread out, improving the seal. B—When installing the fasteners on a round cover, tighten in a star or crisscross pattern.

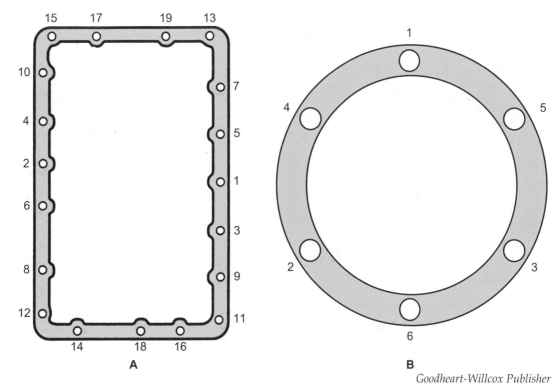

Goodheart-Willcox Publisher

Figure 8-3. A spaghetti gasket used on an intake manifold is shown here. Some spaghetti gaskets are simply sections of flexible rubber that strongly resemble spaghetti. They are extremely easy to overtighten.

Goodheart-Willcox Publisher

Apply Room Temperature Vulcanizing (RTV) Adhesive/Sealant

> **Note**
>
> There are two general classes of RTV sealants: silicone and acrylic. Silicone based RTV is more flexible, while acrylic based RTV can be cleaned using soap and water. Silicone RTV is usually used for automotive sealing. RTV can be used to attach or seal gaskets, or used in place of a gasket. RTV is destroyed by high temperatures. Do not attempt to use RTV to seal exhaust system parts. The following steps apply to silicone based RTV.

> **Caution**
>
> Apply RTV only in a well-ventilated area.

- [ ] 1. Ensure that the temperature of the sealing surfaces are between –35°F (–37°C) and 140°F (60°C).
- [ ] 2. Clean and dry both sides of the sealing surfaces. Use a residue-free solvent for best results.
- [ ] 3. Put on gloves.
- [ ] 4. Cut RTV applicator nozzle to desired RTV bead size.

> **Note**
>
> If the RTV is being used to make a gasket, cut the nozzle to obtain a 1/16″ to 1/4″ (1.5 to 6.5 mm) bead.

- [ ] 5. Apply RTV to one surface of the parts to be sealed. Apply in an even, continuous bead.
- [ ] 6. Assemble parts as soon as RTV has been applied.

Job 8—Replace a Gasket (continued)

☐ 7. As soon as application is complete, replace cap on RTV applicator.

☐ 8. Remove excess RTV from hands with a dry towel, and then wash hands with hand cleaner. Clean application tools with solvent.

☐ 9. Allow the RTV to cure (become tack free). This usually occurs in one hour or less.

Note

If RTV is being used as an adhesive or to seal widely separated surfaces, clamp the surfaces together for 20–30 minutes or until silicone is firm.

☐ 10. Allow 24 hours for full cure and maximum strength under normal conditions. Allow more time in cold or very dry conditions.

☐ 11. After curing is complete, trim excess RTV with a sharp knife.

☐ 12. Operate the vehicle and check for leaks.

Job Wrap Up

☐ 1. Return all tools and equipment to storage.

☐ 2. Clean the work area.

☐ 3. Did you encounter any problems during this procedure? Yes ___ No ___
If Yes, describe the problems: _____
_____
_____
What did you do to correct the problems?_____
_____
_____

☐ 4. Have your instructor check your work and sign this job sheet.

Performance Evaluation—Instructor Use Only

Did the student complete the job in the time allotted? Yes ___ No ___
If No, which steps were not completed?_____
How would you rate this student's overall performance on this job?____
5–Excellent, 4–Good, 3–Satisfactory, 2–Unsatisfactory, 1–Poor
Comments: _____
_____
_____

INSTRUCTOR'S SIGNATURE_____

Notes

Job
Replace a Seal

After completing this job, you will be able to remove and install a seal on an automotive part.

Instructions

As you read the job instructions, answer the questions and perform the tasks. Print your answers neatly and use complete sentences. Consult the proper service literature and ask your instructor for help as needed.

> **Warning**
> ⚠ Before performing this job, review all pertinent safety information in the text and discuss safety procedures with your instructor.

Procedures

1. Obtain a vehicle to be used in this job. Your instructor may direct you to perform this job on a shop vehicle or engine.
2. Gather the tools needed to perform the following job.

Replace a Seal

1. Remove shafts and other parts that restrict access to the lip seal to be replaced.

> **Caution**
> ◇ Drain oil to a level below the seal if necessary.

2. Remove the lip seal by one of the following methods:
   - Prying the seal from the housing. See **Figure 9-1**.
   - Driving the seal from the back side of the housing.
   - Using a special removal tool to remove the seal.

   Describe the method used to remove the lip seal._____

   _____

Figure 9-1. If the seal will not be reused, pry it from the housing with a large screwdriver or pry bar. Be careful not to damage the seal housing during removal.

Goodheart-Willcox Publisher

3. Obtain a replacement seal and compare it with the old seal.

   Is the replacement seal correct? Yes ___ No ___

   If No, what should you do next? _____

   _____

4. Thoroughly clean the seal housing to remove oil, sludge and carbon deposits, and old sealer.

5. Inspect the seal housing for cracks, gouges, and dents at the sealing area. **Figure 9-2** shows a cracked seal housing.

   Describe the condition of the housing and the old seal: _____

   _____

   _____

6. Inspect the shaft at the sealing area. Look for nicks, burrs, and groove wear.

   Describe the condition of the shaft at the sealing area: _____

   _____

   _____

   _____

> **Note**
>
> Defective housings should be repaired or replaced. Defective shafts should also be replaced. Consult your instructor to determine what additional steps, if any, need to be taken.

Job 9—Replace a Seal (continued)

Figure 9-2. This seal housing is visibly cracked. A damaged seal housing must be properly repaired or replaced.

Crack in housing

Goodheart-Willcox Publisher

☐ 7. Lightly lubricate the lip of the seal as shown in **Figure 9-3**. Use the same type of lubricant as is used in the device being serviced.

☐ 8. If specified by the seal manufacturer, lightly coat the outside diameter of the seal with nonhardening sealer.

Figure 9-3. Lubricate the sealing lip before installation.

Goodheart-Willcox Publisher

9. Install the new seal using one of the following methods:
   - Drive the seal into place with a seal driver, **Figure 9-4**.
   - Carefully tap the seal into place with a hammer.

> **Caution**
>
> When installing a seal by tapping it into place with a hammer, lightly tap on alternating sides of the seal.

Describe the method used to install the seal: _____

_____

_____

> **Caution**
>
> Some technicians prefer to drive the seal into place using a hammer and a block of wood. This should only be done when no other method is available. Wood fragments can enter the bore and cause damage.

10. Reinstall the shaft and other parts as necessary.
11. Check that the shaft turns freely after all parts are installed.
12. Add fluid as needed. Then, operate the unit and check for leaks.

Job Wrap Up

1. Return all tools and equipment to storage.
2. Clean the work area.

Figure 9-4. A typical seal driver.

Goodheart-Willcox Publisher

Job 9—Replace a Seal (continued)

☐   3.   Did you encounter any problems during this procedure? Yes ___ No ___

     If Yes, describe the problems: _____

     _____

     _____

     What did you do to correct the problems?_____

     _____

     _____

☐   4.   Have your instructor check your work and sign this job sheet.

Performance Evaluation—Instructor Use Only

Did the student complete the job in the time allotted? Yes ___ No ___

If No, which steps were not completed?_____

How would you rate this student's overall performance on this job?_____

5–Excellent, 4–Good, 3–Satisfactory, 2–Unsatisfactory, 1–Poor

Comments: _____

_____

_____

INSTRUCTOR'S SIGNATURE _____

Notes

Job
Replace a Timing Belt

10

After completing this job, you will be able to replace a valve timing belt.

Instructions

As you read the job instructions, answer the questions and perform the tasks. Print your answers neatly and use complete sentences. Consult the proper service literature and ask your instructor for help as needed.

> ### Warning
> ⚠ Before performing this job, review all pertinent safety information in the text and discuss safety procedures with your instructor.

Procedures

 1. Obtain an engine to be used in this job. Your instructor may direct you to perform this job on a shop engine.
   Make of engine:_____
   Number of cylinders:_____
   Cylinder arrangement (V-type, inline, etc.):_____
   Cooling system: Liquid ___ Air ___

2. Gather the tools needed to perform the following tasks.

3. Look up the following torque specifications in the service manual. Record the information in the appropriate spaces.
   Intake manifold/plenum fasteners: _____ ft-lb _____ N·m
   Rocker arm fasteners (if applicable): _____ ft-lb _____ N·m
   Valve cover fasteners: _____ ft-lb _____ N·m
   Timing mechanism fasteners: _____ ft-lb _____ N·m
   Front cover fasteners: _____ ft-lb _____ N·m

> **Note**
> Some belt-driven overhead camshaft engines may have as many as four camshaft sprockets.

☐ 4. Remove the front timing cover, coolant pump and other parts covering the timing belt and gears as needed.

☐ 5. Align the camshaft and crankshaft sprocket timing marks for removal.

> **Note**
> Some camshaft sprockets will be pushed out of position by valve spring tension when the timing belt is removed. A special tool must be installed before belt removal to prevent unwanted sprocket movement.

☐ 6. Remove or otherwise release the pressure on the belt tensioner.

☐ 7. Remove the timing belt from the sprockets.

☐ 8. Visually inspect the condition of the drive sprockets.

☐ 9. Check the timing belt condition. Most checks can be made visually. A worn belt will have cracks and, possibly, missing teeth.

☐ 10. Check the condition of the belt tensioner.

a. Check the tensioner for obvious physical damage.

b. When possible, check the tensioner spring pressure with the proper special tool.

c. Check hydraulic tensioners for leaks, lack of oil, or other damage.

☐ 11. Compare the old and new belts.

☐ 12. Place the new timing belt in position over the sprockets. Be careful to maintain the alignment of the timing marks. If necessary, rotate the crankshaft and camshaft(s) until the timing marks are aligned.

☐ 13. Re-engage the tensioner on the timing belt and tighten any fasteners as needed.

☐ 14. Check and adjust belt tension using one of the following methods, as outlined by the manufacturer's instructions:

> **Note**
> Belt tension is not adjustable on many engines.

a. Measure belt deflection with a special tool and adjust the tensioner as required. Adjustment devices include slotted holes in the tensioner, adjusting screws, or shims.

b. Loosen tensioner fasteners just enough to allow tensioner movement.

c. Adjust the tensioner using one of the following methods:
- Adjust the tensioner until the belt can be twisted to a 90° angle.
- Use a torque wrench to adjust the tensioner to the proper torque value.
- Align marks on the tensioner with marks on the engine block or head.

Method used: _____

d. Tighten tensioner fasteners just enough to allow tensioner movement.

Job 10—Replace a Timing Belt (continued)

☐ 15. After all parts are installed, recheck the timing marks to ensure that they are in position.

☐ 16. If necessary, index the camshaft position sensor(s) using manufacturer's procedures.

☐ 17. If necessary, scrape the timing cover, coolant pump, and block mating surfaces to remove old gasket material.

☐ 18. If applicable, place the timing cover gaskets and any oil seals on the engine block. Use the proper type of sealant, if required.

☐ 19. Place the timing cover on the block.

☐ 20. Install and tighten the timing cover fasteners to the proper torque in the correct sequence.

Job Wrap Up

☐ 1. Return all tools and equipment to storage.

☐ 2. Clean the work area.

☐ 3. Did you encounter any problems during this procedure? Yes ___ No ___
   If Yes, describe the problems: _____
   _____
   _____
   What did you do to correct the problems?_____
   _____
   _____

☐ 4. Have your instructor check your work and sign this job sheet.

Performance Evaluation—Instructor Use Only

Did the student complete the job in the time allotted? Yes ___ No ___
If No, which steps were not completed?_____
How would you rate this student's overall performance on this job?_____
5–Excellent, 4–Good, 3–Satisfactory, 2–Unsatisfactory, 1–Poor
Comments: _____
_____
_____
INSTRUCTOR'S SIGNATURE_____

Notes

Job
Repair Damaged Threads

After completing this job, you will be able to repair a variety of damaged threads and chase threads in a bore.

Instructions

As you read the job instructions, answer the questions and perform the tasks. Print your answers neatly and use complete sentences. Consult the proper service literature and ask your instructor for help as needed.

> **Warning**
>
> Before performing this job, review all pertinent safety information in the text and discuss safety procedures with your instructor.

Procedures

☐ 1. Obtain a piece of metal or a part with a threaded bore that has stripped threads.

☐ 2. Gather the tools needed to perform the following job.

Repair External Threads

> **Note**
>
> Most stripped external threads occur on capscrews, bolts, or other parts that are usually replaced when damaged. Occasionally, the technician will be asked to repair damaged external threads. The usual reason for repairing an external thread is to remove burrs. External threads may also be repaired if hammering or cross-threading has damaged the beginning thread.

☐ 1. Carefully inspect the external threads and determine whether they can be repaired.
   - Are large sections of the threads missing? Yes ___ No ___
   - Have large sections of the thread been cross-threaded? Yes ___ No ___
   - Are the threads badly damaged throughout their length? Yes ___ No ___
   - Are the threads badly damaged at the spot where they will be under the most tension? Yes ___ No ___

   A Yes answer to any of these questions usually means that the threads cannot safely be repaired and the part must be replaced.

   Can the threads be repaired? Yes ___ No ___

   Warning

   ⚠ Do not attempt to repair badly damaged external threads, or damaged threads on critical parts. Part failure and possible injury could result.

☐ 2. Use one of the following methods to repair an external thread.

   Die Method

   a. Install the correct size die in the die stock.

   b. Place the die and die stock over the external threads to be repaired.

   c. Lubricate the external threads.

   d. Begin turning the die stock over the threads to remove burrs or straighten a cross-threaded or damaged beginning thread.

   e. After the damaged threads are repaired, remove the die and die stock by turning it in the opposite direction.

   f. Thoroughly clean and reinspect the threads.

   Can the part be reused? Yes ___ No ___

   Thread Chaser Method

   Note

   📄 Some thread chasers clamp over the damaged thread. Use the die method to operate this type of thread chaser.

   ---

   a. Lubricate the external threads.

   b. Select the proper size thread chaser. Most file-type thread chasers will be four-sided, with a different thread on each side of one end, and four other thread sizes on the other end.

   c. Place the thread chaser on the damaged threads. Make sure that the high points of the chaser rest over the low points of the thread.

   d. Slowly draw the thread chaser over the damaged threads, stopping frequently to inspect the work.

   e. Thoroughly clean the threads and reinspect.

   Can the part be reused? Yes ___ No ___

Job 11—Repair Damaged Threads (continued)

Repair Internal Threads

> **Note**
> Stripped threads are usually found in aluminum assemblies, but can occur in any type of metal. Thread repair kits contain the needed drills, taps, thread repair inserts, and special mandrels for installing the inserts.

☐ 1. Determine the size and pitch of the stripped thread.

☐ 2. If necessary, place rags around the stripped thread to catch metal chips.

☐ 3. Select the proper drill bit according to the instructions of the thread-repair kit manufacturer.

☐ 4. Drill out the stripped threads and clean the metal chips from the hole.

☐ 5. Tap the hole with the appropriate tap from the thread-repair kit. Be sure to lubricate the tap before beginning the tapping operation.

☐ 6. Clean the threads to remove any remaining chips.

☐ 7. Thread the repair insert onto the correct mandrel. The insert tang should be engaged with the matching slot on the mandrel.

☐ 8. If installing the insert into an iron or steel part, lubricate it with engine oil. Do not lubricate the insert if it is to be installed in an aluminum part.

☐ 9. Turn the mandrel to advance it into the tapped hole.

☐ 10. Back the mandrel out of the hole when the insert reaches the bottom.

☐ 11. If the tang did not break off when the mandrel was removed, lightly tap it with a drift punch and hammer to remove it.

Remove a Broken Fastener

☐ 1. Consult with your instructor to obtain a part with a broken fastener. Remove the fastener using one of the following methods. Place a check mark next to the method used.

> **Note**
> Sometimes it is necessary to use more than one removal method, depending on fastener tightness and how much of the fastener remains above the part.

☐ Clamp the fastener with locking pliers and turn to remove the fastener.

☐ Grind flats on each side of the fastener, and use an adjustable wrench to remove the fastener.

☐ Cut a slot in the top of the fastener, and use a screwdriver to remove the fastener.

☐ Heat the area surrounding the fastener with a torch and remove the fastener.

> **Note**
> Work quickly to remove the fastener, before the surrounding area cools.

☐ Drill out the center of the fastener and use an extractor to remove the fastener.

☐ Weld a nut to the top of the fastener and turn the nut with a wrench.

Describe the procedure(s) you used and the results: _____

_____

_____

_____

Were the threads of the part holding the broken fastener damaged? Yes ___ No ___

If Yes, what did you do to correct the problem? _____

_____

_____

Job Wrap Up

☐ 1. Return all tools and equipment to storage.

☐ 2. Clean the work area.

☐ 3. Did you encounter any problems during this procedure? Yes ___ No ___

If Yes, describe the problems: _____

_____

_____

What did you do to correct the problems?_____

_____

_____

☐ 4. Have your instructor check your work and sign this job sheet.

Performance Evaluation—Instructor Use Only

Did the student complete the job in the time allotted? Yes ___ No ___

If No, which steps were not completed?_____

How would you rate this student's overall performance on this job?_____

5–Excellent, 4–Good, 3–Satisfactory, 2–Unsatisfactory, 1–Poor

Comments: _____

_____

INSTRUCTOR'S SIGNATURE _____

Job

Adjust Valves

12

After completing this job, you will be able to adjust valves with mechanical and hydraulic valve lifters.

Instructions

As you read the job instructions, answer the questions and perform the tasks. Print your answers neatly and use complete sentences. Consult the proper service literature and ask your instructor for help as needed.

> **Warning**
>
> Before performing this job, review all pertinent safety information in the text and discuss safety procedures with your instructor.

Procedures

☐ 1. Obtain a vehicle to be used in this job. Your instructor may direct you to perform this job on a shop vehicle or engine.

☐ 2. Gather the tools needed to perform the following job.

☐ 3. Remove the engine valve cover(s) to reveal the valve adjustment device.

> **Note**
>
> On some overhead camshaft engines, clearance is adjusted by changing lifters or adding shims at the lifters. Consult the manufacturer's service information for these procedures.

☐ 4. Determine whether the engine uses mechanical or hydraulic valve lifters.
Mechanical ___ Hydraulic ___

> **Note**
>
>
>
> The following sections provide instructions for adjusting valves with mechanical lifters and adjusting valves with hydraulic lifters. Use the procedure that is appropriate for the type of lifters used in your vehicle. Skip the procedure that does not apply.

Adjust Valves—Mechanical Valve Lifters

☐ 1. Obtain the proper valve-clearance specifications.

Specifications for intake valve: _____ inches or millimeters (circle one).

Does the specification call for the engine to be warmed up? Yes ___ No ___

Specifications for exhaust valve: _____ inches or millimeters (circle one).

Does the specification call for the engine to be warmed up? Yes ___ No ___

☐ 2. Turn the engine until the camshaft lobe for the valve to be adjusted points away from the lifter.

☐ 3. Loosen the adjuster locknut.

☐ 4. Insert the proper thickness feeler gauge between the end of the valve stem and the rocker arm. See **Figure 12-1**.

☐ 5. Turn the adjuster while moving the feeler gauge between the valve and rocker arm. When there is a light drag on the feeler gauge, clearance is correct.

☐ 6. Tighten the adjuster locknut while holding the adjuster in position.

☐ 7. Recheck adjustment to ensure that the adjuster did not move when the locknut was tightened.

☐ 8. Repeat steps 2 through 7 for the other engine valves.

☐ 9. Reinstall the valve cover using a new gasket as necessary.

☐ 10. Start the engine and listen for noise in the valve train.

Are any valves noisy (clattering or tapping sounds)? Yes ___ No ___

If Yes, recheck the clearance specifications and repeat the procedure.

Figure 12-1. Insert the feeler gauge between the rocker arm and the valve stem. The cam lobe must be at its lowest point (putting no pressure on the valve train).

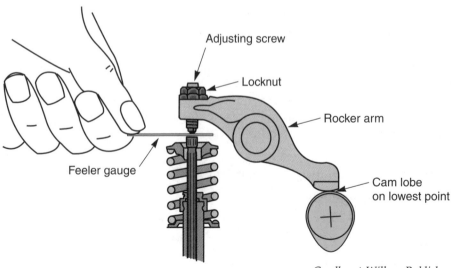

Goodheart-Willcox Publisher

Job 12—Adjust Valves (continued)

Adjust Valves—Hydraulic Valve Lifters

☐ 1. Install oil deflector clips or other shielding to reduce oil spray.

☐ 2. Start the engine.

☐ 3. Loosen the valve adjuster locknut on the first valve to be adjusted. Note that not all rocker assemblies are equipped with valve adjuster locknuts.

☐ 4. Back off the valve adjuster until the valve begins to make a clattering noise. See **Figure 12-2**.

☐ 5. Tighten the adjuster until the noise just stops.

☐ 6. Tighten the adjuster an additional number of turns as specified by the service literature. If the rocker assembly is equipped with a valve adjuster locknut, retighten it. Be careful not to allow the valve adjuster to rotate.

☐ 7. Repeat steps 3 through 6 for all other engine valves.

☐ 8. Reinstall the valve cover using a new gasket as necessary.

Figure 12-2. Adjust the valve until it just stops clattering, then turn in the adjuster an additional number of turns. This adjusting nut is an interference fit and does not use a locknut.

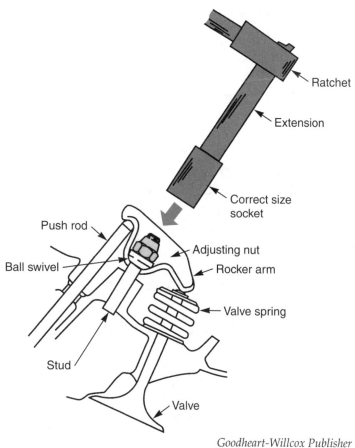

Goodheart-Willcox Publisher

Job Wrap Up

☐ 1. Return all tools and equipment to storage.

☐ 2. Clean the work area.

☐ 3. Did you encounter any problems during this procedure? Yes ___ No ___

If Yes, describe the problems: _____

_____

_____

What did you do to correct the problems?_____

_____

_____

☐ 4. Have your instructor check your work and sign this job sheet.

Performance Evaluation—Instructor Use Only

Did the student complete the job in the time allotted? Yes ___ No ___

If No, which steps were not completed?_____

How would you rate this student's overall performance on this job?_____

5–Excellent, 4–Good, 3–Satisfactory, 2–Unsatisfactory, 1–Poor

Comments: _____

_____

_____

INSTRUCTOR'S SIGNATURE _____

Job

Inspect and Test Cooling System Components

13

After completing this job, you will be able to inspect and test components of a vehicle's cooling system.

Instructions

As you read the job instructions, answer the questions and perform the tasks. Print your answers neatly and use complete sentences. Consult the proper service literature and ask your instructor for help as needed.

> **Warning**
>
> ⚠ Before performing this job, review all pertinent safety information in the text and discuss safety procedures with your instructor.

Procedures

☐ 1. Obtain a vehicle to be used in this job. Your instructor may direct you to perform this job on a shop vehicle or engine.

☐ 2. Gather the tools needed to perform the following job.

☐ 3. Determine the type of antifreeze used in the vehicle cooling system.

Antifreeze type: _____

☐ 4. Open the hood and inspect the condition of the cooling system hoses, including heater hoses. Examine the hoses for bulging, leaks, or fraying. Ensure the hoses do not contact any moving parts. Squeeze the hoses to check for hardness, cracks, or softness.

Were any problems found? Yes ___ No ___

If Yes, describe the problem(s):_____

_____

☐ 5. Determine the condition of the vehicle's belts. Examine the belts for glazing, fraying, or oil contamination. If applicable, check the condition of the belt tensioner.

Were any problems found? Yes ___ No ___

If Yes, describe the problem(s):_____

_____

6. Visually check the radiator's condition. Make sure the radiator fins are free of leaves and other debris, the radiator's cooling fins are not damaged, and there are no obvious leaks.

   Were any problems found? Yes ___ No ___

   If Yes, describe the problems: _____

   _____

7. Check the condition of the coolant recovery system. Inspect the coolant recovery tank, cap, and hoses for damage.

   Were any problems found? Yes ___ No ___

   If Yes, describe the problems: _____

   _____

8. Ensure that the engine and cooling system are sufficiently cool to allow the radiator or coolant recovery reservoir cap to be safely removed.

9. Place a rag over the radiator, slowly turn it to allow pressure to escape, then remove the cap and check its condition. If the system uses a pressurized coolant recovery reservoir, remove the cap on the reservoir. Replace the cap if it is corroded or if the rubber seal is hard, cracked, or otherwise damaged. If the cap is a plastic type, such as those used on pressurized coolant recovery reservoirs, check it for cracks and missing plastic sections.

   Is the cap in good condition? Yes ___ No ___

10. Check the coolant level. If the cooling system has a coolant recovery system, the coolant level should be at the top of the filler neck. If the vehicle does not have a coolant recovery system the coolant level should be about 3" (76 mm) below the filler neck.

    Is the coolant level correct? Yes ___ No ___

11. Visually check the coolant for rust.

    Is the coolant rusty? Yes ___ No ___

12. Check degree of freeze protection (antifreeze percentage) with an antifreeze tester. Follow the directions provided by the tester manufacturer.

    Antifreeze will protect to _____ °F or °C (circle one).

Pressure Test the Pressure Cap

1. Obtain a cooling system pressure tester.

2. Check the condition of the radiator cap by installing it on the tester, **Figure 13-1**. Pressure caps on a pressurized coolant recovery reservoir may require special adapters.

3. Pump up the tester pressure until it levels off. A pressure specification should be printed somewhere on the cap. The radiator should hold this pressure without allowing it to drop.

   Did the radiator cap pass the pressure test? Yes ___ No ___

   If No, replace the radiator cap.

Vacuum Test the Pressure Cap

1. Obtain a vacuum pump and radiator cap vacuum test adapter.

2. Install the cap in the adapter and connect the adapter to the vacuum pump.

Job 13—Inspect and Test Cooling System Components (continued)

Figure 13-1. Install the pressure cap on the pressure tester. Adapters may be needed.

Jack Klasey

☐ 3. Apply vacuum to the radiator cap. The cap should allow vacuum to build up to approximately 2–5 inches Hg, then release and allow air to flow through the cap. Does the cap allow vacuum to build up then release? Yes ___ No ___ If No, replace the radiator cap.

Pressure Test the Cooling System

☐ 1. Remove the radiator cap from the pressure tester and install the pressure tester on the radiator filler neck. See **Figure 13-2**.

☐ 2. Pump the pressure tester handle until the cooling system has been pressurized to the rating on the radiator cap. If the system is very low on coolant, add water to make the job of pressurizing easier.

Figure 13-2. Install the pressure tester on the radiator fill neck.

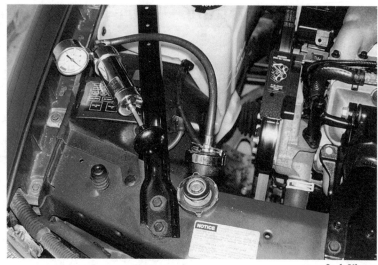

Jack Klasey

> **Note**
>
> It may be necessary to remove the cap from the radiator filler neck to add water to a system using a pressurized coolant recovery reservoir. After adding water, reinstall the radiator cap and continue with the other pressure testing steps.

☐ 3. Carefully observe the cooling system for leaks. If no leaks are visible and the pressure holds for two minutes, the system is not leaking.

Did the cooling system pass the pressure test? Yes ___ No ___

If No, explain why the cooling system failed:_____

_____

_____

> **Note**
>
> If you add water to the cooling system for diagnostic testing, make sure you drain and refill the system with the proper antifreeze mixture before releasing the vehicle to its owner.

Job Wrap Up

☐ 1. Return all tools and equipment to storage.

☐ 2. Clean the work area.

☐ 3. Did you encounter any problems during this procedure? Yes ___ No ___

If Yes, describe the problems: _____

_____

_____

What did you do to correct the problems?_____

_____

_____

☐ 4. Have your instructor check your work and sign this job sheet.

Performance Evaluation—Instructor Use Only

Did the student complete the job in the time allotted? Yes ___ No ___

If No, which steps were not completed?_____

How would you rate this student's overall performance on this job?_____

5–Excellent, 4–Good, 3–Satisfactory, 2–Unsatisfactory, 1–Poor

Comments: _____

_____

_____

INSTRUCTOR'S SIGNATURE _____

Job
Service Belt Drives

14

After completing this job, you will be able to observe belt and pulley alignment, replace V-belts, and serpentine belts, and replace a belt tensioner.

Instructions

As you read the job instructions, answer the questions and perform the tasks. Print your answers neatly and use complete sentences. Consult the proper service literature and ask your instructor for help as needed.

> **Warning**
> ⚠ Before performing this job, review all pertinent safety information in the text and discuss safety procedures with your instructor.

Procedures

☐ 1. Obtain a vehicle to be used in this job. Your instructor may direct you to perform this job on a shop vehicle.

☐ 2. Gather the tools needed to perform the following job.

Check Belt and Pulley Alignment

 1. Determine the type and number of belts on the engine.

Number of V-belts: ___

Number of serpentine belts: ___

☐ 2. Observe the condition of the drive belts and pulleys. Place a check mark next to all that apply:

V-belt Condition
- ☐ Good.
- ☐ Worn.
- ☐ Glazed.
- ☐ Cracked.
- ☐ Oil contaminated.

Pulley Condition
- ☐ Good.
- ☐ Worn.
- ☐ Grooved.

Serpentine Belt Condition
- ☐ Good.
- ☐ Worn.
- ☐ Glazed.
- ☐ Cracked.
- ☐ Oil contaminated.
- ☐ Pilling in pulley grooves.

Pulley Condition:
- ☐ Good.
- ☐ Worn.

☐ 3. Sight along the pulley and belt assembly at right angles to the engine.

Do the pulleys and belt(s) appear to be in alignment? Yes ___ No ___

If No, what could be the cause? _____

_____

☐ 4. Start the engine and observe belt and pulley operation.

Do all pulleys turn evenly with no wobbling or noise? Yes ___ No ___

If no, what could be the cause? _____

_____

Replace a V-Belt

☐ 1. Determine which belt must be replaced. V-belts are used to drive combinations of accessories, including the coolant pump, alternator, air conditioning compressor, power steering pump, and air pump. Some or all of these accessories must be loosened to remove a particular belt. Sometimes one or more serviceable belts must be removed to remove the defective belt.

Which accessories are driven by the belt that will be replaced? _____

_____

_____

☐ 2. Loosen the fasteners holding the accessory driven by the belt. You may need a droplight so that you can find all of the fasteners.

Job 14—Service Belt Drives (continued)

☐ 3. Push the accessory toward the engine to remove tension on the belt.

☐ 4. Remove the belt from the pulleys.

☐ 5. Compare the old and new belts.

Is the new belt the correct replacement? Yes ___ No ___

> **Note**
> Even a slight difference in size means that the new belt is unusable.

☐ 6. Slip the new belt over the pulleys, making sure that it is fully seated in the pulley grooves.

☐ 7. Pull the accessories away from the engine to place slight tension on the belt.

☐ 8. Adjust belt tension. Use a belt tension gauge to measure exact tension. If a gauge is not available, use the belt deflection method to adjust the belt. The belt should deflect from 1/2″ to 5/8″ (10 mm to 15 mm) with 25 pounds (10 kg) of applied pressure. The belts should only be tight enough to prevent slipping or squealing. Excessive tension on the belt places stress on the accessory bearings, which will quickly wear out.

> **Note**
> Since one hand needs to be free to tighten the fasteners, you may need to use a lever to hold the accessory in the proper position as the fasteners are tightened.

☐ 9. Start the vehicle and check belt operation.

Replace a Serpentine Belt

> **Note**
> This procedure assumes that the vehicle has one serpentine belt. If you must remove other belts in order to replace the serpentine belt, use this procedure to remove serpentine belts or the previous procedure to remove V-belts.

☐ 1. Open the vehicle hood and determine whether the engine contains a label showing serpentine belt routing, or obtain service literature showing serpentine belt routing for the vehicle on which you are working.

☐ 2. Locate the belt-tensioning device and determine which tool(s) are needed to remove tension. This may be simple hand tools or a special tool.

Tool(s) needed to remove tension: _____

☐ 3. Remove tension from the belt using the proper tool(s), **Figure 14-1**.

☐ 4. Remove the serpentine belt.

Figure 14-1. Serpentine belt tension can usually be removed by inserting a 3/8″ or 1/2″ ratchet or flex handle into a square hole in the tensioner and pulling away from the direction of tension. Sometimes a special tool is needed to remove belt tension.

Goodheart-Willcox Publisher

☐ 5. Release the belt-tensioning device.

☐ 6. Turn the pulley of the belt-tensioning device.

Is any roughness noted? Yes ___ No ___

If Yes, the pulley should be replaced. Consult your instructor before proceeding.

☐ 7. Compare the old and new belts.

Are the belts the same size? Yes ___ No ___

If No, obtain the correct belt before proceeding.

☐ 8. Refer to the proper belt routing diagram and place the new belt in position.

☐ 9. Pull the belt-tensioning device away from the belt to allow the belt to be installed.

☐ 10. Finish installing the new belt, making sure that the belt is properly positioned over the pulleys.

☐ 11. Release the belt-tensioning device.

☐ 12. Start the engine and check belt operation.

Replace a Serpentine Belt Tensioner

> **Note**
>
> Refer to the previous procedures to remove the serpentine belt.

☐ 1. Once the belt tension is removed, locate the fasteners holding the tensioner assembly to the engine.

☐ 2. Remove the fasteners holding the tensioner assembly to the engine.

Job 14—Service Belt Drives (continued)

☐ 3. Compare the removed tensioner with the new tensioner.

Do the old and new tensioners match? Yes ___ No ___

If No, why are they different?_____

☐ 4. If the tensioner pulley is being replaced, remove it from the tensioner body, install the new pulley.

If the entire tensioner assembly is being replaced, place the tensioner assembly on the engine and loosely install the fasteners.

☐ 5. Tighten the fasteners to the proper torque.

☐ 6. Reinstall the serpentine belt.

☐ 7. Start the engine and check belt and tensioner operation.

Job Wrap Up

☐ 1. Return all tools and equipment to storage.

☐ 2. Clean the work area.

☐ 3. Did you encounter any problems during this procedure? Yes ___ No ___

If Yes, describe the problems: _____

_____

_____

What did you do to correct the problems?_____

_____

_____

☐ 4. Have your instructor check your work and sign this job sheet.

Performance Evaluation—Instructor Use Only

Did the student complete the job in the time allotted? Yes ___ No ___

If No, which steps were not completed?_____

How would you rate this student's overall performance on this job?_____

5–Excellent, 4–Good, 3–Satisfactory, 2–Unsatisfactory, 1–Poor

Comments: _____

_____

_____

INSTRUCTOR'S SIGNATURE _____

Notes

Job

Remove and Replace a Thermostat

15

After completing this job, you will be able to remove and replace a thermostat.

Instructions

As you read the job instructions, answer the questions and perform the tasks. Print your answers neatly and use complete sentences. Consult the proper service literature and ask your instructor for help as needed.

Warning

⚠ Before performing this job, review all pertinent safety information in the text and discuss safety procedures with your instructor.

Procedures

☐ 1. Obtain a vehicle to be used in this job. Your instructor may direct you to perform this job on a shop vehicle.

☐ 2. Gather the tools needed to perform the following job.

☐ 3. Ensure that the engine and cooling system are sufficiently cool to allow the radiator cap to be safely removed.

☐ 4. Remove the radiator cap, and then locate the radiator drain plug.

☐ 5. Place a suitable container under the drain plug.

☐ 6. Open the radiator drain plug. Ensure that coolant drains into the container.

Warning

⚠ Clean up any coolant spills. Antifreeze is poisonous to people and animals.

☐ 7. Allow coolant to drain out so that the level of coolant in the engine is below the level of the thermostat. It is not necessary to remove all of the coolant.

8. Loosen the upper radiator hose clamp and remove the hose from the thermostat housing.

9. Remove the fasteners holding the thermostat housing to the engine and remove the housing. The thermostat should now be visible. See **Figure 15-1**.

10. Remove the thermostat from the engine.

11. Remove any gasket material from the engine and the thermostat housing sealing areas. If seals are used instead of gaskets, remove them and make sure the seal grooves are clean. You may wish to stuff a rag in the thermostat housing to prevent any debris from entering.

> **Note**
>
> The following step is optional and may be assigned by your instructor.

12. Test the thermostat by suspending it in a water-filled container over a burner or other source of heat. The thermostat should not touch the sides of the container. Place a thermometer in the water and observe the thermostat as the water is heated. If the thermostat does not begin to open at the rated temperature or is not fully open before the water begins boiling, it is defective.

13. If the thermostat is being replaced, compare the old and new thermostats. The new thermostat should be the same size as the original thermostat. The thermostat opening temperature should match the manufacturer's specifications. The thermostat opening temperature is usually stamped on the thermostatic element, as shown in **Figure 15-2**.

Do the sizes match? Yes ___ No ___

Does the opening temperature match? Yes ___ No ___

Figure 15-1. On V-type engines, the thermostat is usually located between the cylinder banks at the front of the engine. On inline engines, thermostats are usually near the upper radiator hose at the front of the engine.

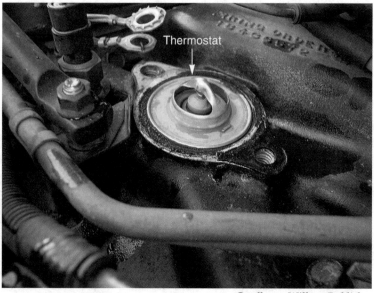

Goodheart-Willcox Publisher

Job 15—Remove and Replace a Thermostat (continued)

Figure 15-2. The opening temperature is usually stamped on the thermostatic element of the thermostat. Most thermostats will have both Fahrenheit and Celsius figures.

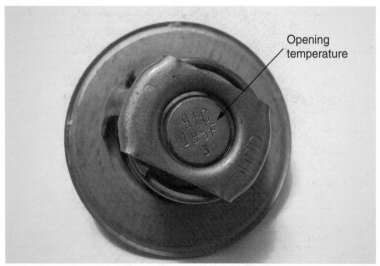

Goodheart-Willcox Publisher

> **Caution**
>
> Do not install a thermostat with a lower operating temperature than the original thermostat. This will affect emission control operations and may set a trouble code on OBD II-equipped vehicles.

14. Place the thermostat in position. The heat-sensing element should face the interior of the engine.

    Is the thermostat installed properly? Yes ___ No ___

15. If specified, coat the thermostat housing and engine sealing surfaces with nonhardening sealer.

16. Install the thermostat gasket on the engine.

17. Place the thermostat housing on the engine and install the housing fasteners.

18. Tighten the thermostat housing fasteners in an alternating pattern to prevent distortion. Be careful not to overtighten the fasteners. Overtightening the housing can cause distortion and leaks, and may break the housing.

19. Refill the system with the proper kind of coolant and bleed the system as described in Job 16. Many modern vehicles use special long-life coolant. Do not mix coolant types.

20. Start the engine and check for leaks and proper thermostat operation.

21. Clean up any coolant spills.

Job Wrap Up

1. Return all tools and equipment to storage.

2. Clean the work area.

☐ 3. Did you encounter any problems during this procedure? Yes ___ No ___

   If Yes, describe the problems: _____

   _____

   _____

   What did you do to correct the problems?_____

   _____

   _____

☐ 4. Have your instructor check your work and sign this job sheet.

Performance Evaluation—Instructor Use Only

Did the student complete the job in the time allotted? Yes ___ No ___

If No, which steps were not completed?_____

How would you rate this student's overall performance on this job?_____

5–Excellent, 4–Good, 3–Satisfactory, 2–Unsatisfactory, 1–Poor

Comments: _____

_____

INSTRUCTOR'S SIGNATURE _____

After completing this job, you will be able to flush and bleed a cooling system.

Instructions

As you read the job instructions, answer the questions and perform the tasks. Print your answers neatly and use complete sentences. Consult the proper service literature and ask your instructor for help as needed.

> **Warning**
>
> ⚠ Before performing this job, review all pertinent safety information in the text and discuss safety procedures with your instructor.

Procedures

☐ 1. Obtain a vehicle on which cooling system service can be performed. Your instructor may direct you to perform this job on a shop vehicle.

☐ 2. Gather the tools needed to perform the following job.

☐ 3. Determine the type of antifreeze to be used in the vehicle's cooling system.
Antifreeze type: _____

Flush and Bleed the Cooling System

> **Note**
>
> Many shops have pressure flushing and refilling machines. To use such a machine, use the manufacturer's procedures rather than the steps given here.

☐ 1. Ensure that the engine and cooling system are sufficiently cool to allow the radiator cap to be safely removed.

☐ 2. Remove the radiator cap, then locate the radiator drain plug. Locate any coolant drain plugs on the engine.

☐ 3. Place a suitable container under the drain plug(s).

☐ 4. Open the radiator drain plug and any coolant drain plugs on the engine. Make sure that coolant drains into the containers.

> ### Warning
> ⚠ Clean up any coolant spills. Antifreeze is poisonous to people and animals.

☐ 5. Allow the coolant to drain into the container(s) until coolant stops coming from the drain plugs.

☐ 6. Close the drain plugs.

☐ 7. Refill the cooling system with water and flushing agent. Carefully follow the directions provided by the manufacturer of the flushing agent.

☐ 8. Start the engine and allow it to idle for the recommended time. Turn the vehicle heater to high and closely monitor the level in the radiator.

☐ 9. After the recommended time has elapsed, turn the engine off.

☐ 10. Repeat steps 4 through 9 until the water from the drain plugs is clear. The length of this procedure varies depending on the condition of the cooling system and the number of times the cooling system must be flushed to remove all of the cleaning agent.

☐ 11. Refill the cooling system with a 50-50 mixture of the proper type of antifreeze and clean water.

What type of antifreeze does this engine require? _____

_____

> ### Caution
> ◇ Many modern vehicles take special long-life coolant. Always install the proper type of coolant. Do not mix coolant types.

☐ 12. Bleed the system using one of the following procedures, depending on the relative placement of the engine and radiator:

- **Radiator higher than engine:** Fill the system to about 3″ (76 mm) below the top of the filler neck. Allow the engine to reach operating temperature. When the thermostat opens, the radiator level will drop. Add more coolant until the level is at the top of the filler neck (coolant recovery system) or 3″ (76 mm) below the filler neck (no coolant recovery system).

- **Engine higher than radiator:** Fill the system to about 3″ (76 mm) below the top of the filler neck. Allow the engine to reach operating temperature. When the thermostat opens, the radiator level will drop. Open the bleed valve(s) on the engine and add more coolant until the coolant begins to exit from the bleeder valve. Close the bleeder valve and add coolant to fill the radiator. On some vehicles the bleeder may need to be opened and closed several times to remove all of the air from the system.

☐ 13. Install the radiator cap.

Job 16—Flush and Bleed a Cooling System (continued)

☐ 14. Add coolant to the cold level on the coolant recovery reservoir.

☐ 15. Clean up any spilled coolant.

Job Wrap Up

☐ 1. Return all tools and equipment to storage.

☐ 2. Clean the work area.

☐ 3. Did you encounter any problems during this procedure? Yes ___ No ___

If Yes, describe the problems: _____

_____

_____

What did you do to correct the problems?_____

_____

_____

☐ 4. Have your instructor check your work and sign this job sheet.

Performance Evaluation—Instructor Use Only

Did the student complete the job in the time allotted? Yes ___ No ___

If No, which steps were not completed?_____

How would you rate this student's overall performance on this job?____

5–Excellent, 4–Good, 3–Satisfactory, 2–Unsatisfactory, 1–Poor

Comments: _____

_____

_____

INSTRUCTOR'S SIGNATURE _____

Notes

Job

Change Oil and Filter

17

After completing this job, you will be able to perform an oil and filter change.

Instructions

As you read the job instructions, answer the questions and perform the tasks. Print your answers neatly and use complete sentences. Consult the proper service literature and ask your instructor for help as needed.

> **Warning**
>
> ⚠ Before performing this job, review all pertinent safety information in the text and discuss safety procedures with your instructor.

Procedures

☐ 1. Obtain a vehicle to be used in this job. Your instructor may direct you to perform this job on a shop vehicle or engine.

☐ 2. Gather the tools needed to perform the following job.

Change Oil and Filter

> **Caution**
>
> ◇ Before performing any service or test driving any vehicle, always place disposable covers over the upholstery and steering wheel and place mats on the carpet to prevent stains.

☐ 1. Obtain the correct oil filter and type and grade of motor oil.

Brand, grade, and weight of oil: _____

Brand and stock number of oil filter: _____

☐ 2. Run the engine until it reaches operating temperature.

☐ 3. Raise the vehicle on a lift or raise it with a jack and secure it on jack stands. The vehicle should be level when raised to allow all of the oil to drain from the pan.

> **Warning**
>
> ⚠ The vehicle must be raised and supported in a safe manner. Always use approved lifts or jacks and jack stands. See **Figure 17-1**.

☐ 4. Place the oil drain pan under the engine oil pan. **Figure 17-2** shows a typical oil drain pan.

☐ 5. Remove the oil drain plug. A few engines have two drain plugs.

> **Warning**
>
> ⚠ Avoid contact with hot oil. You could be severely burned.

Figure 17-1. When raising a vehicle, make sure the lift pads are positioned at recommended lift points.

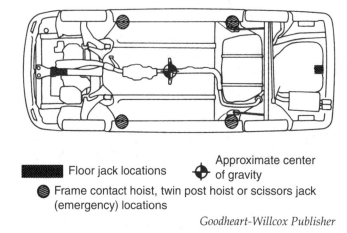

■ Floor jack locations

⊕ Approximate center of gravity

● Frame contact hoist, twin post hoist or scissors jack (emergency) locations

Goodheart-Willcox Publisher

Figure 17-2. The oil pan should be large enough to fit under both the oil drain and the oil filter.

Oil drain plug

Oil drain pan

Goodheart-Willcox Publisher

Job 17—Change Oil and Filter (continued)

☐ 6. Inspect the drain plug. The seal should be undamaged to prevent leaks. Check the drain plug's threads for damage. If the drain plug is damaged, replace it.

Are the drain plug threads and seal OK? Yes ___ No ___

☐ 7. Loosen the oil filter using a filter wrench and remove the filter from the engine. If necessary reposition the oil drain pan under the filter or use a second drain pan.

☐ 8. Wipe off the oil filter mounting base and check that the old filter seal is not stuck on the base.

☐ 9. Check the new filter to ensure that it is the correct replacement.

☐ 10. Fill the new filter with the correct grade of motor oil. If the oil filter is mounted with the opening down, skip this step.

☐ 11. Smear a thin film of clean engine oil on to the new oil filter's rubber seal, as shown in **Figure 17-3**.

☐ 12. Screw on the new oil filter and hand tighten it.

☐ 13. Turn the filter an additional 1/2 to 3/4 turn.

☐ 14. Install and tighten the oil drain plug.

> **Note**
>
> Some vehicles have a crush washer on the oil drain plug that should be replaced any time the oil drain plug is removed.

☐ 15. Remove the oil filler cap from the engine.

Figure 17-3. Use clean oil to lightly lubricate the filter seal.

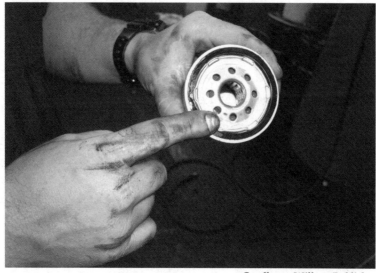

Goodheart-Willcox Publisher

Caution

⚠️ Before performing any work under the hood of a vehicle, always place covers over the fenders to prevent scratches and dings.

☐ 16. Open the first oil container and pour the oil into the filler opening in the engine. Carefully monitor the filler opening to ensure that oil does not spill out.

☐ 17. Repeat step 16 until the engine is filled to the proper level.

☐ 18. Replace the filler cap and wipe any spilled oil from the engine.

☐ 19. Start the engine and watch the oil pressure light or gauge. The light should go out or the gauge should begin to register within 10 to 20 seconds. If it does not, stop the engine immediately and locate the problem.

☐ 20. Raise the vehicle and check for leaks from the oil filter and drain plug.

Are there any leaks? Yes ___ No ___

If you found leaks, what did you do to correct them?_____

_____

_____

_____

☐ 21. Lower the vehicle and stop the engine.

☐ 22. Allow the engine to sit for several minutes.

☐ 23. Recheck the oil level.

Is the level correct? Yes ___ No ___

If the level is low, add oil until the dipstick reads full.

Note

📄 Before returning a vehicle to a customer, always inspect the work area and passenger compartment to ensure that all tools, parts, and debris related to the service have been picked up. Some companies may want the disposable floor mats and protective covers left in place until the customer takes possession of the vehicle. Always prepare the vehicle in accordance with your company or school's policy.

Job Wrap Up

☐ 1. Return all tools and equipment to storage.

☐ 2. Clean the work area.

☐ 3. Did you encounter any problems during this procedure? Yes ___ No ___

If Yes, describe the problems: _____

_____

_____

What did you do to correct the problems?_____

_____

_____

☐ 4. Have your instructor check your work and sign this job sheet.

Name_____ Date _____

Instructor_____ Period _____

Performance Evaluation—Instructor Use Only

Did the student complete the job in the time allotted? Yes ___ No ___

If No, which steps were not completed?_____

How would you rate this student's overall performance on this job?____

5–Excellent, 4–Good, 3–Satisfactory, 2–Unsatisfactory, 1–Poor

Comments: _____

_____

_____

INSTRUCTOR'S SIGNATURE _____

Notes

Job

18

Perform General Automatic Transmission and Transaxle Service Tasks

After completing this job, you will determine the type of transmission or transaxle installed in the selected vehicle. You will also be able to check fluid level, determine the correct fluid to be added to the unit, and add fluid as needed. In addition, you will able to check for sources of transmission or transaxle fluid leaks.

Instructions

As you read the job instructions, answer the questions and perform the tasks. Print your answers neatly and use complete sentences. Consult the proper service literature and ask your instructor for help as needed.

> ### Warning
> Before performing this job, review all pertinent safety information in the text and discuss safety procedures with your instructor.

Procedures

☐ 1. Obtain a vehicle to be used in this job. Your instructor may direct you to perform this job on a shop vehicle.

☐ 2. Determine the following vehicle information:

Manufacturer:_____

Model: _____

Model year: _____

☐ 3. Once the vehicle make and model have been established, identify the type of transmission/transaxle being serviced.

How was the type of transmission/transaxle determined?

☐ Service information.

☐ Pan shape.

☐ Other (explain): _____

Is the unit a rear-wheel drive transmission? Yes ___ No ___

Is the unit a transaxle? Yes ___ No ___

Is the unit a CVT? Yes ___ No ___

Is the unit a hybrid vehicle transmission? Yes ___ No ___

☐ 4. Briefly describe the operational characteristics of the transmission or transaxle being serviced.

_____

_____

_____

_____

_____

_____

☐ 5. Consult the vehicle service history (if available):

Has the transmission or transaxle been serviced in the past? Yes ___ No ___

If Yes, state briefly what was done: _____

_____

☐ 6. Determine the fluid type.

> **Note**
>
> Modern transmissions and transaxles use many different types of transmission fluids. Proper fluid type is extremely important to transmission/transaxle performance and durability. Adding the wrong fluid can damage internal components.

Locate a source of fluid information and place a check mark in the appropriate box:

☐ Listed in owner's manual.

☐ Stamped on dipstick.

☐ Listed in service information.

Type of service information: _____

☐ Listed on website.

Type of website: _____

> **Note**
>
> Check with your instructor to determine whether the website is reliable.

☐ Other (explain): _____

_____

Type of fluid needed for this job: _____

Indicate where the proper type of fluid can be obtained.

☐ Auto parts store.

☐ Vehicle dealer.

☐ Lubricant outlet.

☐ Other (explain): _____

☐ 7. Start the engine and allow it to reach operating temperature. Ensure that the transmission fluid temperature is also at operating temperature. If necessary, attach a scan tool to monitor transmission/transaxle fluid temperature.

Job 18—Perform General Automatic Transmission and Transaxle Service Tasks (continued)

> **Note**
>
> To properly check the fluid level, the transmission fluid must reach normal operating temperature, usually about 180°F (82°C). It may be necessary to drive the vehicle several miles to reach the proper temperature.

☐ 8. Ensure that the vehicle is parked on a level surface. If the vehicle must be raised to check the fluid, make sure that it is raised evenly. Do not raise one side of the vehicle to check as this will cause inaccurate readings.

☐ 9. Place your foot on the brake pedal and apply the parking brake.

☐ 10. Shift the transmission/transaxle through all ranges, and then place it in park. Do not turn off the engine.

☐ 11. Check the fluid level. Use one of the following methods, depending on transmission or transaxle design. Consult the proper service information for exact instructions, and check the procedure used.

    ☐ **Transmission/transaxle with dipstick.**

    • Remove the dipstick and note the fluid level: Normal ___ High ___ Low ___

    ☐ **Transmission/transaxle with fill plug on top of case.**

    • Remove the fill plug and insert the dipstick tool until it bottoms on the oil pan.

    • Remove tool and note the fluid level: Normal ___ High ___ Low ___

    ☐ **Transmission/transaxle with fill plug on side of case.**

    • Remove the fill plug and, depending on the factory procedure, note whether a slight amount of fluid drips out of the fill hole. Yes ___ No ___

    or

    • The fluid just wets the bottom of threads. Yes ___ No ___

    ☐ **Fill plug in oil pan.** See **Figure 18-1.**

    • Remove plug and note whether a slight amount of fluid drips out of the fill hole. Yes ___ No ___

Figure 18-1. Note the differences between the fill and drain plugs on this transmission pan. For checking the oil level, be sure not to loosen the drain plug, as this will allow all fluid to drain from the pan.

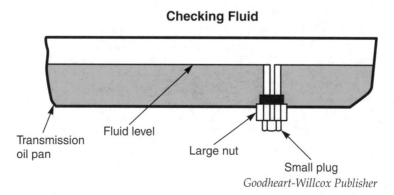

Checking Fluid

Transmission oil pan

Fluid level

Large nut

Small plug

Goodheart-Willcox Publisher

☐ 12. Check fluid condition by observing dipstick or, if a dipstick is not used, by obtaining a small sample of the fluid. Indicate the fluid condition by placing checkmarks in the appropriate boxes:

    ☐ Normal color and smell.

    ☐ Overheated (dark color).

    ☐ Burned smell.

    ☐ Debris in fluid.

    ☐ Water or coolant in fluid (strawberry milkshake look).

    ☐ Other (explain): _____

Does fluid level and condition indicate a problem? Yes ___ No ___

If Yes, could this be the cause of a transmission/transaxle problem? Yes ___ No ___

☐ 13. If the fluid is low, check for leaks.

Look for obvious leaks at the case, pan, and wherever seals or gaskets are used.

Were any leaks found? Yes ___ No ___

If Yes, where? _____

_____

Use other methods as necessary to locate hard-to-find leaks:

    ☐ Powder.

    ☐ Black light.

    ☐ Other (describe): _____

Were any leaks found? Yes ___ No ___

If Yes, describe the location: _____

_____

☐ 14. If the fluid level is low, add fluid as needed. Indicate which filling procedure is used.

    ☐ If the transmission/transaxle has a dipstick or uses a dipstick tool, use a funnel to add fluid through the filler tube, frequently rechecking the level as fluid is added.

    ☐ If the unit does not have a dipstick, use a suction gun to add fluid. Draw fluid from the container and add it through the filler hole. If a special dipstick tool is used, add fluid and recheck with the tool. In most transmission/transaxles without dipsticks, the fluid level is correct when a small amount of fluid drips from the opening. If no fluid exits, add more fluid. If fluid exits in a steady stream after addition, wait until flow is reduced to slight dripping before reinstalling the filler plug.

☐ 15. Road test the vehicle.

Job 18—Perform General Automatic Transmission and Transaxle Service Tasks (continued)

Job Wrap Up

☐ 1. Return all tools and equipment to storage.

☐ 2. Clean the work area.

☐ 3. Did you encounter any problems during this procedure? Yes ___ No ___

   If Yes, describe the problems: _____

   _____

   _____

   What did you do to correct the problems?_____

   _____

   _____

☐ 4. Have your instructor check your work and sign this job sheet.

Performance Evaluation—Instructor Use Only

Did the student complete the job in the time allotted? Yes ___ No ___

If No, which steps were not completed?_____

How would you rate this student's overall performance on this job?_____

5–Excellent, 4–Good, 3–Satisfactory, 2–Unsatisfactory, 1–Poor

Comments: _____

_____

_____

INSTRUCTOR'S SIGNATURE _____

Notes

Job

19

Adjust Transmission Linkage and Neutral Safety Switch/Range Switch

After completing this job, you will be able to adjust transmission linkages and neutral safety and range switches.

Instructions

As you read the job instructions, answer the questions and perform the tasks. Print your answers neatly and use complete sentences. Consult the proper service literature and ask your instructor for help as needed.

> ### Warning
> ⚠ Before performing this job, review all pertinent safety information in the text and discuss safety procedures with your instructor.

Procedures

> ### Note
> 📄 There are many variations in automatic transmission design. The following procedure is to be used as a general guide only. Always consult the manufacturer's service manual for exact linkage and switch adjustment procedures and specifications.

 1. Obtain a vehicle to be used in this job. Your instructor may direct you to perform this job on a shop vehicle.

☐ 2. Gather the tools needed to perform the following job.

Adjust Manual Shift Linkage

 1. Make sure the transmission shift selector lever is in *Park* or another position as specified by the manufacturer.

☐ 2. Raise the vehicle in a safe manner.

> **Note**
>
> The shift selector indicator adjuster is located under the hood on some transaxle-equipped vehicles. On other vehicles, the shift selector indicator adjusters are located under the vehicle instrument panel or in the center console. It is unnecessary to raise these vehicles, **Figure 19-1**.

☐ 3. Locate the adjuster lock button or lock nut.

Where is the adjuster locking device located? _____

What type of locking device is used? _____

☐ 4. Pull the lock button up or loosen the lock nut.

☐ 5. Use the outer manual lever on the transmission case to place the transmission or transaxle in the same gear as the shift selector lever.

☐ 6. Push the lock button down or tighten the adjuster lock nut.

☐ 7. Recheck the shift selector lever operation and indicator position.

☐ 8. Lower the vehicle and road test it, carefully observing transmission operation.

Adjust Neutral Safety Switch/Mechanically Operated Range Switch

☐ 1. Place the transmission in *Neutral*, apply the parking brake, and block the drive wheels.

☐ 2. Determine the neutral safety switch/range switch problem:

Does the starter crank with the shift selector in *Park* and *Neutral*? Yes ___ No ___

Does the starter crank with the shift selector in any gear other than *Park* and *Neutral*? Yes ___ No ___

☐ 3. Locate the neutral safety switch/range switch on the vehicle. The switch could be installed on the steering column, linkage, or at the transmission manual shaft.

☐ 4. Loosen the switch fasteners.

Figure 19-1. This manual linkage adjuster is located near the air cleaner in the engine compartment. Other linkage adjusters can only be reached by raising the vehicle.

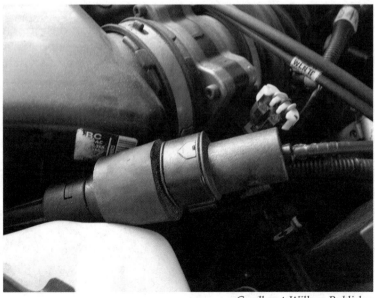

Goodheart-Willcox Publisher

Job 19—Adjust Transmission Linkage and Neutral Safety Switch/ Range Switch (continued)

☐ 5. Move the switch in small amounts until the starter cranks in *Park* and *Neutral* and does not crank in any other gear.

☐ 6. Tighten the switch fasteners and recheck operation.

Job Wrap Up

☐ 1. Return all tools and equipment to storage.

☐ 2. Clean the work area.

☐ 3. Did you encounter any problems during this procedure? Yes ___ No ___

If Yes, describe the problems: _____

_____

_____

What did you do to correct the problems?_____

_____

_____

☐ 4. Have your instructor check your work and sign this job sheet.

Performance Evaluation—Instructor Use Only

Did the student complete the job in the time allotted? Yes ___ No ___

If No, which steps were not completed?_____

How would you rate this student's overall performance on this job?_____

5–Excellent, 4–Good, 3–Satisfactory, 2–Unsatisfactory, 1–Poor

Comments: _____

_____

_____

INSTRUCTOR'S SIGNATURE _____

Notes

Job

Inspect Powertrain Mounts

20

After completing this job, you will be able to check powertrain mounts on front-wheel and rear-wheel drive vehicles.

Instructions

As you read the job instructions, answer the questions and perform the tasks. Print your answers neatly and use complete sentences. Consult the proper service literature and ask your instructor for help as needed.

> **Warning**
>
> ⚠ Before performing this job, review all pertinent safety information in the text and discuss safety procedures with your instructor.

Procedures

☐ 1. Obtain a vehicle to be used in this job. Your instructor may direct you to perform this job on a shop vehicle.

☐ 2. Gather the tools needed to perform the following job.

Preliminary Check

☐ 1. Open the hood of the vehicle.

☐ 2. Apply the parking brake.

☐ 3. Have an assistant start the engine and tightly press on the brake pedal while placing the engine in drive.

☐ 4. Have the assistant slightly open the throttle.

> **Note**
>
> If the engine rises more than 1″ (25.4 mm) in the following steps, a motor mount may be broken or soft. If this occurs, make a visual inspection of the mounts using the procedure presented later in this job.

5. Observe the engine as the throttle is opened with the brakes applied.

   Did the engine move excessively? Yes ___ No ___

   If Yes, perform a visual inspection of the motor mounts.

6. Continue to observe the engine as you have your assistant place the transmission in reverse and slightly open the throttle while keeping the brakes engaged.

   Did the engine move excessively? Yes ___ No ___

   If Yes, perform a visual inspection of the motor mounts.

Visual Inspection

1. Make sure that there is sufficient illumination to see the mount. If necessary, have an assistant hold a light in position to illuminate the mount. Mount locations vary. **Figure 20-1** and **Figure 20-2** show the general location of motor and drive train mounts on front-wheel and rear-wheel drive vehicles.

2. Carefully pry on the engine to raise it in the area of a solid mount. Check for cracked rubber as you move the mount.

   Did you find any cracked rubber in the mount? Yes ___ No ___

   If Yes, replace the mount using the procedures outlined in Job 21.

3. Check fluid-filled mounts for exterior oil leakage.

   Did you detect any oil leakage? Yes ___ No ___

   If Yes, replace the mount using the procedures outlined in Job 21.

4. Check the mounts for loose fasteners.

   Did you find any loose fasteners? Yes ___ No ___

   If Yes, tighten the fasteners to the proper torque.

Figure 20-1. Location of mounts on a rear-wheel drive vehicle. Most rear-wheel drive vehicles will have mounts in these general locations.

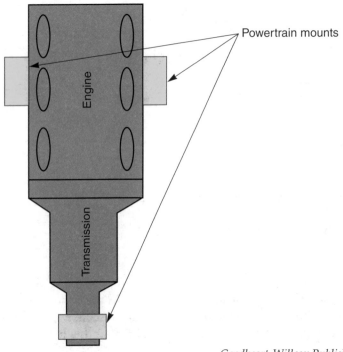

Goodheart-Willcox Publisher

Job 20—Inspect Powertrain Mounts (continued)

Figure 20-2. Location of mounts on a front-wheel drive vehicle. Mount locations on front-wheel drive vehicles vary between makers, and even between engines from the same maker. Always check the service literature for the exact mount locations.

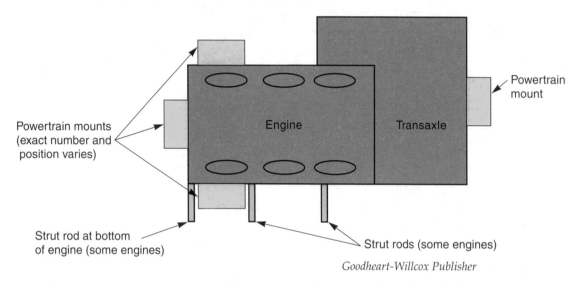

Powertrain mount

Powertrain mounts (exact number and position varies)

Engine

Transaxle

Strut rod at bottom of engine (some engines)

Strut rods (some engines)

Goodheart-Willcox Publisher

Job Wrap Up

☐ 1. Return all tools and equipment to storage.

☐ 2. Clean the work area.

☐ 3. Did you encounter any problems during this procedure? Yes ___ No ___
If Yes, describe the problems: _____

_____

What did you do to correct the problems?_____

_____

☐ 4. Have your instructor check your work and sign this job sheet.

Performance Evaluation—Instructor Use Only

Did the student complete the job in the time allotted? Yes ___ No ___
If No, which steps were not completed?_____
How would you rate this student's overall performance on this job?____
5–Excellent, 4–Good, 3–Satisfactory, 2–Unsatisfactory, 1–Poor
Comments: _____

_____

INSTRUCTOR'S SIGNATURE_____

Notes

Job 21

Replace and Align Powertrain Mounts

After completing this job, you will be able to replace and align powertrain mounts on front-wheel drive and rear-wheel drive vehicles.

Instructions

As you read the job instructions, answer the questions and perform the tasks. Print your answers neatly and use complete sentences. Consult the proper service literature and ask your instructor for help as needed.

> **Warning**
>
> ⚠ Before performing this job, review all pertinent safety information in the text and discuss safety procedures with your instructor.

Procedures

☐ 1. Obtain a vehicle to be used in this job. Your instructor may direct you to perform this job on a shop vehicle.

☐ 2. Gather the tools needed to perform the following job.

Replace Powertrain Mounts

☐ 1. Raise the vehicle as necessary to gain access to the powertrain mount to be replaced.

> **Warning**
>
> ⚠ The vehicle must be raised and supported in a safe manner. Always use approved lifts or jacks and jack stands.

☐ 2. Place a jack stand under the engine or transmission/transaxle near the powertrain mount to be replaced.

> **Caution**
>
> Place the jack stand so that it will not damage the underside of the engine or transmission/transaxle. If necessary place a wood block or other protective device on the jack stand.

> **Note**
>
> On some front-wheel drive vehicles, an engine-lifting device can be used to raise the engine and remove pressure on the mounts.

- [ ] 3. Lower the vehicle just enough to remove engine and drive train weight from the mount to be replaced.
- [ ] 4. Lightly shake the vehicle to ensure that the jack stand is solidly placed.
- [ ] 5. Remove the fasteners holding the mount to the engine and vehicle.
- [ ] 6. Compare the old and new mounts to ensure that the new mount is correct.
- [ ] 7. Place the new mount in position and install the fasteners loosely.
- [ ] 8. Once all fasteners are in place, tighten them to the proper torque.
- [ ] 9. Raise the vehicle and remove the jack stand.

> **Note**
>
> If necessary, align the new powertrain mount using the following procedure.

Adjust Powertrain Mounts on Rear-Wheel Drive Vehicles

> **Note**
>
> Many rear-wheel drive powertrain mounts are not adjustable. Some rear mounts can be shimmed to correct drive shaft angle problems.

- [ ] 1. Loosen the mounting bolts.
- [ ] 2. Move the tailshaft until it is centered in the drive shaft tunnel.
- [ ] 3. Retighten the mounting bolts.

Adjust Powertrain Mounts on Front-Wheel Drive Vehicles

- [ ] 1. Observe the marks made by the cradle mounting bolts and washers. If the original marks made by the washers are not completely covered, the cradle is incorrectly positioned.

    Is the cradle properly positioned? Yes ___ No ___

> **Note**
>
> If the cradle is correctly positioned, skip steps 2 through 4.

Job 21—Replace and Align Powertrain Mounts (continued)

☐ 2. Loosen the cradle fasteners.

☐ 3. Move the cradle to its original position.

☐ 4. Tighten the cradle fasteners.

☐ 5. Measure the mount adjustment. On many vehicles mount adjustment is checked by measuring the length of the CV axle on the same side as the adjustable mount. If the length of the CV axle is correct, the mount is properly adjusted. On other vehicles the difference between the mount and a stationary part of the vehicle frame must be measured. Sometimes the only procedure is to loosen the fasteners and allow the mount to assume its normal unloaded position.

Briefly describe the mount adjustment method: _____

_____

_____

Is the mount adjustment correct? Yes ___ No ___.

If Yes, skip steps 6 through 10, if your instructor approves.

☐ 6. Remove the load on the mount by raising the engine and transaxle assembly with a floor jack.

> Caution
>
> ⚠ Raise the assembly only enough to unload the mount. Be careful not to damage the oil pan.

☐ 7. Loosen the adjustable mount fasteners.

☐ 8. Reposition the mount as needed.

☐ 9. Measure the mount using the same method used in step 5.

Is the mount adjustment correct? Yes ___ No ___

If No, repeat steps 8 and 9.

☐ 10. Tighten the mount fasteners.

What is the proper fastener torque? _____

☐ 11. Remove the jack from under the engine and transaxle.

Job Wrap Up

☐ 1. Return all tools and equipment to storage.

☐ 2. Clean the work area.

3. Did you encounter any problems during this procedure? Yes ___ No ___
   If Yes, describe the problems: _____
   _____

   What did you do to correct the problems? _____
   _____
   _____

4. Have your instructor check your work and sign this job sheet.

Performance Evaluation—Instructor Use Only

Did the student complete the job in the time allotted? Yes ___ No ___
If No, which steps were not completed? _____
How would you rate this student's overall performance on this job? ____
5–Excellent, 4–Good, 3–Satisfactory, 2–Unsatisfactory, 1–Poor
Comments: _____
_____

INSTRUCTOR'S SIGNATURE _____

Job 22

Change Transmission/ Transaxle Oil and Filter

After completing this job, you will be able to change the oil and filter on an automatic transmission or transaxle.

Instructions

As you read the job instructions, answer the questions and perform the tasks. Print your answers neatly and use complete sentences. Consult the proper service literature and ask your instructor for help as needed.

> **Warning**
>
> ⚠ Before performing this job, review all pertinent safety information in the text and discuss safety procedures with your instructor.

Procedures

☐ 1. Obtain a vehicle to be used in this job. Your instructor may direct you to perform this job on a shop vehicle.

☐ 2. Gather the tools needed to perform the following job.

Preliminary Checks

☐ 1. Locate the transmission/transaxle dipstick and check the fluid level as specified by the vehicle manufacturer.

> **Note**
>
> Some newer vehicles do not have a dipstick. Check the owner's manual or service literature for checking procedures. Some vehicles without a dipstick require the use of a scan tool to check oil level. Other vehicles are checked by noting whether the fluid wets the bottom of the filler plug's opening threads.

☐ 2. Check the fluid condition by examining the fluid on the dipstick, if used.

☐ 3. Add fluid if needed. Transmissions without a dipstick are usually refilled through a filler plug.

> **Caution**
>
> ⬙ Be sure to add the transmission fluid specified by the vehicle manufacturer.

☐ 4. Road test the vehicle and determine whether a problem is evident at this point.

☐ 5. Based on the results of the road test, determine if the transmission/transaxle needs further checking or if a fluid and filter change is all that is required.

Change Transmission/Transaxle Oil and Filter

☐ 1. Raise the vehicle.

> **Warning**
>
> ⚠ The vehicle must be raised and supported in a safe manner. Always use approved lifts or jacks and jack stands.

☐ 2. Position a drain pan at the rear of the transmission/transaxle oil pan.

☐ 3. Remove all but the front four transmission/transaxle oil pan attaching screws.

☐ 4. Pry on the pan to loosen the gasket and allow the pan to drop at the rear.

> **Warning**
>
> ⚠ Transmission fluid may begin to drain at this point. If the fluid is hot, be careful to avoid contacting it because it may cause burns.

☐ 5. Loosen the front four screws to allow the pan to drop further and the fluid to drain.

☐ 6. When the fluid stops draining, remove the four front screws and remove the pan.

☐ 7. Check the bottom of the pan for excessive amounts of sludge or metal, **Figure 22-1**. Inspect the contents of the pan, and place a check mark next to each type of problem found:

    ☐ Sludge buildup greater than 1/4" (6.4 mm).

    ☐ Varnish buildup (baked on fluid resembling household varnish).

    ☐ Many metal particles.

> **Note**
>
> 🗐 Consult your instructor if excessive sludge, varnish, or metal is found. The transmission may require further repair.

☐ 8. Remove the old transmission oil filter. Some filters are held in place with clips, while others are attached with threaded fasteners.

Job 22—Change Transmission/Transaxle Oil and Filter (continued)

Figure 22-1. After removing the oil pan, check for sludge, varnish, or metal particles.

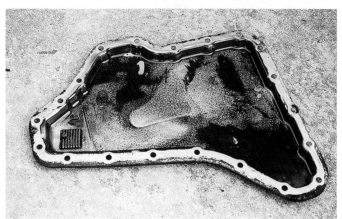

Goodheart-Willcox Publisher

> **Note**
>
> Allow the old transmission fluid to drain from the valve body before installing the new filter. This prevents the old contaminated fluid from soaking the new filter.

☐ 9. If the torque converter has drain plugs, remove them and allow fluid to drain from the converter into the drip pan.

☐ 10. Install the new transmission oil filter in the correct position.

☐ 11. Reinstall the torque converter drain plugs, if applicable.

☐ 12. Check the oil pan for warping or dents. Straighten or replace the pan as needed.

☐ 13. Scrape all old gasket material from the transmission or transaxle oil pan and the case.

> **Note**
>
> Some new vehicles have a reusable gasket that does not have to be replaced. Check the service literature to determine whether your unit has this type of gasket.

☐ 14. Install a new gasket on the transmission oil pan, using a light coat of gasket sealer on the pan side of the gasket.

☐ 15. Correctly position the oil pan on the transmission case.

☐ 16. Install the transmission oil pan attaching fasteners and torque them to specifications. If the pan has a tightening sequence, follow it, otherwise start at the middle of each side of the pan and work toward the corners.

☐ 17. Lower the vehicle.

☐ 18. Refill the transmission with the proper type of fluid, being careful not to overfill. What type of fluid did you use? _____

> **Note**
>
> Transmissions or transaxles without dipsticks may require special filling procedures. Some units have a fluid level sensor in the case, and fluid level can only be read with a scan tool. On other transmissions or transaxles, the fluid level is read by noting whether the fluid wets the bottom threads of the fill plug, similar to the checking procedure for a manual transmission or rear axle. Check the manufacturer's service literature for exact procedures.

☐ 19. Start the vehicle and shift through all gear positions.

☐ 20. Recheck the fluid level according to the manufacturer's instructions.

☐ 21. Check for fluid leaks from the transmission oil pan.

☐ 22. Road test the vehicle, carefully observing transmission operation.

☐ 23. Recheck the fluid level and add fluid if necessary.

☐ 24. Raise the vehicle and inspect the transmission or transaxle for leaks.

> **Note**
>
> See Job 25 for detailed procedures for the different methods of leak detection. The procedures in that job can be used to check automatic transmissions and transaxles for leaks.

Job Wrap Up

☐ 1. Return all tools and equipment to storage.

☐ 2. Clean the work area.

☐ 3. Did you encounter any problems during this procedure? Yes ___ No ___

If Yes, describe the problems: _____

_____

_____

What did you do to correct the problems?_____

_____

_____

☐ 4. Have your instructor check your work and sign this job sheet.

Performance Evaluation—Instructor Use Only

Did the student complete the job in the time allotted? Yes ___ No ___

If No, which steps were not completed?_____

How would you rate this student's overall performance on this job?_____

5–Excellent, 4–Good, 3–Satisfactory, 2–Unsatisfactory, 1–Poor

Comments: _____

_____

_____

INSTRUCTOR'S SIGNATURE _____

After completing this job, you will be able to identify operating principles and major parts of CVT and dual clutch transmissions and transaxles, and hybrid vehicle drive trains.

Instructions

Read each question carefully before answering. Print your answers neatly and use complete sentences. Consult the proper service literature and ask your instructor for help as needed.

Questions

Continuously Variable Transmission (CVT)

_____ 1. A basic CVT has two pulleys and one segmented _____.

_____ 2. A CVT has a(n) _____ number of possible gear ratios.

_____ 3. True or False? CVTs are usually installed on larger vehicles with more powerful engines.

_____ 4. A CVT has at least one planetary gearset to obtain _____ gear.

_____ 5. True or False? Any type of modern transmission fluid can be used to refill a CVT.

_____ 6. CVT pulleys are operated by _____.
   A. electric solenoids
   B. electric motors
   C. hydraulic pressure
   D. All of the above.

Dual Clutch Transmission

_____ 7. Technician A says that all odd numbered gears of a dual clutch transmission are controlled by one of the clutches. Technician B says that all even numbered gears of a dual clutch transmission are controlled by one of the clutches. Who is right?
   A. A only.
   B. B only.
   C. Both A and B.
   D. Neither A nor B.

_____ 8. True or False? Dual clutch transmissions are manufactured in manual and automatic forms.

_____ 9. True or False? In reverse on a dual clutch transmission, both clutches are applied.

_____ 10. True or False? All dual clutch transmissions use at least one planetary gearset.

_____ 11. Dual clutch transmission gears are selected by internal _____.

_____ 12. Dual clutch transmissions may use wet or dry _____, depending on make.

Hybrid Drive Trains

_____ 13. True or False? A hybrid vehicle drive train may use planetary gearsets.

_____ 14. True or False? The parts of a hybrid drive train can include more than one motor, as well as an internal combustion engine, both connected by the drive train components.

_____ 15. On some hybrids, the engine can be off or on independently of _____ movement.

_____ 16. On almost all hybrids, the engine is turned off when the vehicle is _____.

_____ 17. Which of the following is a feature of hybrid vehicle regenerative braking?
   A. Slows the vehicle.
   B. Makes electricity.
   C. Charges the battery.
   D. All of the above.

Matching

Match the type of hybrid with its description

_____ 18. There is no connection between the engine and the drive wheels.

_____ 19. The engine can drive the vehicle by itself.

_____ 20. Motor or engine can drive vehicle by itself.

A. Series hybrid

B. Series-parallel hybrid

C. Parallel hybrid

Job 23—Describe Operating Principles of Nontraditional Transmissions/Transaxles (continued)

Job Wrap Up

☐ 1. Return all service literature to storage.

☐ 2. Have your instructor check your work and sign this job sheet.

Performance Evaluation—Instructor Use Only

Did the student complete the job in the time allotted? Yes ___ No ___

If No, which steps were not completed?_____

How would you rate this student's overall performance on this job?____

5–Excellent, 4–Good, 3–Satisfactory, 2–Unsatisfactory, 1–Poor

Comments: _____

_____

_____

INSTRUCTOR'S SIGNATURE _____

Notes

Job

Check Drive Train Unit Fluid Level

24

After completing this job, you will be able to check the fluid level in various drive train components. You will also be able to drain and refill drive train components.

Instructions

As you read the job instructions, answer the questions and perform the tasks. Print your answers neatly and use complete sentences. Consult the proper service literature and ask your instructor for help as needed.

> **Warning**
> Before performing this job, review all pertinent safety information in the text and discuss safety procedures with your instructor.

Procedures

> **Note**
> This job applies to all drive train units except automatic transmissions and transaxles.

☐ 1. Obtain a vehicle to be used in this job. Your instructor may direct you to perform this job on a shop vehicle or engine.

☐ 2. Gather the tools needed to perform the following job.

☐ 3. Obtain the correct type of replacement fluid.

☐ 4. Safely raise vehicle as necessary.

☐ 5. Remove filler plug. See **Figures 24-1** for typical filler plug locations.

☐ 6. Check fluid level. Fluid level is satisfactory if a small amount of fluid drips from the filler plug opening, or if the bottom threads of the opening are wet with oil.

Figure 24-1. Filler and drain plug locations vary from unit to unit. A—Typical transmission filler plug. Note the location high on the transmission case. B—Rear axle filler plug. This rear axle also has a drain plug, located at the lower right side of the housing. The vent is visible at the upper right side of the housing.

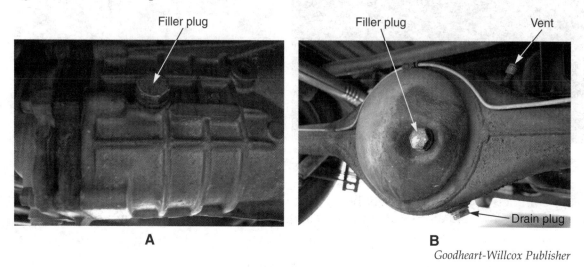

A   B

Goodheart-Willcox Publisher

> **Note**
>
> An excessively high fluid level, especially when combined with milky looking fluid, indicates that water has entered the unit, usually as a result of driving through high water. This fluid and water mix must be removed from the unit as soon as possible. Consult your instructor as to what further steps should be taken.

- [ ] 7. If necessary, add fluid as explained in the next section of this job.
- [ ] 8. Reinstall filler plug.
- [ ] 9. Inspect the unit for the following.
  - Fluid leaks: No ___ Yes ___

  If Yes, location: _____
  - Vent condition: Good ___ Damaged ___ Missing ___
  - Housing condition: Good ___ Damaged ___

  Describe any damage found: _____

  _____

  If any problems are found, discuss repair options with your instructor.
- [ ] 10. Lower the vehicle
- [ ] 11. Start the engine and check drive train unit operation

Drain and Refill Drive Train Unit

- [ ] 1. Obtain a vehicle to be used in this job.
- [ ] 2. Obtain the correct type of replacement fluid.
- [ ] 3. Safely raise vehicle as necessary.
- [ ] 4. Place drain pan under unit to be serviced.

Job 24—Check Drive Train Unit Fluid Level (continued)

☐ 5. Remove drain plug. Sometimes a housing or pan cover bolt is the drain plug. Allow fluid to drain into pan until all fluid is removed.

   If the unit does not have a drain plug, place the suction gun hose through filler plug and use the suction gun to draw fluid from unit.

☐ 6. Install the drain plug if applicable. Use sealer if recommended by the manufacturer.

☐ 7. Remove the filler plug.

☐ 8. Clean the suction gun as necessary to remove old fluid, and then use the suction gun to install new fluid through the filler plug opening.

☐ 9. Check that fluid level is correct.

☐ 10. Replace the filler plug.

☐ 11. Lower the vehicle

☐ 12. Start the engine and check drive train unit operation

Job Wrap Up

☐ 1. Return all tools and equipment to storage.

☐ 2. Clean the work area.

☐ 3. Did you encounter any problems during this procedure? Yes ___ No ___

   If Yes, describe the problems: _____

   _____

   What did you do to correct the problems?_____

   _____

☐ 4. Have your instructor check your work and sign this job sheet.

Performance Evaluation—Instructor Use Only

Did the student complete the job in the time allotted? Yes ___ No ___
If No, which steps were not completed?_____
How would you rate this student's overall performance on this job?_____
5–Excellent, 4–Good, 3–Satisfactory, 2–Unsatisfactory, 1–Poor
Comments: _____

_____

INSTRUCTOR'S SIGNATURE _____

Notes

Job

Diagnose Drive Train Component Leakage

25

After completing this job, you will be able to locate and diagnose leaks in drive train components.

Instructions

As you read the job instructions, answer the questions and perform the tasks. Print your answers neatly and use complete sentences. Consult the proper service literature and ask your instructor for help as needed.

> **Warning**
> ⚠ Before performing this job, review all pertinent safety information in the text and discuss safety procedures with your instructor.

Procedures

☐ 1. Obtain a vehicle to be used in this job. Your instructor may direct you to perform this job on a shop vehicle.

☐ 2. Gather the tools needed to perform the following job

Visually Check for Leakage

 1. If possible, determine from the owner what unit is leaking.

> **Note**
> 📄 Usually the owner will not know what is leaking and will only be aware of oil spots on the pavement, oil on the underside of vehicle, or a performance problem related to a low oil level.

 2. Raise the vehicle.

> ### Warning
> ⚠ The vehicle must be raised and supported in a safe manner. Always use approved lifts or jacks and jack stands.

☐ 3. Obtain a drop light or other source of illumination.

☐ 4. Observe the underside of the vehicle for evidence of oil or grease. Slight seepage is normal.

Is excessive oil or grease observed? Yes ___ No ___

If Yes, where does the oil/grease appear to be coming from? _____

_____

> ### Note
> 📄 Airflow under the vehicle will blow leaking oil backward. The leak may be some distance forward from where the oil appears.

Use the Powder Method to Check for Leakage

☐ 1. Refill the unit to be checked with the proper lubricant. This step applies to drive train parts with a reservoir for liquid lubricant, such as the transmission, transaxle, transfer case, and rear axle assembly.

☐ 2. Thoroughly clean the area around the suspected leak.

☐ 3. Apply talcum powder to the area around the suspected leak.

☐ 4. Lower the vehicle from the lift and operate the vehicle for several miles, or carefully run it on the lift for 10–15 minutes.

☐ 5. Raise the vehicle, if necessary, and check the area around the suspected leak.

Does the powder show streaks of lubricant? Yes ___ No ___

If Yes, where does the lubricant appear to be coming from?_____

_____

If No, repeat this procedure on another suspected component, or attempt to locate the leak using the black light method.

Use the Black Light Method to Check for Leakage

☐ 1. Refill the unit to be checked with the proper lubricant, and add fluorescent dye to the unit through the dipstick or filler plug, being careful not to spill dye on the outside of the case.

☐ 2. Thoroughly clean the area around the suspected leak.

☐ 3. Lower the vehicle from the lift and operate the vehicle for several miles, or carefully run it on the lift for 10–15 minutes.

☐ 4. Raise the vehicle, if necessary.

Job 25—Diagnose Drive Train Component Leakage (continued)

☐ 5. Turn on the black light and direct it toward the area around the suspected leak. See **Figure 25-1**.

Does the black light show the presence of dye? Yes ___ No ___

If Yes, where does the dye and lubricant appear to be coming from? _____

_____

If No, repeat this procedure on another suspected component, or attempt to locate the leak using another detection method.

Repair the Leak

☐ 1. Consult your instructor about the steps to take to correct the leak. Steps may include some of the following actions:

- Tightening fasteners.
- Replacing gasket or seal. See Jobs 8 and 9.
- Replacing a cracked, broken, or punctured part.

What steps should be taken to correct the leak? _____

_____

_____

_____

Figure 25-1. Fluorescent dye and a black light can be used to locate leaks.

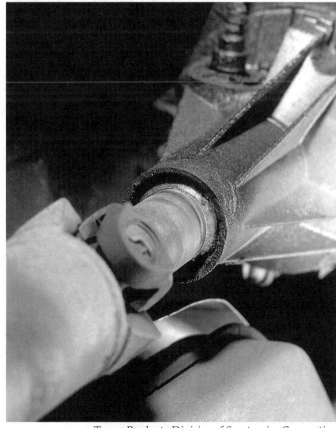

Tracer Products Division of Spectronics Corporation

☐ 2. Make repairs as needed.

☐ 3. Recheck the unit for leaks.

Is the unit leaking? Yes ___ No ___

If No, go to the *Job Wrap Up*. If Yes, repeat one of the leak detection procedures until the leak has been located and corrected.

Job Wrap Up

☐ 1. Return all tools and equipment to storage.

☐ 2. Clean the work area.

☐ 3. Did you encounter any problems during this procedure? Yes ___ No ___

If Yes, describe the problems: _____

_____

_____

What did you do to correct the problems?_____

_____

_____

☐ 4. Have your instructor check your work and sign this job sheet.

Performance Evaluation—Instructor Use Only

Did the student complete the job in the time allotted? Yes ___ No ___

If No, which steps were not completed?_____

How would you rate this student's overall performance on this job?____

5–Excellent, 4–Good, 3–Satisfactory, 2–Unsatisfactory, 1–Poor

Comments: _____

_____

_____

INSTRUCTOR'S SIGNATURE_____

Job

Bleed a Hydraulic Clutch System

26

After completing this job, you will be able to bleed a hydraulic clutch system.

Instructions

As you read the job instructions, answer the questions and perform the tasks. Print your answers neatly and use complete sentences. Consult the proper service literature and ask your instructor for help as needed.

> **Warning**
>
> Before performing this job, review all pertinent safety information in the text and discuss safety procedures with your instructor.

Procedures

☐ 1. Obtain a vehicle to be used in this job. Your instructor may direct you to perform this job on a shop vehicle.

☐ 2. Gather the tools needed to perform the following job.

> **Caution**
>
> Brake fluid can damage paint. Cover painted surfaces near the master cylinder before beginning this procedure.

> **Warning**
>
> Use the proper type of fluid in the clutch hydraulic system. Most systems use DOT 3 or 4 brake fluid. Fluid type is usually stamped on the reservoir cover. Always use the correct type of fluid.

☐ 3. Locate the clutch master cylinder and check the fluid level in the reservoir. See **Figure 26-1**.

Is the level near the full mark? Yes ___ No ___

If Yes, go to step 5. If No, add fluid and go to step 4.

☐ 4. If the fluid level was low, check for leaks by carefully looking for obvious signs of leakage at the hydraulic clutch master cylinder, slave cylinder, and all hoses and lines for leaks.

Were any leaks found? Yes ___ No ___

If Yes, where? _____

If Yes, consult with your instructor about what steps should be taken to correct the leak(s).

If No, go to step 5.

☐ 5. Place a drip pan under the master and slave cylinders.

☐ 6. Have an assistant depress and hold the clutch pedal.

☐ 7. Open the bleeder on the master cylinder.

Does only fluid exit, or does air exit also? Exiting air will make a spitting sound and will show up as bubbles in the fluid.

    ☐ Fluid only.

    ☐ Air and fluid.

☐ 8. Close the bleeder screw before allowing your assistant to release the pedal. Once the bleeder screw is seated, have your assistant pump and then depress and hold the clutch pedal.

☐ 9. Repeat steps 7 and 8 until only fluid exits from the bleeder.

Note

Keep the clutch master cylinder reservoir filled with the proper fluid during this procedure.

Figure 26-1. Check the fluid in the clutch master cylinder reservoir before proceeding. In this photograph, the smaller reservoir next to the brake fluid reservoir is the clutch master cylinder reservoir.

Goodheart-Willcox Publisher

Job 26—Bleed a Hydraulic Clutch System (continued)

☐ 10. Road test the vehicle and check clutch operation.

☐ 11. If the clutch pedal operation continues to feel soft or spongy, repeat steps 6 through 10 until the pedal becomes firm.

Job Wrap Up

☐ 1. Return all tools and equipment to storage.

☐ 2. Clean the work area.

☐ 3. Did you encounter any problems during this procedure? Yes ___ No ___
If Yes, describe the problems: _____
_____
_____

What did you do to correct the problems?_____
_____
_____

☐ 4. Have your instructor check your work and sign this job sheet.

Performance Evaluation—Instructor Use Only

Did the student complete the job in the time allotted? Yes ___ No ___
If No, which steps were not completed?_____
How would you rate this student's overall performance on this job?_____
5–Excellent, 4–Good, 3–Satisfactory, 2–Unsatisfactory, 1–Poor
Comments: _____
_____
_____

INSTRUCTOR'S SIGNATURE _____

Notes

Job

27

Remove, Inspect, and Reinstall a CV Axle

After completing this job, you will be able to remove, inspect, and reinstall a CV axle.

Instructions

As you read the job instructions, answer the questions and perform the tasks. Print your answers neatly and use complete sentences. Consult the proper service literature and ask your instructor for help as needed.

> ### Warning
> ⚠ Before performing this job, review all pertinent safety information in the text and discuss safety procedures with your instructor.

Procedures

☐ 1. Obtain a vehicle to be used in this job. Your instructor may direct you to perform this job on a shop vehicle.

☐ 2. Gather the tools needed to perform the following job.

> ### Note
> The following is a general procedure for CV axle service, including typical CV joint repair and CV joint boot replacement. Some Rzeppa and tripod joints are not repaired, and the entire assembly, including the boot, must be replaced. Also, some boots are made in two pieces and can be changed without removing the axle from the vehicle. Always consult the manufacturer's service manual for exact CV joint repair or boot replacement procedures.

Remove a CV Axle

☐ 1. Disconnect the battery negative cable.

☐ 2. Place the vehicle transmission in neutral.

3. Loosen the nut holding the CV axle stub shaft to the wheel hub and bearing assembly.

4. Raise the vehicle.

> ### Warning
>
> ⚠ The vehicle must be raised and supported in a safe manner. Always use approved lifts or jacks and jack stands.

5. Remove the wheel from the axle to be serviced.

6. Cover the outer CV boot with a shop cloth or boot protector.

7. If needed, remove the tie rod end nut and use a ball joint separator to free the tie rod end from the steering knuckle.

8. Remove the stub shaft nut. A special deep socket may be needed to remove the nut, **Figure 27-1**.

> ### Note
>
> On some vehicles it is necessary to remove the brake rotor, caliper, and wheel speed sensor to gain access to the CV axle shaft assembly.

9. Remove the CV axle shaft assembly from the steering knuckle. Some shafts will slide from the hub, while others must be pressed out.

> ### Note
>
> Removal of the CV axle shaft assembly from the steering knuckle may require the removal of the tie rod end, strut assembly, or lower ball joint. Consult the proper manufacturer's service manual for exact procedures.

Figure 27-1. A special deep socket is sometimes needed to remove the stub shaft nut. These sockets are usually sold in sets of three—30 mm, 32 mm, and 36 mm.

Goodheart-Willcox Publisher

Job 27—Remove, Inspect, and Reinstall a CV Axle (continued)

☐ 10. Remove the CV axle shaft assembly from the transaxle with a suitable puller or pry bar. If the transaxle uses a stub shaft that is attached to the CV axle by flanges, remove the bolts attaching the flanges.

> **Note**
> Cap the transaxle opening to prevent oil loss.

Repair a CV Joint and Replace the Boot

☐ 1. Lightly clamp the shaft in a vise with soft jaws.

☐ 2. Remove the clamps from the boot of the CV joint to be serviced (or from the boot to be replaced).

☐ 3. Pull the boot back from the CV joint and remove enough grease to further disassemble the CV joint.

☐ 4. If applicable, remove the clip holding the CV joint to the axle shaft.

☐ 5. Place alignment marks on the joint housing and the axle shaft to aid in reassembly.

☐ 6. Pull or tap the CV joint from the axle shaft.

☐ 7. Remove the CV joint boot from the axle shaft.

> **Note**
> If only the boot is being replaced, skip ahead to step 14.

☐ 8. Disassemble the CV joint by one of the following procedures, depending on the CV joint type.

List the type of joint(s) to be serviced: _____

Rzeppa Joint

a. Tap the bearing cage downward with a brass drift, **Figure 27-2**, until the ball on the opposite side can be removed through the cage opening.

b. Repeat the previous step until all balls are removed.

c. Remove the cage and inner race from the housing.

Tripod Joint

a. Remove the snap ring or clip holding the joint together, **Figure 27-3**.

b. Pull the tripod assembly from the housing.

c. Remove the tripod assembly from the shaft. Tripod joints may be held in place by a clip or may be pressed on the shaft. Consult the service information for exact procedures to avoid damaging the joint or shaft.

Figure 27-2. Tap the bearing cage downward until the first ball can be removed. Repeat the process until all balls are out.

Goodheart-Willcox Publisher

Figure 27-3. Many tripod joints are held in place by a clip, as shown here, or a retaining collar.

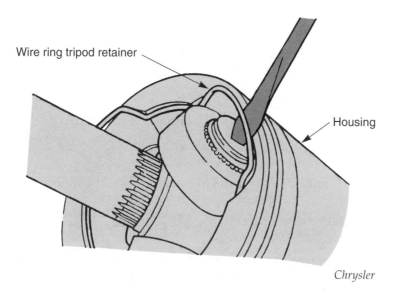

Chrysler

> **Note**
>
> Some CV joints are not serviceable and must be replaced as a unit.

☐ 9. Wash all parts in solvent and dry with compressed air.

☐ 10. Inspect all internal CV joint parts for excessive wear, cracked or chipped parts, or scoring.

Describe their condition:_____

_____

_____

Job 27—Remove, Inspect, and Reinstall a CV Axle (continued)

☐ 11. Check the joint splines and threads for damage.

Describe their condition:_____

_____

☐ 12. Report any CV joint component defects that you found to your instructor. Then, determine which parts must be replaced.

☐ 13. Obtain the proper replacement parts and compare them with the old parts to ensure that they are the correct replacements.

☐ 14. Lightly lubricate all CV joint parts before proceeding.

☐ 15. Align and install all CV joint parts according to the manufacturer's instructions.

☐ 16. If the CV joint boot uses a one-piece clamp, slide the clamp onto the axle shaft. Often it is easier to place the clamps on the boot before installing it.

☐ 17. Install the CV joint boot on the axle shaft.

> **Note**
> It may be necessary to position the small end of the boot lip face in line with a mark or groove on the shaft.

☐ 18. Place the small clamp over the groove at the small end of the boot and tighten it by hand.

☐ 19. Place sufficient grease in the boot cavity to provide the CV joint with lubrication during vehicle operation.

> **Caution**
> CV joints must be lubricated with special grease, usually supplied with the replacement joint parts or boot. Do not use ordinary chassis or wheel bearing grease.

☐ 20. Position the CV joint over the splines of the axle shaft.

☐ 21. Engage the splines and tap the joint into position with a wooden or rubber hammer.

☐ 22. Install the joint-to-shaft clip, if used.

☐ 23. Pull the CV joint boot over the CV joint housing. Ensure that the boot end fits snugly into the matching groove in the housing.

> **Caution**
> Ensure that the boot is not twisted or otherwise deformed during the installation process.

☐ 24. Place the large clamp over the groove in the boot. Tighten the clamp by hand.

☐ 25. Fully tighten both boot clamps using the correct special tool.

> **Caution**
>
> ⚠ Do not cut through the boot by overtightening the clamp.

☐ 26. Check for free movement of the CV joint and otherwise ensure that it is properly assembled.

Install CV Axle

☐ 1. Install the inboard stub shaft of the CV axle assembly into the transaxle.

☐ 2. Install the outboard stub shaft of the CV axle assembly into the steering knuckle.

☐ 3. Install the stub shaft nut on the outboard shaft.

☐ 4. Adjust front wheel bearing preload, if necessary.

☐ 5. Install brake rotor, caliper, and wheel speed sensor as needed.

☐ 6. Reinstall the wheel.

☐ 7. Lower the vehicle.

☐ 8. Install the battery negative cable.

☐ 9. Start the engine.

☐ 10. Check brake operation.

☐ 11. Road test the vehicle.

Job Wrap Up

☐ 1. Return all tools and equipment to storage.

☐ 2. Clean the work area.

☐ 3. Did you encounter any problems during this procedure? Yes ___ No ___

If Yes, describe the problems: _____

_____

_____

What did you do to correct the problems?_____

_____

_____

☐ 4. Have your instructor check your work and sign this job sheet.

Performance Evaluation—Instructor Use Only

Did the student complete the job in the time allotted? Yes ___ No ___

If No, which steps were not completed?_____

How would you rate this student's overall performance on this job?_____

5–Excellent, 4–Good, 3–Satisfactory, 2–Unsatisfactory, 1–Poor

Comments: _____

_____

INSTRUCTOR'S SIGNATURE _____

Job

28

Remove, Inspect, and Reinstall U-Joints and a Drive Shaft

After completing this job, you will be able to remove and replace a drive shaft and U-joints.

Instructions

As you read the job instructions, answer the questions and perform the tasks. Print your answers neatly and use complete sentences. Consult the proper service literature and ask your instructor for help as needed.

> **Warning**
> ⚠ Before performing this job, review all pertinent safety information in the text and discuss safety procedures with your instructor.

Procedures

> **Note**
> 📄 The procedures presented in this job also apply to the front drive shaft of a four-wheel drive vehicle.

☐ 1. Obtain a vehicle to be used in this job. Your instructor may direct you to perform this job on a shop vehicle.

☐ 2. Gather the tools needed to perform the following job.

Remove the Drive Shaft

☐ 1. Place the vehicle's transmission in neutral.

☐ 2. Raise the vehicle.

> **Warning**
> ⚠ The vehicle must be raised and supported in a safe manner. Always use approved lifts or jacks and jack stands.

3. Place match marks on the drive shaft and differential yokes to aid drive shaft reinstallation.

> **Caution**
>
> If the vehicle has a two piece drive shaft, mark the front and rear shafts so they can be reinstalled in the same position.

4. Remove the fasteners holding the rear of the drive shaft to the rear axle assembly. This is accomplished on most drive shafts by one of the following methods:

   Remove the nuts and bolts holding the companion flange to the pinion flange. Then, separate the companion flange from the pinion flange.

   or

   Remove two U-bolts secured with nuts or two straps secured with cap screws.

> **Caution**
>
> Do not let loose bearing cups fall off their trunnions once the U-bolts or straps are removed.

5. If the vehicle has a two piece drive shaft, loosen and remove the center support bolts.

6. Remove the drive shaft assembly from the vehicle.

> **Note**
>
> On some vehicles with two piece drive shafts, the rear section of the drive shaft is removed first, and then the center support and front drive shaft section are removed.

7. Cap the rear of the transmission once the drive shaft is removed to prevent oil loss.

Repair a Cross-and-Roller U-Joint

> **Note**
>
> This procedure details the general removal and installation of a U-joint. If there is any variation between the procedures given here and the procedures in the manufacturer's service literature, use the manufacturer's procedure.

1. Attempt to rotate the two sides of the U-joint, **Figure 28-1**. Note any roughness, excessive play, noise, or binding.

   Describe the condition of the U-joints: _____

   _____

2. Place the drive shaft on a stand or workbench so that the shaft is horizontal.

3. Clamp the yoke of the U-joint to be replaced in a vise.

Job 28—Remove, Inspect, and Reinstall U-Joints and a Drive Shaft (continued)

Figure 28-1. Attempt to move the drive shaft yokes by hand to detect problems.

Goodheart-Willcox Publisher

☐ 4. Mark the drive shaft yokes so they can be reassembled in the same position relative to each other. See **Figure 28-2**. This step is not necessary on a rear U-joint with only one yoke.

Figure 28-2. Mark the drive shaft yokes so that they can be reassembled in the same position as they were originally.

Goodheart-Willcox Publisher

5. Remove the bearing cup retaining devices. Removal methods vary depending on the retaining device used:

- Use a hammer and a small chisel to remove C-clips.
- Use pliers to remove snap rings.
- Use a heat gun or torch to soften injected plastic retainers.

6. Obtain a piece of pipe (or similar tool) having an inside diameter slightly larger in size than a bearing cup. Obtain a socket or other metal piece with an outside diameter slightly smaller in size than a bearing cup.

7. Remove the bearing cup, using one of the following methods:

> **Caution**
>
> Be careful not to lose any needle bearings when you remove the bearing cups.

Press Method

a. Position the front yoke in a press to drive the bearing cups from the yoke. You can press the cups out with a vise, a C-clamp, or an arbor press.

b. Place the small diameter pressing tool against one of the front yoke bearing cups.

c. Place the larger-diameter tool over the opposite cup and against the yoke itself.

d. Slowly operate the press until the bearing cup is driven from the yoke as far as it will go. The small pressing tool will drive the bearing cup that is opposite it into the larger-diameter tool.

Hammer Method

> **Warning**
>
> Do not use a socket as a driver. Hammer blows can shatter a socket.

a. Place one of the front yoke bearing cups on top of the small pressing tool.

b. Place the larger-diameter tool over the top bearing cup and against the yoke.

c. Strike the larger-diameter tool with a hammer. This will cause the top cup to move up and out of the yoke and into the larger-diameter tool.

d. Rotate the drive shaft 180° and place the slip yoke in a vise.

e. With the slip yoke clamped across its lugs in a vise, place the larger-diameter tool over the top cup of the front yoke and against the yoke.

f. Strike the larger-diameter tool with a hammer. This will cause the front yoke lug to flex downward and the cup to move up out of the yoke and into the receiving piece (the larger-diameter tool).

C-Frame Driver Method

a. Place a C-frame driver (U-joint removal/installation tool) around the front drive shaft yoke, **Figure 28-3**.

b. Turn the driver handle to press the cup from the yoke.

Job 28—Remove, Inspect, and Reinstall U-Joints and a Drive Shaft (continued)

Figure 28-3. Install the C-frame driver around the drive shaft yoke.

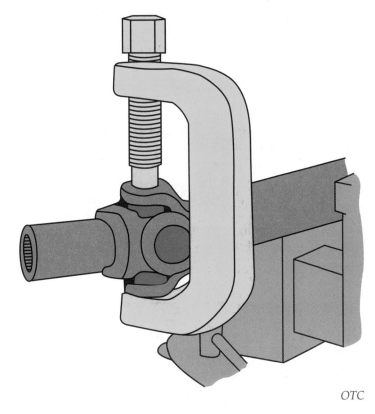

OTC

☐ 8. If you are using the press or C-frame driver methods, repeat step 7 to remove the opposite bearing cup. To remove the remaining cup, place the small driver tool on the exposed trunnion and the large driver tool over the remaining cup.

☐ 9. Remove the slip yoke and U-joint from the drive shaft by slipping the front yoke lugs from the U-joint cross.

☐ 10. If necessary, complete the removal of the yoke bearing cups by tapping them out with a hammer.

☐ 11. Remove the bearing cups from the slip yoke by repeating steps 7 through 10.

☐ 12. Visually examine the U-joint and other drive shaft components, looking for the following:

- Damaged or rusty needle bearings or bearing cups.
- Worn, rough, rusty, or out-of-round U-joint trunnions.
- Cracked, spalled, or pitted U-joint cross.
- Burred yokes, caused by bearing cup removal, or damaged yokes.
- Worn or damaged slip yoke splines.
- Bent drive shaft.
- Excessive pinion flange or companion flange runout.

Inspect components using special measuring instruments, as required.
Describe the condition of the components: _____

_____

_____

_____

_____

☐ 13. Report any drive shaft component defects to your instructor and determine which parts must be replaced.

> **Note**
>
> If either the cross or the bearings are worn, replace both. Never install new bearings on an old cross, or vice versa.

☐ 14. Obtain the proper replacement parts and compare them with the old parts to ensure that they are the correct replacements.

☐ 15. If bearing needles are loose, begin bearing cup installation by lining the cup with the needles, using grease to hold them in place. Then, install a new seal.

☐ 16. Push a bearing cup about one fourth of its length into either lug of the front yoke.

> **Note**
>
> Check for proper cup/yoke alignment and make sure the bearing needles are still in place.

☐ 17. Place the cross into the partially installed bearing cup.

☐ 18. Hammer or press the cup onto the cross trunnion, until the bearing cup is flush with the outside of the yoke and fully seated on the cross trunnion.

☐ 19. Repeat steps 15 through 18 to install the opposite bearing cup.

☐ 20. Install the retainer, snap rings, or clips, to ensure that the bearing cups are fully seated.

> **Note**
>
> If snap rings are used, install the ring gap so it points away from the yoke opening.

☐ 21. Check for free movement of the U-joint.

☐ 22. Repeat steps 15 through 21 to install the bearing cups in the slip yoke, making sure to align the match marks made before disassembly.

☐ 23. Ensure that the snap rings or clips are fully seated in their grooves.

Install the Drive Shaft

☐ 1. Lightly lubricate the outside of the slip yoke with automatic transmission fluid or gear oil, depending on the type of transmission the vehicle has.

Job 28—Remove, Inspect, and Reinstall U-Joints and a Drive Shaft (continued)

☐ 2. Slide the slip yoke onto the transmission output shaft, being careful not to damage the rear seal.

> **Note**
>
> Ensure that the extension bushing and rear seal are in good condition before installing the slip yoke.

☐ 3. If the drive shaft has a center support bearing, align the center support with the cross-member and loosely install the center support bearing fasteners.

☐ 4. Install the rear drive shaft on the differential yoke. Make sure you align the match marks that were made during disassembly.

☐ 5. If the drive shaft is a two-piece type, be sure to align the front and rear drive shaft yokes, sometimes called phasing the drive shaft. A slip yoke installed between the two drive shafts may have a large spline that matches a missing spline in the shaft. This prevents improper installation.

> **Warning**
>
> ⚠ If the yokes are not aligned, the drive shaft will vibrate severely.

☐ 6. Tighten the drive shaft yoke and center support fasteners.

☐ 7. Once all drive shaft parts are installed, tighten the fasteners to the proper torque and check drive shaft alignment.

☐ 8. Lower the vehicle.

☐ 9. Road test the vehicle.

Job Wrap Up

☐ 1. Return all tools and equipment to storage.

☐ 2. Clean the work area.

☐ 3. Did you encounter any problems during this procedure? Yes ___ No ___

If Yes, describe the problems: _____

_____

_____

What did you do to correct the problems?_____

_____

_____

☐ 4. Have your instructor check your work and sign this job sheet.

Performance Evaluation—Instructor Use Only

Did the student complete the job in the time allotted? Yes ___ No ___

If No, which steps were not completed?_____

How would you rate this student's overall performance on this job?_____

5–Excellent, 4–Good, 3–Satisfactory, 2–Unsatisfactory, 1–Poor

Comments: _____

_____

_____

INSTRUCTOR'S SIGNATURE _____

Job

Inspect and Replace Wheel Studs

29

After completing this job, you will be able to inspect and replace wheel studs.

Instructions

As you read the job instructions, answer the questions and perform the tasks. Print your answers neatly and use complete sentences. Consult the proper service literature and ask your instructor for help as needed.

> **Warning**
>
> ⚠ Before performing this job, review all pertinent safety information in the text and discuss safety procedures with your instructor.

Procedures

☐ 1. Obtain a vehicle to be used in this job. Your instructor may direct you to perform this job on a shop vehicle.

☐ 2. Gather the tools needed to perform this job.

☐ 3. Raise the vehicle.

> **Warning**
>
> ⚠ The vehicle must be raised and supported in a safe manner. Always use approved lifts or jacks and jack stands.

Inspect Wheel Studs

☐ 1. Remove the wheel on the axle containing the stud(s) to be inspected or replaced.

☐ 2. Check the wheel studs for the following conditions. Check all that apply.

   ☐ Stripped threads.

   ☐ Corrosion.

   ☐ Broken stud.

Replace a Wheel Stud

☐ 1. If necessary, remove the rotor and splash shield to allow the stud to be removed from the rear of the wheel assembly.

☐ 2. Knock out the damaged stud with a large hammer.

or

Use a special stud removal tool to press out the damaged stud.

☐ 3. Compare the old and new studs.

> **Note**
>
> If the studs do not match, obtain the correct stud before proceeding. Stud length, diameter, and thread size must all match. Never attempt to install an incorrect stud.

☐ 4. Place the new stud in position on the hub.

☐ 5. Lightly lubricate the stud splines.

☐ 6. Install washers and a lug nut on the stud as shown in **Figure 29-1**.

☐ 7. Slowly tighten the nut to draw the stud into the hub.

☐ 8. Check that the stud is fully seated in the hub. The back of the wheel stud should be even with the other studs installed in the hub.

☐ 9. Remove the nut and washers from the stud.

☐ 10. Install the wheel.

Job Wrap Up

☐ 1. Return all tools and equipment to storage.

☐ 2. Clean the work area.

Figure 29-1. Arrange washers and a lug nut on the new wheel stud as shown. Tighten the lug nut to draw the new stud into position.

Goodheart-Willcox Publisher

Job 29—Inspect and Replace Wheel Studs (continued)

☐ 3. Did you encounter any problems during this procedure? Yes ___ No ___

   If Yes, describe the problems: _____

   _____

   _____

   What did you do to correct the problems?_____

   _____

   _____

☐ 4. Have your instructor check your work and sign this job sheet.

Performance Evaluation—Instructor Use Only

Did the student complete the job in the time allotted? Yes ___ No ___

If No, which steps were not completed?_____

How would you rate this student's overall performance on this job?_____

5–Excellent, 4–Good, 3–Satisfactory, 2–Unsatisfactory, 1–Poor

Comments: _____

_____

_____

INSTRUCTOR'S SIGNATURE _____

Notes

Job

30

Inspect a Transfer Case and Locking Hubs

After completing this job, you will be able to inspect a transfer case and locking hubs on a four-wheel drive vehicle.

Instructions

As you read the job instructions, answer the questions and perform the tasks. Print your answers neatly and use complete sentences. Consult the proper service literature and ask your instructor for help as needed.

> **Warning**
>
> ⚠ Before performing this job, review all pertinent safety information in the text and discuss safety procedures with your instructor.

Procedures

> **Note**
>
> The following procedure is a general guide only. Always refer to the manufacturer's service literature for specific procedures.

☐ 1. Obtain a vehicle to be used in this job. Your instructor may direct you to perform this job on a shop vehicle.

☐ 2. Gather the tools needed to perform the following job.

Inspect a Transfer Case

☐ 1. Check the general condition of the transfer case by performing the following inspections:

    ☐ Check the case for cracks, extreme corrosion, and loose fasteners.

    ☐ Check for worn or damaged mounts.

    ☐ Check the input and output shafts and flanges for damage or loose fasteners.

    ☐ Check the linkage for binding, damage, or missing parts.

    ☐ Check for plugged or missing vent tube(s) and related hoses.

Is any damage found? Yes ___ No ___

If Yes, describe the problem: _____

_____

_____

_____

☐ 2. Check for leaks at the following points:

    ☐ Front and rear pinion seals.

    ☐ Case gaskets.

    ☐ Linkage and sensor gaskets and seals.

Are any leaks found? Yes ___ No ___

If Yes, describe the problem: _____

_____

_____

☐ 3. Check the fluid level and the general condition of the fluid.

Is the fluid level OK? Yes ___ No ___

Describe the fluid condition: _____

_____

_____

Were any transfer case problems found while performing the above steps?
Yes ___ No ___

If Yes, what should be done to correct them? _____

_____

_____

Inspect Locking Hubs

> **Note**
>
> There are many types of locking hubs. Consult the proper service information to determine the exact type of hub used.

☐ 1. Raise the vehicle so the front and rear wheels are off the ground

☐ 2. Make visual inspection of the locking hubs as needed. Look for:

- Damaged parts.
- Lubricant leaks.

Describe any problems found: _____

_____

_____

Job 30—Inspect a Transfer Case and Locking Hubs (continued)

☐ 3. Turn the ignition switch to the *On* position but do not start the vehicle.

☐ 4. Place the vehicle in four-wheel drive.

☐ 5. Check the locking hubs for engagement of both front wheels.

This can be done by turning one front wheel and ensuring that the other wheel turns. Check the service literature for other possible checking methods.

☐ 6. Start the engine and place the vehicle in drive or first gear as necessary, allowing the front wheels to rotate.

> **Warning**
>
> ⚠ Avoid contacting spinning tires and drive train parts.

☐ 7. Check for noises and vibrations.

Describe any problems found: _____

_____

Job Wrap Up

☐ 1. Return all tools and equipment to storage.

☐ 2. Clean the work area.

☐ 3. Did you encounter any problems during this procedure? Yes ___ No ___

If Yes, describe the problems: _____

_____

_____

What did you do to correct the problems?_____

_____

_____

☐ 4. Have your instructor check your work and sign this job sheet.

Performance Evaluation—Instructor Use Only

Did the student complete the job in the time allotted? Yes ___ No ___

If No, which steps were not completed?_____

How would you rate this student's overall performance on this job?____

5–Excellent, 4–Good, 3–Satisfactory, 2–Unsatisfactory, 1–Poor

Comments: _____

_____

INSTRUCTOR'S SIGNATURE _____

Notes

After completing this job, you will be able to safely disable and enable an air bag system.

Instructions

As you read the job instructions, answer the questions and perform the tasks. Print your answers neatly and use complete sentences. Consult the proper service literature and ask your instructor for help as needed.

> **Warning**
>
> Before performing this job, review all pertinent safety information in the text and discuss safety procedures with your instructor.

Procedures

☐ 1. Before beginning this job, review the following important air bag safety rules:
- Do not place the air bag module where temperatures will exceed 175°F (79.4°C).
- If you drop any part of the air bag system, replace the part.
- When carrying a live air bag module, point the bag and trim cover away from you.
- Do not carry an air bag by the connecting wires.
- Place a live air bag module on a bench with the bag and trim cover facing up.
- Do not test an air bag with electrical test equipment unless the manufacturer's instructions clearly call for such testing.

> **Warning**
>
> Always obtain the proper service literature and follow manufacturer's procedures exactly before attempting to disable any air bag system.

☐ 2. Obtain a vehicle to be used in this job. Your instructor may direct you to perform this job on a shop vehicle.

☐ 3. Gather the tools needed to perform this job.

Disable an Air Bag System

☐ 1. Turn the steering wheel to the straight-ahead position.

☐ 2. Lock the ignition and remove the ignition key.

☐ 3. Locate and remove the air bag fuses. Check the service information, as there may be more than one system fuse.

☐ 4. Locate the air bag connectors under the dashboard. Check the service manual for the exact connector locations. Newer connectors are yellow, but older systems may use another color for the connectors. **Figure 31-1** shows a common air bag connector location.

☐ 5. Disconnect the air bag connectors. To access the connectors, it may be necessary to remove the trim parts from the lower dashboard or center console. Some air bag connectors have a locking pin to ensure that the connector does not come apart accidentally. This pin must be removed to separate the connector. Use the service literature to confirm that you are disconnecting the proper connectors.

> **Warning**
>
> Although the air bags are disabled, they can still inflate without warning. Follow all safety rules.

Enable Air Bag Systems

☐ 1. Make sure that the key is removed from the ignition switch.

☐ 2. Reconnect the air bag connectors and reinstall any trim pieces that were removed.

☐ 3. Reinstall the air bag system fuses.

☐ 4. Position yourself in the passenger compartment so that you are away from the air bags. This will keep you from being injured if the system accidentally deploys.

Figure 31-1. The location of one typical air bag connector is shown here. Note the yellow color of the connector and wires.

Goodheart-Willcox Publisher

Job 31—Disable and Enable an Air Bag System (continued)

☐ 5. Turn the ignition switch to the *On* position.

☐ 6. Allow the air bag system self-diagnostic program to run. This will ensure that the system is operating correctly.

Job Wrap Up

☐ 1. Return all tools and equipment to storage.

☐ 2. Clean the work area.

☐ 3. Did you encounter any problems during this procedure? Yes ___ No ___

If Yes, describe the problems: _____

_____

_____

What did you do to correct the problems? _____

_____

_____

☐ 4. Have your instructor check your work and sign this job sheet.

Performance Evaluation—Instructor Use Only

Did the student complete the job in the time allotted? Yes ___ No ___

If No, which steps were not completed? _____

How would you rate this student's overall performance on this job? ____

5–Excellent, 4–Good, 3–Satisfactory, 2–Unsatisfactory, 1–Poor

Comments: _____

_____

_____

INSTRUCTOR'S SIGNATURE _____

Notes

Job

Inspect Steering and Suspension Systems

32

After completing this job, you will be able to inspect steering and suspension systems for problems.

Instructions

As you read the job instructions, answer the questions and perform the tasks. Print your answers neatly and use complete sentences. Consult the proper service literature and ask your instructor for help as needed.

> **Warning**
>
> ⚠ Before performing this job, review all pertinent safety information in the text and discuss safety procedures with your instructor.

Procedures

☐ 1. Obtain a vehicle to be used in this job. Your instructor may direct you to perform this job on a shop vehicle.

☐ 2. Gather the tools needed to perform this job.

Identify the Complaint

☐ 1. Obtain a description of the problem from the vehicle operator.

Problem as described by the operator: _____

_____

☐ 2. Obtain the proper service literature for the vehicle.

☐ 3. Check ride height according to manufacturer's procedures and record the results below. Indicate the units of measurement.

Left Front
Specification:_____ inches/mm
Actual:_____ inches/mm

Right Front
Specification:_____ inches/mm
Actual:_____ inches/mm

Left Rear
Specification:_____ inches/mm
Actual:_____ inches/mm

Right Rear
Specification:_____ inches/mm
Actual:_____ inches/mm

Does any ride height measurement exceed the manufacturer's specifications?
Yes ___ No ___

☐ 4. Road test the vehicle to duplicate the original complaint.

Describe abnormal sounds and indicate the conditions under which they occur:

_____

_____

_____

Describe any vibrations, shocks or bumping/looseness sensations, body sway on turns or at cruising speeds, wander or loose sensation at cruising speeds, or sensations of harshness and the conditions under which the problems occur:

_____

_____

_____

Did the road test confirm that the problem described by the operator exists?
Yes ___ No ___

If the answer to the question in steps 3 or 4 is Yes, go to step 5.

If the answer is No, discuss your findings with your instructor before proceeding.

☐ 5. Raise the front of the vehicle so the front suspension is correctly suspended for checking the ball joints. Make sure the steering linkage is free to turn.

> **Warning**
>
> ⚠ Raise and support the vehicle in a safe manner. Always use approved lifts or jacks and jack stands.

☐ 6. Shake each front wheel and note any looseness.

a. Grasp the wheel at the top and bottom and shake it in and out to check the suspension parts. See **Figure 32-1**.
Does the right wheel feel loose? Yes ___ No ___
Does the left wheel feel loose? Yes ___ No ___

b. Grasp the wheel at the front and back and shake it back and forth to check the steering linkage parts, **Figure 32-2**.
Does the right wheel feel loose? Yes ___ No ___
Does the left wheel feel loose? Yes ___ No ___

c. On some MacPherson strut vehicles, grasp the wheel at approximately 45° from the top and bottom and shake it in and out to check the suspension.
Does the right wheel feel loose? Yes ___ No ___
Does the left wheel feel loose? Yes ___ No ___

Job 32—Inspect Steering and Suspension Systems (continued)

Figure 32-1. When checking for loose suspension parts, grasp the wheel at the top and bottom, and try to shake it. Slight movement is normal.

Goodheart-Willcox Publisher

Figure 32-2. When checking the steering linkage for looseness, try to move the wheel back and forth.

Goodheart-Willcox Publisher

7. Have a helper shake each front wheel while you observe the front suspension.
   Were any parts loose? Yes ___ No ___
   If Yes, list them in the following blanks.
   Front left side:_____
   Front right side: _____

Check Suspension Parts

☐ 1. Check all front suspension parts and their mounts for damage and complete the following chart. Write "NA" in the first blank when the part is not used on the vehicle you are checking.

	Passed	Worn/Loose	Bent/Broken	Leaking
Upper ball joints				
Upper control arms				
Lower ball joints				
Lower control arms				
Control arm bushings				
Rebound bumpers				
Steering knuckle				
Strut rod				
Strut rod bushings				
Stabilizer bar				
Stabilizer bar bushings				
Shock absorbers				
Strut cartridges				
Springs/torsion bars				
Insulators				
Fasteners				
Frame/subframe				

☐ 2. Obtain a dial indicator and use it to check ball joint play.

> **Note**
>
> Checking ball joint play may not be necessary on the vehicle you are servicing. Check with your instructor.

Specified maximum ball joint play:_____

Actual ball joint play:_____

Is ball joint play within specifications? Yes ___ No ___

☐ 3. If not already done, raise the rear of the vehicle so the rear suspension parts can be checked.

Job 32—Inspect Steering and Suspension Systems (continued)

> **Warning**
>
> ⚠ Raise and support the vehicle in a safe manner. Always use approved lifts or jacks and jack stands.

☐ 4. Check all rear suspension parts and their mounts for damage and complete the following chart. Write "NA" in the first blank when the part is not used on the vehicle you are checking.

	Passed	Worn/Loose	Bent/Broken	Leaking
Upper ball joints				
Upper control arms				
Lower ball joints				
Lower control arms				
Control arm bushings				
Rebound bumpers				
Strut rod				
Strut rod bushings				
Stabilizer bar				
Stabilizer bar bushings				
Shock absorbers				
Strut cartridges				
Springs/torsion bars				
Insulators				
Fasteners				
Axle				

☐ 5. If the vehicle is equipped with rear lower ball joints, check them for looseness as specified by the service manual.

Specified maximum ball joint play:_____

Actual ball joint play:_____

Is ball joint play within specifications? Yes ___ No ___

Check Steering Parts

☐ 1. Check the steering linkage, steering gear, and steering shaft for damage. Complete the following chart. Write "NA" in the first column when the part is not used on the vehicle you are checking.

	Passed	Worn/Loose	Bent/Broken	Leaking
Steering arms				
Outer tie rod ends				
Inner tie rod ends				
Pitman arm				
Idler arm				
Relay rod/drag link				
Steering gear				
Steering coupler				
Steering shaft				
Power steering pump				
Power steering belt				
Power steering hoses				
Fasteners				

> ### Note
> In many vehicles equipped with power steering, a power steering pressure switch sends a signal to the ECM when the system pressure exceeds a preset limit. In response, the ECM will raise the idle speed or turn off the air conditioning compressor to prevent the engine from stalling. If the engine is experiencing performance problems that seem to coincide with steering actions, suspect the power steering pressure switch.

☐ 2. If necessary, check the rear steering linkage for damage. Complete the following chart. Write "NA" in the first column when the part is not used on the vehicle you are checking.

	Passed	Worn/Loose	Bent/Broken	Leaking
Steering arms				
Outer tie rod ends				
Inner tie rod ends				
Steering gear				
Power steering hoses				
Hydraulic valves				
Electrical controls				
Fasteners				

Job 32—Inspect Steering and Suspension Systems (continued)

☐ 3. Discuss with your instructor the results obtained in the preceding charts. Determine which suspension and steering parts are defective.

List the defective parts:_____

_____

_____

☐ 4. After obtaining your instructor's approval, make needed repairs based on your front and rear suspension inspections.

What repairs were made?_____

_____

_____

_____

☐ 5. Recheck the condition of the suspension and steering system. If the problem has been corrected, continue on to the Job Wrap Up. If the problem still exists, repeat the procedures in this job until the problem is located and corrected.

Job Wrap Up

☐ 1. Return all tools and equipment to storage.

☐ 2. Clean the work area.

☐ 3. Did you encounter any problems during this procedure? Yes ___ No ___

If Yes, describe the problems: _____

_____

_____

What did you do to correct the problems?_____

_____

_____

☐ 4. Have your instructor check your work and sign this job sheet.

Performance Evaluation—Instructor Use Only

Did the student complete the job in the time allotted? Yes ___ No ___
If No, which steps were not completed?_____
How would you rate this student's overall performance on this job?____
5–Excellent, 4–Good, 3–Satisfactory, 2–Unsatisfactory, 1–Poor
Comments: _____

_____

_____

INSTRUCTOR'S SIGNATURE _____

Notes

Job

33

Checking Power Steering Fluid Level and Finding Leaks

After completing this job, you will be able to check power steering fluid level and condition. You will also be able to use a variety of methods to find the source of power steering system leaks.

Instructions

As you read the job instructions, answer the questions and perform the tasks. Print your answers neatly and use complete sentences. Consult the proper service literature and ask your instructor for help as needed.

> **Warning**
> ⚠ Before performing this job, review all pertinent safety information in the text and discuss safety procedures with your instructor.

Procedures

☐ 1. Obtain a vehicle to be used in this job. Your instructor may direct you to perform this job on a shop vehicle.

☐ 2. Gather the tools needed to perform this job.

> **Note**
> 📄 For information on removing, inspecting, replacing, and adjusting a power steering pump belt, refer to Job 14.

Check Power Steering Fluid Level and Condition

 1. Refer to the service literature to determine the type of power steering fluid used in the vehicle.

Type of power steering fluid: _____

 2. Locate the power steering reservoir. Some power steering reservoirs surround the pump, **Figure 33-1**, while others are located remotely, **Figure 33-2**.

Figure 33-1. Some power steering systems have a separate reservoir. Note that the pump itself is out of sight under the alternator.

Goodheart-Willcox Publisher

Figure 33-2. This reservoir is part of the power steering pump assembly. Note the pump pulley directly under the reservoir.

Goodheart-Willcox Publisher

3. Remove the cap and observe the fluid level. Most power steering reservoirs have the dipstick built into the cap. A few reservoirs are made of clear plastic and the cap does not have to be removed to observe fluid level.

   Is the fluid level low? Yes ___ No ___

4. Place some of the fluid on a clean white rag and check for the following conditions.

   • Discoloration.

   • Burned odor.

   Describe the condition of the power steering fluid: _____

Job 33—Checking Power Steering Fluid Level and Finding Leaks (continued)

Find Power Steering System Leaks

Visual Observation Method

☐ 1. Visually observe the power steering system components for evidence of fluid leakage. It may be necessary to raise the vehicle to observe all power steering components.

Did you notice any fluid leaks? Yes ___ No ___

If Yes, where does the fluid appear to be coming from?_____

_____

> **Note**
>
> Slight seepage from power steering components is normal.

Powder Method

☐ 1. Make sure the power steering system has enough fluid. Add fluid as necessary.

☐ 2. Thoroughly clean the area around the suspected leak.

☐ 3. Apply talcum powder to the area around the suspected leak.

☐ 4. Start and run the vehicle in the shop 10–15 minutes, turning the steering wheel occasionally. You can also start the vehicle and drive it for several miles before moving on to the next step.

> **Warning**
>
> ⚠ Never operate a vehicle in an enclosed area without proper ventilation. A running engine emits carbon monoxide, a deadly gas that builds up quickly.

☐ 5. Raise the vehicle (if necessary) and check the area around the suspected leak.

> **Warning**
>
> ⚠ Raise and support the vehicle in a safe manner. Always use approved lifts or jacks and jack stands.

Does the powder show fluid streaks? Yes ___ No ___

If Yes, where does the fluid appear to be coming from?_____

_____

Black Light Method

☐ 1. Make sure the power steering system has enough fluid. Add fluid if necessary.

☐ 2. Add fluorescent dye to the power steering reservoir, being careful not to spill dye on the outside of the reservoir.

3.   Start the vehicle and run it in the shop 10–15 minutes, turning the steering wheel occasionally.

> **Warning**
>
> ⚠ Never operate a vehicle in an enclosed area without proper ventilation.

4.   Turn on the black light and direct it toward the area around the suspected leak. See **Figure 33-3**.

Does the black light show the presence of dye? Yes ___ No ___

If Yes, where does the dye appear to be coming from? _____

_____

5.   Consult your instructor for the steps to take to correct the leak. Steps may include some of the following:

• Tightening fasteners.

• Replacing a gasket or seal. See Jobs 8 and 9.

• Replacing a cracked, broken, or punctured hose.

Steps to be taken:_____

_____

_____

6.   Make repairs as needed.

7.   Recheck the system for leaks.

Figure 33-3. Hard-to-find power steering fluid leaks can often be spotted with fluorescent dye and a black light.

Tracer Products Division of Spectronics Corporation

Job 33—Checking Power Steering Fluid Level and Finding Leaks (continued)

Job Wrap Up

- ☐ 1. Return all tools and equipment to storage.
- ☐ 2. Clean the work area.
- ☐ 3. Did you encounter any problems during this procedure? Yes ___ No ___

   If Yes, describe the problems: _____

   _____

   _____

   What did you do to correct the problems?_____

   _____

   _____

- ☐ 4. Have your instructor check your work and sign this job sheet.

Performance Evaluation—Instructor Use Only

Did the student complete the job in the time allotted? Yes ___ No ___

If No, which steps were not completed?_____

How would you rate this student's overall performance on this job?_____

5–Excellent, 4–Good, 3–Satisfactory, 2–Unsatisfactory, 1–Poor

Comments: _____

_____

_____

INSTRUCTOR'S SIGNATURE _____

Notes

Job
Inspect and Service Power Steering System Hoses

34

After completing this job, you will be able to check the condition of power steering hoses. You will also be able to replace low- and high-pressure power steering hoses.

Instructions

As you read the job instructions, answer the questions and perform the tasks. Print your answers neatly and use complete sentences. Consult the proper service literature and ask your instructor for help as needed.

> ### Warning
> ⚠ Before performing this job, review all pertinent safety information in the text and discuss safety procedures with your instructor.

Procedures

☐ 1. Obtain a vehicle to be used in this job. Your instructor may direct you to perform this job on a shop vehicle.

☐ 2. Gather the tools needed to perform this job.

Check Power Steering Hose Condition

☐ 1. Safely raise vehicle on lift as necessary.

☐ 2. Inspect hoses for defects.

Are there any leaks? Yes ___ No ___

If Yes, location: _____

Are the coverings damaged or frayed? Yes ___ No ___

If Yes, location: _____

Are there any bulging or swollen hose segments? Yes ___ No ___

If Yes, location: _____

Are there other problems, such as damaged fittings? Yes ___ No ___

If Yes, describe the problem and its location: _____

_____

☐ 3. Check with your instructor to see if there are further steps that should be taken.

Remove and Replace Power Steering Hose

☐ 1. Safely raise vehicle on lift as necessary.

☐ 2. Place a drain pan under the hose to be replaced.

☐ 3. Remove hose fasteners:

- **High-pressure hose.** Loosen and remove fittings using tubing wrenches.
- **Low-pressure (return) hose.** Remove clamps as necessary

☐ 4. Remove hose from power steering fittings.

☐ 5. Compare the old and new hoses.

Do the hoses match? Yes ___ No ___

If No, in what way(s) do they differ?_____

_____

☐ 6. Place new hose in position on power steering fittings, making sure that it does not contact any moving parts.

☐ 7. Tighten fittings or clamps as applicable.

☐ 8. Lower vehicle.

☐ 9. Refill and bleed power steering system as explained in Job 35.

☐ 10. Recheck power steering system operation.

Job Wrap Up

☐ 1. Return all tools and equipment to storage.

☐ 2. Clean the work area.

☐ 3. Did you encounter any problems during this procedure? Yes ___ No ___

If Yes, describe the problems: _____

_____

What did you do to correct the problems?_____

_____

☐ 4. Have your instructor check your work and sign this job sheet.

Performance Evaluation—Instructor Use Only

Did the student complete the job in the time allotted? Yes ___ No ___

If No, which steps were not completed?_____

How would you rate this student's overall performance on this job?_____

5–Excellent, 4–Good, 3–Satisfactory, 2–Unsatisfactory, 1–Poor

Comments: _____

_____

INSTRUCTOR'S SIGNATURE _____

Job

Flush, Fill, and Bleed a Power Steering System

35

After completing this job, you will be able to replace a power steering filter. You will also be able flush, fill, and bleed air from a power steering system.

Instructions

As you read the job instructions, answer the questions and perform the tasks. Print your answers neatly and use complete sentences. Consult the proper service literature and ask your instructor for help as needed.

> **Warning**
>
> ⚠ Before performing this job, review all pertinent safety information in the text and discuss safety procedures with your instructor.

Procedures

 1. Obtain a vehicle to be used in this job. Your instructor may direct you to perform this job on a shop vehicle.

2. Gather the tools needed to perform this job.

Replace Power Steering System Filter

1. Drain fluid from the power steering system as necessary.
2. Place a drip pan under the vehicle.
3. Remove the clamps holding the filter to the return hose and remove the filter.

   or

   Remove the housing containing the filter and remove the filter.
4. Install the new filter.

> **Note**
>
> If the filter is an in-line type, make sure that it is installed so that fluid will flow through the filter in the proper direction.

☐ 5. Refill and bleed the power steering system as necessary.

☐ 6. Recheck power steering system operation.

Flush, Fill, and Bleed Power Steering System

☐ 1. Place a pan under the power steering reservoir.

☐ 2. Remove the return hose at the reservoir and allow fluid to drain from the reservoir and hose into the pan.

☐ 3. Plug the return port and add fluid to the reservoir. Be sure to use the proper type of fluid.

   What type of fluid was added? _____

☐ 4. Start the engine and add clean fluid to the reservoir as the old fluid flows from the return hose.

☐ 5. When only clean fluid flows from the return hose, turn off the engine.

☐ 6. Remove the plug from the return port and reinstall the return hose.

☐ 7. Refill the reservoir with the proper type of fluid.

☐ 8. Start the engine and add fluid to the reservoir until it stabilizes at the full mark.

☐ 9. Stop the engine and wait approximately two minutes.

☐ 10. Add fluid to the reservoir, if necessary.

☐ 11. Start the engine and turn the steering wheel from side to side for about one minute.

> **Caution**
>
> Raise the wheels off the ground or move the vehicle a few feet after making each complete turn to avoid rubbing flat spots on the tires.

☐ 12. Repeat steps 9–11 until the fluid has no visible bubbles or foam.

Job Wrap Up

☐ 1. Return all tools and equipment to storage.

☐ 2. Clean the work area.

☐ 3. Did you encounter any problems during this procedure? Yes ___ No ___

   If Yes, describe the problems: _____

   _____

   What did you do to correct the problems?_____

   _____

☐ 4. Have your instructor check your work and sign this job sheet.

Job 35—Flush, Fill, and Bleed a Power Steering System (continued)

Performance Evaluation—Instructor Use Only

Did the student complete the job in the time allotted? Yes ___ No ___

If No, which steps were not completed?_____

How would you rate this student's overall performance on this job?_____

5–Excellent, 4–Good, 3–Satisfactory, 2–Unsatisfactory, 1–Poor

Comments: _____

_____

_____

INSTRUCTOR'S SIGNATURE _____

Notes

Job

Inspect and Replace Shock Absorbers

36

After completing this job, you will be able to replace front or rear shock absorbers.

Instructions

As you read the job instructions, answer the questions and perform the tasks. Print your answers neatly and use complete sentences. Consult the proper service literature and ask your instructor for help as needed.

> **Warning**
>
> ⚠ Before performing this job, review all pertinent safety information in the text and discuss safety procedures with your instructor.

Procedures

- [ ] 1. Obtain a vehicle to be used in this job. Your instructor may direct you to perform this job on a shop vehicle.
- [ ] 2. Gather the tools needed to perform this job

Check Shock Absorbers

- [ ] 1. Vigorously bounce one corner of the vehicle up and down by hand; then remove your hand at the bottom of a down stroke. If the vehicle bounces more than once after your hand is removed, the shock absorber is worn out. Perform the bounce test on all four corners of the vehicle.
- [ ] 2. Visually inspect the shock absorbers for the following problems:
  - Dents or other damage to the shock absorber body.
  - Bent shaft.
  - Leaks. See **Figure 36-1**.
  - Damaged, worn, or loose bushings.
  - Damaged, worn, or loose mountings and fasteners.

Figure 36-1. This shock absorber is obviously leaking and should be replaced.

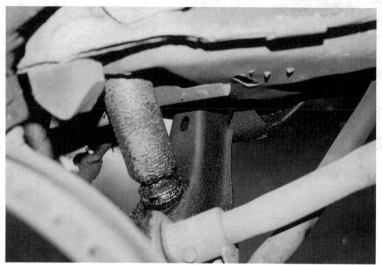

Goodheart-Willcox Publisher

> **Note**
>
> On some vehicles, the shock absorber must be removed to make these inspections.

Describe your findings:_____

Do the shock absorbers require replacement? Yes ___ No ___

Replace Shock Absorbers

☐ 1. Raise the vehicle on a lift or with a floor jack and jack stands.

> **Warning**
>
> Raise and support the vehicle in a safe manner. Always use approved lifts or jacks and jack stands.

☐ 2. If replacing shock absorbers on a rear axle, make sure the axle will not drop when the shock absorbers are removed. If necessary, support the rear axle with jack stands.

> **Note**
>
> If the rear shock absorbers are air operated, depressurize the system and remove the air lines at this time.

☐ 3. Remove the fasteners holding the shock absorber to the vehicle. See **Figure 36-2**.
Describe how the shock absorbers are attached to the vehicle:
Upper: _____
Lower: _____

☐ 4. Remove the shock absorber from the vehicle.

☐ 5. Compare the old and new shock absorbers.

Job 36—Inspect and Replace Shock Absorbers (continued)

Figure 36-2. Shock absorber mountings vary from one type of vehicle to another. This illustration shows the attachment methods used on most modern shock absorbers.

 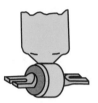 

| Bushing | Bushing with sleeve | Bushing with mounting bars | Two-piece frame bushing |

Goodheart-Willcox Publisher

Note

If the shock absorbers do not match, obtain the correct shocks before proceeding. Shock absorbers that are the incorrect length will not operate properly.

☐ 6. Place the new shock absorber in position.

Note

It may be necessary to compress the new shock absorber slightly to place it in position.

☐ 7. Install the shock absorber fasteners.

☐ 8. Repeat steps 2–7 for other shock absorbers to be changed.

☐ 9. Lower the vehicle and check shock absorber operation.

Job Wrap Up

☐ 1. Return all tools and equipment to storage.

☐ 2. Clean the work area.

☐ 3. Did you encounter any problems during this procedure? Yes ___ No ___

If Yes, describe the problems: _____

_____

_____

What did you do to correct the problems?_____

_____

_____

☐ 4. Have your instructor check your work and sign this job sheet.

Performance Evaluation—Instructor Use Only

Did the student complete the job in the time allotted? Yes ___ No ___
If No, which steps were not completed?_____
How would you rate this student's overall performance on this job?_____
5–Excellent, 4–Good, 3–Satisfactory, 2–Unsatisfactory, 1–Poor
Comments: _____
_____
_____
INSTRUCTOR'S SIGNATURE _____

Job

Check Electric/ Electronic Power Steering

37

After completing this job, you will be able to check electric/electronic power steering, including those systems used on hybrid vehicles.

Instructions

As you read the job instructions, answer the questions and perform the tasks. Print your answers neatly and use complete sentences. Consult the proper service literature and ask your instructor for help as needed.

> **Warning**
>
> Before performing this job, review all pertinent safety information in the text and discuss safety procedures with your instructor.

Procedures

☐ 1. Obtain a vehicle to be used in this job. Your instructor may direct you to perform this job on a shop vehicle.

☐ 2. Gather the tools needed to perform this job.

Inspect and Test Electric/Electronic Power Steering

☐ 1. Road test the vehicle to verify problems and determine steering effort required to turn the wheels from side to side.

☐ 2. Ensure that binding or looseness problems involve the electric power steering system and are not mechanical.

> **Caution**
>
> Some manufacturers recommend removing the power steering control fuse and road testing the vehicle to isolate problems. Do not, however, remove any fuses before retrieving trouble codes.

☐ 3. Use the scan tool to retrieve trouble codes.

List the retrieved codes: _____

_____

☐ 4. Check service information to determine whether any of the codes are electric power steering–related codes. Do the steering trouble codes involve any of the following?

Steering angle sensors? Yes ___ No ___

If Yes, list: _____

Torque sensors? Yes ___ No ___

If Yes, list: _____

Motor amperage? Yes ___ No ___

If Yes, list: _____

☐ 5. Use the scan tool to check sensor inputs, motor amperage draw, and other parameters as necessary.

Results of tests:_____

_____

_____

☐ 6. Consult with your instructor about needed repairs.

Job Wrap Up

☐ 1. Return all tools and equipment to storage.

☐ 2. Clean the work area.

☐ 3. Did you encounter any problems during this procedure? Yes ___ No ___

If Yes, describe the problems: _____

_____

_____

What did you do to correct the problems?_____

_____

_____

☐ 4. Have your instructor check your work and sign this job sheet.

Performance Evaluation—Instructor Use Only

Did the student complete the job in the time allotted? Yes ___ No ___

If No, which steps were not completed?_____

How would you rate this student's overall performance on this job?_____

5–Excellent, 4–Good, 3–Satisfactory, 2–Unsatisfactory, 1–Poor

Comments: _____

_____

INSTRUCTOR'S SIGNATURE_____

Job

Check a Power Steering Pressure Switch

38

After completing this job, you will explain the purpose of a power steering pressure switch and check the switch for proper operation.

Instructions

As you read the job instructions, answer the questions and perform the tasks. Print your answers neatly and use complete sentences. Consult the proper service literature and ask your instructor for help as needed.

> **Warning**
>
> ⚠ Before performing this job, review all pertinent safety information in the text and discuss safety procedures with your instructor.

Questions

Identify the Purpose of the Power Steering Pressure Switch

_____ 1. True or False? The power steering pressure switch is a type of on-off switch.

_____ 2. The power steering pressure switch tells the vehicle ECM that the power steering system pressure is _____.

_____ 3. The ECM compensates for high power steering system pressure by raising the engine _____.

Procedures

Test Power Steering Pressure Switch

☐ 1. Obtain a vehicle to be used in this job. Your instructor may direct you to perform this job on a shop vehicle.

☐ 2. Gather the tools needed to perform this job.

☐ 3. Locate the power steering pressure switch.

☐ 4. Disconnect the electrical connector at the power steering pressure switch.

☐ 5. Obtain an ohmmeter with appropriate leads.

☐ 6. Set the ohmmeter to its highest setting and zero the ohmmeter as necessary.

☐ 7. Attach the ohmmeter leads to the pressure switch leads.

☐ 8. Record the ohmmeter reading:_____Ω.

> ### Note
> The reading could be very low or infinity, depending on switch design.

☐ 9. Have an assistant start the engine and turn the steering wheel to its furthest position (lock) in either direction.

☐ 10. Record the ohmmeter reading: _____Ω.
    Is this reading different from the reading in step 8? Yes ___ No ___
    If No, the switch is defective.

☐ 11. Disconnect the ohmmeter and consult your instructor as to what further steps to take.

Job Wrap Up

☐ 1. Return all tools and equipment to storage.

☐ 2. Clean the work area.

☐ 3. Did you encounter any problems during this procedure? Yes ___ No ___
    If Yes, describe the problems: _____
    _____
    _____
    What did you do to correct the problems?_____
    _____
    _____

☐ 4. Have your instructor check your work and sign this job sheet.

Performance Evaluation—Instructor Use Only

Did the student complete the job in the time allotted? Yes ___ No ___
If No, which steps were not completed?_____
How would you rate this student's overall performance on this job?_____
5–Excellent, 4–Good, 3–Satisfactory, 2–Unsatisfactory, 1–Poor
Comments: _____
_____
_____

INSTRUCTOR'S SIGNATURE _____

Job

Perform a Pre-Alignment Inspection

39

After completing this job, you will be able to prepare a vehicle for a two- or four-wheel alignment.

Instructions

As you read the job instructions, answer the questions and perform the tasks. Print your answers neatly and use complete sentences. Consult the proper service literature and ask your instructor for help as needed.

> **Warning**
>
> Before performing this job, review all pertinent safety information in the text and discuss safety procedures with your instructor.

Procedures

- [ ] 1. Obtain a vehicle to be used in this job. Your instructor may direct you to perform this job on a shop vehicle.
- [ ] 2. Gather the tools needed to perform this job.

Preliminaries

- [ ] 1. Consult the driver to determine the exact nature of the complaint or, if there is no complaint, ask why the driver feels that steering/suspension service is necessary.

> **Note**
>
> If necessary, road test the vehicle with the driver to determine the exact nature of the complaint.

☐ 2. Identify the owner's complaint. Check all that apply.
   ☐ Pulling or drifting.
   ☐ Hard steering.
   ☐ Bump steer.
   ☐ Wander.
   ☐ Memory steer.
   ☐ Torque steer.
   ☐ Poor return.
   ☐ Uneven tire wear.
   ☐ Other (describe):_____

   _____

   Briefly describe the results of the road test (if performed): _____

   _____

☐ 3. Determine whether the complaint could be caused by part or alignment concerns. List possible causes of the problem.

   Defective parts (list): _____

   _____

   Incorrect steering geometry (list): _____

   _____

Prepare the Vehicle and Rack for Alignment

☐ 1. Park the vehicle on level pavement.

☐ 2. Check tire condition and pressure, and complete the following tire condition chart:

	Tire Size	Tire Pressure	Tire Condition
Left front			
Left rear			
Right rear			
Right front			

Problems found: _____

_____

What should you do to correct them? _____

_____

Note

If tire pressures are incorrect, or if tires are mismatched, step 3 cannot be performed.

Job 39—Perform a Pre-Alignment Inspection (continued)

☐ 3. Measure vehicle ride height at all four wheels. Record the readings in the following chart:

	Ride Height
Left front	
Left rear	
Right rear	
Right front	

Compare your measurements to specifications. Were any ride height measurements out of specification? Yes ___ No ___

Is there more than 1/4″ (0.6 mm) variation from side to side or from front and rear? Yes ___ No ___

If the answer to either of the above questions is Yes, consult your instructor before proceeding.

☐ 4. Make sure the lift is in safe working order.

☐ 5. Drive the vehicle onto the lift and raise the lift to a comfortable working height.

☐ 6. Raise the vehicle so the front suspension is correctly suspended for checking the ball joints.

☐ 7. Perform the shake test on the front wheels:

Grasp the wheel at the top and bottom and shake it back and forth. This checks the suspension parts.

Do the wheels feel loose? Yes ___ No ___

> **Note**
>
> To check the suspension on some MacPherson strut vehicles, grasp the wheel at approximately 45° from the top and bottom and shake it back and forth.

Grasp the wheel at the front and back and shake it back and forth. This checks steering linkage parts.

Do the wheels feel loose? Yes ___ No ___

☐ 8. If the front wheels feel loose during the shake test, check the individual front suspension and steering parts, wheels, and tires for wear or damage.

Problems found: _____

What should you do to correct them? _____

☐ 9. Make a visual inspection of the front suspension and steering parts. Look carefully for loose or bent parts, loose fasteners, torn boots or seals, and a bent or misaligned frame or subframe/engine cradle.

Problems found: _____

What should you do to correct the problems? _____

> **Note**
>
> Be sure to check the front and rear frame components and cradles for damage.

☐ 10. Make a visual inspection of the rear suspension and steering parts, as well as the rear wheels and tires.

> **Note**
>
> If necessary, raise the rear of the vehicle to check for worn suspension and steering parts. Perform the shake test as described in step 7.

☐ 11. Consult with your instructor concerning needed repairs.

What repairs are needed?_____

_____

_____

_____

Job Wrap Up

☐ 1. Return all tools and equipment to storage.

☐ 2. Clean the work area.

☐ 3. Did you encounter any problems during this procedure? Yes ___ No ___

If Yes, describe the problems: _____

_____

_____

What did you do to correct the problems?_____

_____

_____

☐ 4. Have your instructor check your work and sign this job sheet.

Performance Evaluation—Instructor Use Only

Did the student complete the job in the time allotted? Yes ___ No ___

If No, which steps were not completed?_____

How would you rate this student's overall performance on this job?_____

5–Excellent, 4–Good, 3–Satisfactory, 2–Unsatisfactory, 1–Poor

Comments: _____

_____

INSTRUCTOR'S SIGNATURE _____

Job

Inspect Tires
and Rims

After completing this job, you will be able to inspect tires and rims for damage.

Instructions

As you read the job instructions, answer the questions and perform the tasks. Print your answers neatly and use complete sentences. Consult the proper service literature and ask your instructor for help as needed.

> **Warning**
>
> ⚠ Before performing this job, review all pertinent safety information in the text and discuss safety procedures with your instructor.

Procedures

 1. Obtain a vehicle to be used in this job. Your instructor may direct you to perform this job on a shop vehicle.

☐ 2. Gather the tools needed to perform this job.

Inspect Tires on a Vehicle

 1. Raise the vehicle in a safe manner.

> **Warning**
>
> ⚠ The vehicle must be raised and supported in a safe manner. Always use approved lifts or jacks and jack stands.

2. From the information printed on the sidewall of the tire, fill in the following data for each tire.

	Left Front	Right Front	Left Rear	Right Rear
Manufacturer				
Section width				
Aspect ratio				
Speed rating				
Construction type				
Rim diameter				

Do all tires match? Yes ___ No ___

Maximum tire pressure as listed on the sidewall of the tire: _____

3. Compare the tire pressure specification on the sidewall with the vehicle manufacturer's tire pressure recommendation. Vehicle manufacturer's tire pressure recommendations are listed on the tire loading information sticker. Common sticker locations are the driver's side door, driver's side doorjamb, or inside of the trunk lid.

Vehicle manufacturer's tire pressure recommendation for this vehicle: _____

4. Check tire pressure and fill in the following chart. Add or remove pressure as necessary.

	Left Front	Right Front	Left Rear	Right Rear
Recommended pressure				
Measure pressure				

5. Measure tread depth of all the tires with a tire depth gauge. See **Figure 40-1**. Measure the tread at its deepest and shallowest points. If the tread depth is less than 1/16" (1.59 mm) deep, the tire should be replaced.

	Left Front	Right Front	Left Rear	Right Rear
Maximum tread depth				
Minimum tread depth				

Note

 A quick and relatively accurate method of checking tire wear is to insert a Lincoln penny into the tire tread at various locations with the top of the head pointing downward. If the top of Lincoln's head shows in any of the test locations, the tire is worn out.

Job 40—Inspect Tires and Rims (continued)

Figure 40-1. Use a depth gauge to check tread wear.

> **Note**
>
> Many modern tires have tread ribs at the bottom of the tire tread, at a right angle (90°) to the tread. When the tread wears down so that these ribs can be seen to extend across the tire tread, the tire is worn excessively and should be replaced.

6. Check all the vehicle's tires for abnormal tire wear patterns and compare the vehicle's tire wear patterns to the patterns shown in **Figure 40-2**. Describe the tire wear patterns.

   Left front: _____

   Right front: _____

   Left rear: _____

   Right rear: _____

   What could cause these wear patterns? _____

   _____

7. Check all tires for damage, such as cuts, cracks, and tread separation.

   Is any damage visible? Yes ___ No ___

   If Yes, describe the damage: _____

   _____

Figure 40-2. This figure shows the cause, effect, and correction of several abnormal tire wear patterns.

Condition	Rapid wear at shoulders	Rapid wear at center	Cracked treads	Wear on one side	Feathered edge	Bald spots	Scalloped wear
Effect							
Cause	Under-inflation or lack of rotation	Over-inflation or lack of rotation	Under-inflation or excessive speed	Excessive camber	Incorrect toe	Unbalanced wheel / or tire defect	Lack of rotation of tires or worn or out-of-alignment suspension
Correction	Adjust pressure to specifications when tires are cool. Rotate tires.			Adjust camber to specifications.	Adjust toe-in to specifications.	Dynamic or static balance wheels.	Rotate tires and inspect suspension.

Chrysler

8. Based on the information gathered in steps 5 through 7, decide whether any tire needs replacement.

   Do any tires require replacement? Yes ___ No ___

   If Yes, fill out the form below. Place a check mark next to the tire(s) that need to be replaced and explain why replacement is necessary.

   Left front ___ Reason:_____

   Right front ___ Reason: _____

   Left rear ___ Reason:_____

   Right rear ___ Reason: _____

Check Tire for Air Loss

1. Remove the wheel and tire assembly from the vehicle.

2. Inflate the tire to its maximum allowable air pressure.

3. Place the wheel and tire in a water tank. Most shops will have a special tank for this purpose.

4. Slowly rotate the tire through the water while watching for air bubbles. Bubbles indicate a leak. Carefully check all areas of the tire and wheel, including:

   ☐ Tread area.

   ☐ Sidewalls.

   ☐ Bead area.

   ☐ Rim.

   ☐ Valve and valve core.

   Were any leaks found? Yes ___ No ___

   If Yes, describe the location: _____

   _____

5. If air leaks were found, consult your instructor. Your instructor may direct you to perform Job 42 at this time.

6. If no air leaks were found, reduce tire air pressure to the recommended amount and reinstall the wheel and tire on the vehicle.

Job 40—Inspect Tires and Rims (continued)

Install Wheels

☐ 1. Place the wheel(s) in position on the vehicle.

☐ 2. Install the lug nuts on each wheel using the following method:

- Tighten the lug nuts in an alternating, or star, pattern. Do not tighten the lug nuts in a circle around the rim.

- Tighten the lug nuts in steps. Do not tighten any lug nut down completely before the others have been partially tightened.

☐ 3. Lower the vehicle.

☐ 4. Use a torque wrench to perform the final tightening sequence in an alternating pattern. Check the service information for the proper lug nut torque for the vehicle.

> **Note**
>
> Recheck the lug nut torque of aluminum and magnesium wheels after the vehicle has been driven 25 to 50 miles.

☐ 5. Reinstall the wheel cover(s) if necessary.

Measure Tire Runout

☐ 1. Select a spot on the vehicle to attach a dial indicator.

☐ 2. Mount the dial indicator so its plunger contacts the tire tread.

☐ 3. Zero the dial indicator.

☐ 4. Rotate the wheel slowly by hand.

☐ 5. Observe and record the maximum variation of the dial indicator.

Maximum variation: _____

Is this within specifications? Yes ___ No ___

☐ 6. Reposition the dial indicator so its plunger contacts the tire sidewall.

☐ 7. Zero the dial indicator.

☐ 8. Rotate the wheel slowly by hand. Observe and record the maximum variation of the dial indicator.

Maximum variation: _____

Is this within specifications? Yes ___ No ___

Measure Rim Runout

☐ 1. Remove the tire and rim assembly from the vehicle.

☐ 2. Remove the tire from the rim.

☐ 3. Install the rim assembly on a tire machine so that it can be turned by hand.

☐ 4. Install a dial indicator so the indicator plunger contacts the inner surface of the rim.

☐ 5. Zero the indicator.

☐ 6. Rotate the rim slowly by hand.

☐ 7. Observe and record the maximum variation of the dial indicator.

Maximum variation: _____

Is this within specifications? Yes ___ No ___

☐ 8. Reposition the dial indicator so that its plunger contacts the outer side surface of the rim.

☐ 9. Zero the indicator.

☐ 10. Rotate the rim slowly by hand.

☐ 11. Observe and record the maximum variation of the dial indicator.

Maximum variation: _____

Is this within specifications? Yes ___ No ___

☐ 12. If the tire and/or wheel runout is out of specification, replace the tire and/or wheel as necessary.

Measure Wheel Hub Runout

☐ 1. Remove the tire and rim assembly from the wheel to be checked.

☐ 2. Place the transmission in neutral if a rear hub is to be checked.

☐ 3. Install a dial indicator so the indicator plunger contacts the outer surface of the hub flange.

☐ 4. Zero the indicator.

☐ 5. Rotate the hub slowly by hand.

☐ 6. Observe and record the maximum variation of the dial indicator.

Maximum variation: _____

Is this within specifications? Yes ___ No ___

Job Wrap Up

☐ 1. Return all tools and equipment to storage.

☐ 2. Clean the work area.

☐ 3. Did you encounter any problems during this procedure? Yes ___ No ___

If Yes, describe the problems: _____

_____

_____

What did you do to correct the problems?_____

_____

_____

☐ 4. Have your instructor check your work and sign this job sheet.

Performance Evaluation—Instructor Use Only

Did the student complete the job in the time allotted? Yes ___ No ___

If No, which steps were not completed?_____

How would you rate this student's overall performance on this job?_____

5–Excellent, 4–Good, 3–Satisfactory, 2–Unsatisfactory, 1–Poor

Comments: _____

_____

_____

INSTRUCTOR'S SIGNATURE _____

After completing this job, you will able to rotate and balance tires.

Instructions

As you read the job instructions, answer the questions and perform the tasks. Print your answers neatly and use complete sentences. Consult the proper service literature and ask your instructor for help as needed.

> **Warning**
>
> ⚠ Before performing this job, review all pertinent safety information in the text and discuss safety procedures with your instructor.

Procedures

☐ 1. Obtain a vehicle to be used in this job. Your instructor may direct you to perform this job on a shop vehicle.

☐ 2. Gather the tools needed to perform this job.

Rotate Tires

☐ 1. Remove all the wheel covers, if necessary.

☐ 2. Loosen the lug nuts on all wheels.

☐ 3. Raise the vehicle in a safe manner.

> **Warning**
>
> ⚠ The vehicle must be raised and supported in a safe manner. Always use approved lifts or jacks and jack stands.

☐ 4. Remove all lug nuts.

☐ 5. Rotate the tires. Rotation patterns vary from vehicle to vehicle. Be sure to check the service information for the proper rotation pattern.

6. Reinstall the lug nuts.
7. Lower the vehicle.
8. Tighten the lug nuts to the proper torque.
9. Reinstall the wheel covers if necessary.

Balance Tires

1. Remove the tire and wheel from the vehicle.
2. Remove all wheel weights from the rim.

Static Balance

1. Install the tire and wheel assembly over the center cone of the bubble balancer.
2. Observe the position of the bubble.
3. If the bubble is not centered, place weights on the wheel rim to center the bubble.
4. Once the bubble is centered, affix the weights to the rim.
5. Remove the tire and wheel assembly from the bubble balancer.
6. Install the assembly on the vehicle and tighten the lug nuts to the proper torque.

Dynamic Balance

1. Install the tire on the balance machine, **Figure 41-1**.
2. Set the tire balance machine to the proper wheel rim diameter and width.
3. Start the balance machine and determine whether the rim and tire are turning without excessive wobbling. If excessive wobble is noted, the rim may be improperly installed or it may be bent.

> **Note**
>
> Correct wobble before proceeding. A wobbling tire cannot be balanced. If the rim is bent, it must be replaced.

Figure 41-1. Tire mounted on a balance machine.

Goodheart-Willcox Publisher

Job 41—Rotate and Balance Tires (continued)

☐ 4. Note the amount and location of needed weights by reading the information on the tire balancer console.

☐ 5. Install the weights on the rim.

☐ 6. Start the balance machine and observe whether installing the weights corrected the balance.

   Is the tire balanced? Yes ___ No ___

   If No, remove the weights and repeat steps 3 through 6.

☐ 7. Reinstall the tire and wheel on the vehicle.

Job Wrap Up

☐ 1. Return all tools and equipment to storage.

☐ 2. Clean the work area.

☐ 3. Did you encounter any problems during this procedure? Yes ___ No ___

   If Yes, describe the problems: _____

   _____

   _____

   What did you do to correct the problems?_____

   _____

   _____

☐ 4. Have your instructor check your work and sign this job sheet.

Performance Evaluation—Instructor Use Only

Did the student complete the job in the time allotted? Yes ___ No ___

If No, which steps were not completed?_____

How would you rate this student's overall performance on this job?_____

5–Excellent, 4–Good, 3–Satisfactory, 2–Unsatisfactory, 1–Poor

Comments: _____

_____

_____

INSTRUCTOR'S SIGNATURE _____

Notes

Job

Remove and Install a Tire on a Rim; Repair a Punctured Tire

After completing this job, you will able to mount and dismount tires on rims and repair a tire puncture.

Instructions

As you read the job instructions, answer the questions and perform the tasks. Print your answers neatly and use complete sentences. Consult the proper service literature and ask your instructor for help as needed.

> **Warning**
>
> ⚠ Before performing this job, review all pertinent safety information in the text and discuss safety procedures with your instructor.

Procedures

☐ 1. Obtain a vehicle to be used in this job. Your instructor may direct you to perform this job on a shop vehicle.

☐ 2. Gather the tools needed to perform this job.

Remove a Tire from a Rim

> **Warning**
>
> ⚠ If the vehicle is equipped with a tire pressure monitoring system, remove the tire carefully to ensure that the rim-mounted pressure sensors are not damaged.

☐ 1. Remove the wheel cover of the tire and wheel to be removed.

☐ 2. Remove the valve stem core (or valve stem if stem is to be replaced).

> **Note**
>
> It is easier to remove the valve core or stem when the tire is solidly mounted on the vehicle.

☐ 3. Loosen the lug nuts.

☐ 4. Raise the vehicle.

> **Warning**
>
> ⚠ The vehicle must be raised and supported in a safe manner. Always use approved lifts or jacks and jack stands.

☐ 5. Remove the lug nuts.

☐ 6. Remove the wheel and tire from the vehicle.

☐ 7. Remove any wheel weights with wheel weight pliers.

> **Note**
>
> The wheel weights can be left on the rim if great care is taken not to move them during tire removal and the tire is reinstalled in exactly the same position on the rim.

☐ 8. Position the tire at the tire changing machine bead breaker and use the bead breaker to loosen both tire beads at the wheel flanges, **Figure 42-1**.

Figure 42-1. Many modern wheels are made of aluminum or composite materials and can be damaged if the bead breaker is not properly positioned.

Bead breaker

Goodheart-Willcox Publisher

Job 42—Remove and Install a Tire on a Rim; Repair a Punctured Tire (continued)

> **Caution**
>
> Avoid catching the bead breaker on the edge of the wheel. The bead breaker can bend a steel wheel or break an alloy wheel.

☐ 9. Place the tire and wheel on the tire-changing machine and tightly install the wheel hold-down cone.

☐ 10. Place a generous quantity of rubber lubricant or soapy water on the tire bead and the wheel flange to ease tire removal.

☐ 11. Use the tire-changing machine inner spindle and the tire changer bar to remove the upper tire bead from the wheel.

> **Note**
>
> Use one hand to hold the tire bead in the center of the wheel while removing the opposite side of the tire.

☐ 12. Pull the bottom bead up to the top of the rim and repeat step 11 to remove the bottom tire bead from the wheel. See **Figure 42-2**.

Install a Tire on a Rim

> **Warning**
>
> If the vehicle is equipped with a tire pressure monitoring system, install the tire carefully to ensure that the rim-mounted pressure sensors are not damaged.

Figure 42-2. Removing the upper tire bead. Use caution and wear safety goggles.

Goodheart-Willcox Publisher

☐ 1. Clean the sealing edge of the wheel rim as needed. If the rim is rusted or dirty, clean it with steel wool.

☐ 2. Check the rim for cracks or dents at the sealing surface.

Was any damage found? Yes ___ No ___

If Yes, describe:_____

☐ 3. Check the condition of the valve stem. Bend it sideways and look for weather cracks or splits.

Can the tire valve be reused? Yes ___ No ___

If No, go to step 4.

If Yes, go to step 6.

☐ 4. Check the tire pressure sensor assembly for damage and make sure that it is solidly mounted on the rim. If the sensor and tire valve are a single assembly, visually inspect any mounting hardware and sealing rings.

☐ 5. Install a new tire valve if necessary. Remove the valve core after installing the valve.

☐ 6. Place tire lubricant or soapy water on the tire bead and the flange of the wheel.

☐ 7. Place the tire on top of the wheel.

Caution

Make sure that the tire is facing in the proper direction.

☐ 8. Use the tire-changing machine inner spindle and the tire changer bar to install the lower tire bead on the wheel.

☐ 9. Repeat step 8 to install the top tire bead on the wheel.

☐ 10. Pull up on the installed tire while twisting to partially seal the tire on the upper flange.

☐ 11. Install the air nozzle on the valve stem.

☐ 12. Fill the tire with air.

Note

If air rushes out of the tire as you try to fill it, push in lightly on the leaking part of the tire. If the tire will not hold enough air to expand and seal on the wheel, clamp a bead expander around the outside of the tire to push the tire bead against the wheel flange; then fill the tire with air.

Warning

Release the bead expander as soon as the tire begins to inflate. If this is not done, the expander can break and fly off the tire with dangerous force.

☐ 13. Loosen the wheel hold-down cone as soon as the tire begins to inflate.

Warning

Do not inflate the tire to over 40 psi (276 kPa). Lean away from the tire as it inflates to prevent possible injury.

Job 42—Remove and Install a Tire on a Rim; Repair a Punctured Tire (continued)

☐ 14. Make sure the tire has popped into place over the safety ridges on the rim.

☐ 15. Remove the air nozzle from the valve stem.

☐ 16. Install the valve core.

☐ 17. Inflate the tire to the correct air pressure.

☐ 18. Rebalance the tire if necessary.

☐ 19. Place the tire in position on the vehicle.

☐ 20. Install the lug nuts.

☐ 21. Lower the vehicle.

☐ 22. Use a torque wrench to perform the final tightening sequence in an alternating pattern. Check the service information for the proper lug nut torque for the vehicle.

> **Note**
>
> Recheck the lug nut torque of aluminum and magnesium wheels after the vehicle has been driven 25 to 50 miles.

☐ 23. Reinstall the wheel cover if necessary.

Repair a Tire Puncture

> **Caution**
>
> The following procedure is for repairing a puncture with a combination patch and plug called a mushroom patch. Consult your instructor if another type of patch is to be used. Tires can be repaired with rubber plugs inserted into the puncture, but tire manufacturers do not recommend this type of repair.

☐ 1. Remove the tire and rim assembly from the vehicle.

☐ 2. Remove the tire from the rim.

☐ 3. Inspect the inside of the tire for splits, cracks, punctures, or previous patches.

☐ 4. Locate and remove the puncturing object, then mark the damaged area with a tire crayon or other easily visible marker.

> **Warning**
>
> Do not attempt to repair a puncture on the tire shoulder or sidewall. Flexing will cause the patch to leak immediately. In addition, a puncture on the shoulder or sidewall may have structurally damaged the tire. Replace tires punctured in these areas.

☐ 5. Mount the tire on a tire repair fixture so the puncture area can be easily reached.

☐ 6. Use a scuffing tool to roughen the inside surface of the tire at the puncture site. Roughen an area larger than the size of the patch and remove all rubber particles.

☐ 7. Apply patch cement to the scuffed area.

☐ 8. Place the patch over the puncture area.

☐ 9. Pull the plug portion of the patch through the puncture.

☐ 10. Apply pressure to the patch to seal it to the inner surface of the tire. A special tool called a stitching tool is available for this operation.

☐ 11. Reinstall the tire on the rim and inflate to the proper pressure.

☐ 12. Check for leaks at the puncture to ensure that the repair is successful.

☐ 13. Trim the mushroom patch so that it is even with the tread surface.

☐ 14. Reinstall the tire assembly on the vehicle.

Replace Tire Pressure Monitors

☐ 1. Remove the tire and rim assembly from vehicle.

☐ 2. Depressurize tire and remove the tire from the rim using the proper tire machine.

☐ 3. Remove the pressure sensor assembly from tire valve opening. Install a new pressure sensor assembly in the tire valve opening and tighten the fastener to the correct value.

    or

    Remove the strap holding the pressure sensor assembly on the inner part of the tire rim. Install the replacement pressure sensor assembly. Install and tighten the strap.

☐ 4. Reinstall the tire on the rim and inflate the tire to the proper pressure.

☐ 5. Reinstall the tire and rim assembly on the vehicle and reprogram the sensing system as needed.

Calibrate a Tire Pressure Monitoring System

> **Note**
>
> This procedure can be performed with the vehicle on or off the ground.

☐ 1. On the scan tool or instrument panel display, locate the menu for calibrating the tire pressure monitoring system.

> **Note**
>
> Most tire pressure monitoring systems are accessed through the scan tool. A few systems, however, use the instrument panel display to calibrate the system. Consult the appropriate service literature to determine which is used.

☐ 2. If necessary, attach a scan tool to the vehicle diagnostic connector.

☐ 3. Enter the tire pressure monitoring system calibration mode.

Job 42—Remove and Install a Tire on a Rim; Repair a Punctured Tire (continued)

> **Note**
>
> Most calibration sequences must be completed in a set time period, such as one minute to calibrate the first tire and 30 seconds each to calibrate the remaining tires. If the calibration does not begin within this time frame, the system will abort the calibration procedure and all information will be lost.

☐ 4. Begin the calibration procedure at the first tire indicated by the calibration mode instructions.

> **Note**
>
> Some systems require that a special relearn magnet be placed over the tire valve to recalibrate the system. See the manufacturer's instructions for exact procedures.

☐ 5. Allow the sensor on the first wheel to transmit its code. The horn will sound very briefly to indicate completion of the transmission.

☐ 6. Repeat steps 3 and 4 for all four wheels, and the spare tire if a 5-tire system is used. When one tire calibration sequence is finished, the system software will move to the next tire to be calibrated. Tires are calibrated in a rotating pattern, such as LF, LR, RR, RF. Be sure to move the calibration magnet, if used, to the next tire to be calibrated.

☐ 7. Exit calibration mode.

☐ 8. Drive the vehicle to confirm that the calibration process was successful.

Job Wrap Up

☐ 1. Return all tools and equipment to storage.

☐ 2. Clean the work area.

☐ 3. Did you encounter any problems during this procedure? Yes ___ No ___

If Yes, describe the problems: _____

_____

What did you do to correct the problems?_____

_____

☐ 4. Have your instructor check your work and sign this job sheet.

Performance Evaluation—Instructor Use Only

Did the student complete the job in the time allotted? Yes ___ No ___

If No, which steps were not completed?_____

How would you rate this student's overall performance on this job?____

5–Excellent, 4–Good, 3–Satisfactory, 2–Unsatisfactory, 1–Poor

Comments: _____

_____

_____

INSTRUCTOR'S SIGNATURE _____

Job

Inspect a Brake System

43

After completing this job, you will be able to inspect a vehicle's brake system.

Instructions

As you read the job instructions, answer the questions and perform the tasks. Print your answers neatly and use complete sentences. Consult the proper service literature and ask your instructor for help as needed.

> **Warning**
> Before performing this job, review all pertinent safety information in the text and discuss safety procedures with your instructor.

Procedures

> **Note**
> This procedure addresses inspection of the base brake system. For diagnosis of the power brake system, see Job 51. For inspection of the anti-lock brake system, see Job 54 .

☐ 1. Obtain a vehicle to be used in this job. Your instructor may direct you to perform this job on a shop vehicle.

☐ 2. Gather the tools needed to perform this job.

☐ 3. Obtain a detailed description of the brake problem from the vehicle's operator. Explain the problem as described by the operator:_____

_____

_____

_____

4. Obtain the proper service literature for the vehicle being diagnosed and determine the type of brake system:

☐ Four-wheel disc brakes.

☐ Front disc, rear drum brakes.

☐ Four-wheel drum brakes.

Is the vehicle equipped with ABS? Yes ___ No ___

5. Check the fluid level in the master cylinder. See **Figure 43-1**.

Is the level at or near the top? Yes ___ No ___

6. If the fluid level in the master cylinder is low, visually inspect the entire system for leaks.

Were any leaks found? Yes ___ No ___

Warning

⚠ Do not perform a road test if the vehicle has no brakes or seriously malfunctioning brakes. Always check the brake fluid level before beginning any road test.

---

7. Drive the vehicle on a lightly traveled, level road until a speed of 30 mph (48 kph) is reached.

8. Apply the brakes lightly.

9. Release the brakes and accelerate to 30 mph (48 kph) again.

10. Apply the brakes firmly.

11. Observe whether any of the following occur during braking:

- Pulling to one side: Yes ___ No ___ To which side? _____
- Vibration throughout the vehicle body/seats: Yes ___ No ___
- Brake pedal pulsation: Yes ___ No ___

Figure 43-1. If the master cylinder reservoir is made of translucent plastic, compare the fluid level to markings on the reservoir. If the reservoir is not translucent or there are no markings, the fluid level should be approximately 1/4" (6 mm) from the top of the reservoir opening.

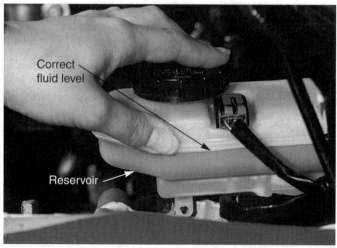

Goodheart-Willcox Publisher

Job 43—Inspect a Brake System (continued)

- Low brake pedal/excessive pedal travel: Yes ___ No ___
- Hard pedal: Yes ___ No ___
- Warning light illumination: Yes ___ No ___
- Noises, such as squealing, grinding, or knocking: Yes ___ No ___

  If Yes, describe: _____

  _____

  _____

- Other apparent brake problems: Yes ___ No ___

  If Yes, describe: _____

  _____

  _____

☐ 12. Release the brakes and accelerate to 60 mph (97 kph).

☐ 13. Ensure that no vehicles are behind you and apply the brakes hard.

☐ 14. Observe the following during hard braking:

- Slight pedal pulsation: Yes ___ No ___
- Straight stop, with no skidding or noise: (slight chirping is normal): Yes ___ No ___
- Wheel lockup on any wheel: Yes ___ No ___
- Illumination of the ABS light (some vehicles): Yes ___ No ___

☐ 15. Stop the vehicle on a slight incline.

☐ 16. Apply the parking brake.

Does the vehicle remain stationary? Yes ___ No ___

☐ 17. Release the parking brake.

Does the parking brake mechanism release easily, allowing the vehicle to move? Yes ___ No ___

☐ 18. Remove the wheels, as well as the drums and/or calipers. Visually inspect the brake system friction materials.

Pad/Shoe Condition					
Pads/Shoes	Worn	Glazed	Cracked	Overheated	Oil- or Brake Fluid-Soaked
Left front					
Right front					
Left rear					
Right rear					
Parking brake (if separate)					

Drum/Rotor Condition				
Drums/Rotors	Worn	Glazed	Cracked	Overheated
Left front				
Right front				
Left rear				
Right rear				
Parking brake (if separate)				

19. Measure the rotors or drums using appropriate micrometers. See **Figure 43-2**.

Rotors/Drums	Specification	Actual Reading	Out-of-Round	Taper
Left front				
Action needed				
Right front				
Action needed				
Left rear				
Action neede				
Right rear				
Action needed				
Parking brake (if separate)				
Action needed				

Figure 43-2. Brake drum diameter can be measured with a drum micrometer. Measure the drum diameter in several locations. Variations in diameter indicate that the drum is out-of-round.

Goodheart-Willcox Publisher

Job 43—Inspect a Brake System (continued)

☐ 20. Use a dial indicator to check the rotors and hubs for warping.

Rotor Runout		
Rotors	Maximum Allowable Variation	Measured Variation
Left front		
Action needed		
Right front		
Action needed		
Left rear		
Action neede		
Right rear		
Action needed		
Parking brake (if separate)		
Action needed		

☐ 21. Visually inspect other brake system components for problems.

> **Note**
> Not every part listed below will be found on every vehicle. Write NA in the space provided if a part is not used.

Brake System Defects			
Front Brakes—Left			
Component	Bent/Broken	Leaking	Other Defect (Describe)
Caliper			
Hardware			
Brake lines/hoses			
Wheel lugs/studs			
Bearings/races			
Seals			

(continued)

Brake System Defects (continued)			
Front Brakes—Right			
Component	Bent/Broken	Leaking	Other Defect (Describe)
Caliper			
Hardware			
Brake lines/hoses			
Wheel lugs/studs			
Bearings/races			
Seals			
Rear Brakes—Left			
Component	Bent/Broken	Leaking	Other Defect (Describe)
Calipers			
Wheel cylinders			
Hardware			
Brake lines/hoses			
Backing plate			
Self-adjuster hardware			
Parking brake cable			
Parking brake lever			
Wheel lugs/studs			
Bearings/races			
Seals			
Rear Brakes—Right			
Component	Bent/Broken	Leaking	Other Defect (Describe)
Calipers			
Wheel cylinders			
Hardware			
Brake lines/hoses			
Backing plate			
Self-adjuster hardware			
Parking brake cable			
Parking brake lever			
Wheel lugs/studs			
Bearings/races			
Seals			

(continued)

Job 43—Inspect a Brake System (continued)

Brake System Defects (continued)			
Hydraulic System			
Component	Stuck	Leaking	Other Defect (Describe)
Master cylinder			
Metering valve			
Proportioning valve			
Combination valve			
Booster and hoses			

Brake Pedal

Is the pedal height correct? Yes ___ No ___

Is the pedal travel/free play about 1/8″ (3.1 mm) when the pedal is pressed down by hand until resistance is felt? Yes ___ No ___

Is the linkage adjustment correct? Yes ___ No ___

Are the linkage and hardware in good condition? Yes ___ No ___

Is the brake light switch adjustment correct? Yes ___ No ___

☐ 22. Attach pressure gauges to the vehicle following instructions in the appropriate service literature.

List the gauge connection point(s):_____

_____

☐ 23. Apply the brakes and record pressure readings.

_____ psi (kPa) with gauge connected to _____.

_____ psi (kPa) with gauge connected to _____.

_____ psi (kPa) with gauge connected to _____.

_____ psi (kPa) with gauge connected to _____.

Do these pressure readings indicate a hydraulic system problem? Yes ___ No ___

☐ 24. Based on the finding in Steps 3 through 23, determine needed repairs.

Parts needed: _____

_____

Services needed (such as machining rotors/drums):_____

_____

Note

If your instructor approves, proceed to the other jobs in this manual and make the needed repairs to the brake system.

☐ 25. Recheck system operation.

Do any brake problems exist? Yes ___ No ___

If Yes, return to the beginning of this job and recheck the brake system.

Job Wrap Up

☐ 1. Return all tools and equipment to storage.

☐ 2. Clean the work area.

☐ 3. Did you encounter any problems during this procedure? Yes ___ No ___

If Yes, describe the problems: _____

_____

_____

What did you do to correct the problems? _____

_____

_____

☐ 4. Have your instructor check your work and sign this job sheet.

Performance Evaluation—Instructor Use Only

Did the student complete the job in the time allotted? Yes ___ No ___

If No, which steps were not completed? _____

How would you rate this student's overall performance on this job? _____

5–Excellent, 4–Good, 3–Satisfactory, 2–Unsatisfactory, 1–Poor

Comments: _____

_____

INSTRUCTOR'S SIGNATURE _____

Job

Inspect Brake Lines, Hoses, and Related Parts

44

After completing this job, you will be able to identify damaged lines, hoses, and related parts. You will also be able to determine what repairs should be made to correct the defects.

Instructions

As you read the job instructions, answer the questions and perform the tasks. Print your answers neatly and use complete sentences. Consult the proper service literature and ask your instructor for help as needed.

> **Warning**
>
> ⚠ Before performing this job, review all pertinent safety information in the text and discuss safety procedures with your instructor.

Procedures

- ☐ 1. Obtain a vehicle to be used in this job. Your instructor may direct you to perform this job on a shop vehicle.
- ☐ 2. Gather the tools needed to perform the following job.
- ☐ 3. Check the master cylinder level.
     Is the fluid at the normal level? Yes ___ No ___
     If No, add fluid before continuing.
- ☐ 4. Safely raise the vehicle.

> **Note**
>
> Some brakes lines, such as those to and from the ABS unit, may be more easily observed from under the hood. For these lines, perform step 5 before raising the vehicle.

☐ 5. Inspect all metal lines for defects.

Are there any leaks? Yes ___ No ___
Location:_____

Are there any dents? Yes ___ No ___
Location:_____

Are there any flattened/crushed areas? Yes ___ No ___
Location:_____

Are there any rust spots on the lines? Yes ___ No ___
Location:_____

Are there any loose fittings? Yes ___ No ___
Location:_____

☐ 6. Inspect all hoses for defects.

Are there any leaks? Yes ___ No ___
Location:_____

Are there any swollen spots? Yes ___ No ___
Location:_____

Are there any cracks? Yes ___ No ___
Location:_____

Note

If a restricted hose is suspected, remove the hose from the vehicle and attach a short length of clean rubber tubing to the fitting on one end of the brake hose. Attempt to blow through the tubing. If any resistance is felt, the hose is restricted.

☐ 7. Inspect the fittings for defects.

Are there any leaks? Yes ___ No ___
Location:_____

Is there any looseness (check with tubing wrench)? Yes ___ No ___
Location:_____

Is there any other damage? Yes ___ No ___
Location:_____

☐ 8. Inspect brake line and hose supports and brackets for defects.

Are any damaged? Yes ___ No ___
Location:_____

Are any bent? Yes ___ No ___
Location:_____

Are there any loose fasteners? Yes ___ No ___
Location:_____

Are any supports or brackets missing? Yes ___ No ___
Location:_____

☐ 9. Consult with your instructor concerning needed repairs or replacements.

What repairs are needed?_____

_____

_____

_____

Job 44—Inspect Brake Lines, Hoses, and Related Parts (continued)

Job Wrap Up

☐ 1. Return all tools and equipment to storage.

☐ 2. Clean the work area.

☐ 3. Did you encounter any problems during this procedure? Yes ___ No ___

If Yes, describe the problems: _____

_____

_____

What did you do to correct the problems?_____

_____

_____

☐ 4. Have your instructor check your work and sign this job sheet.

Performance Evaluation—Instructor Use Only

Did the student complete the job in the time allotted? Yes ___ No ___

If No, which steps were not completed?_____

How would you rate this student's overall performance on this job?____

5–Excellent, 4–Good, 3–Satisfactory, 2–Unsatisfactory, 1–Poor

Comments: _____

_____

_____

INSTRUCTOR'S SIGNATURE _____

Notes

Job

Bleed a Brake System

45

After completing this job, you will be able to bleed and flush the brake hydraulic system and properly handle brake fluids.

Instructions

As you read the job instructions, answer the questions and perform the tasks. Print your answers neatly and use complete sentences. Consult the proper service literature and ask your instructor for help as needed.

> **Warning**
>
> ⚠ Before performing this job, review all pertinent safety information in the text and discuss safety procedures with your instructor.

Procedures

☐ 1. Obtain a vehicle to be used in this job. Your instructor may direct you to perform this job on a shop vehicle.

☐ 2. Gather the tools needed to perform this job.

Fill Brake Fluid Reservoir

> **Caution**
>
> It is very important to handle and store brake fluid properly. Never reuse brake fluid or mix different types of fluid. Keep brake fluid in its original container until used. Also, make sure the brake fluid container is tightly capped after use to prevent moisture and contaminants from entering the fluid.

☐ 1. Remove the cap on the brake fluid reservoir and observe the fluid level.

or

Observe the fluid level in the clear strip on the side of the reservoir.

☐ 2. If necessary, add fluid:

    a. Observe the reservoir cap or the top of the reservoir to determine what type of fluid should be added.

    b. Obtain the proper type of brake fluid.

    c. Remove the brake fluid container cap.

    d. Remove the reservoir cap.

    e. Add fluid to the reservoir until the full or maximum mark is reached.

☐ 3. Reinstall the reservoir cap.

☐ 4. Tightly recap the brake fluid container.

Check Brake Fluid for Moisture Contamination

> **Caution**
>
> ⚠ Do not add fresh fluid before performing this test.

☐ 1. Check for moisture-contaminated fluid using one of the following methods:

Chemically Sensitive Test Strips

    a. Remove the cap on the brake fluid reservoir.

    b. Insert a test strip into the reservoir.

    c. Remove the strip and compare the strip color with the color chart on the strip container.

Does the test strip indicate excessive moisture in the brake fluid? Yes ___ No ___

Electronic Brake Fluid Tester

    a. Remove the cap on the brake fluid reservoir.

    b. Insert the tester probe into the fluid.

    c. Read the tester screen. The tester will display a reading showing the percentage of moisture in the brake fluid.

Does the electronic tester indicate excessive moisture in the brake fluid?
Yes ___ No ___

☐ 2. Report excessive brake fluid moisture to your instructor. Your instructor may direct you to flush the brake system using the procedures in this job.

Bleed Brakes

☐ 1. Remove the master cylinder reservoir cover.

☐ 2. Check the level of fluid in the reservoir.

Is the brake fluid level low? Yes ___ No ___
If Yes, add fluid if necessary.
Type of brake fluid added:_____
Amount of brake fluid added: _____

☐ 3. Tightly close the brake fluid container to ensure that moisture or other contaminants do not enter the fluid.

☐ 4. Replace the reservoir cover.

Job 45—Bleed a Brake System (continued)

Bleed Brakes Manually

> **Note**
>
> If the vehicle is equipped with anti-lock brakes, follow the procedure in the service manual as needed.

☐ 1. Have an assistant pump the brakes slowly several times to build pressure in the hydraulic system.

☐ 2. While the assistant holds the pedal in the applied position, loosen one brake line fitting at the master cylinder. Use a line wrench to prevent fitting damage and place rags under the lines to absorb fluid.

> **Note**
>
> If the master cylinder has bleeder screws, use these instead of opening the lines.

☐ 3. Repeat step 2 at all lines on the master cylinder until only fluid exits when the fittings are loosened.

☐ 4. Raise the vehicle to gain access to the brake bleeder screws.

> **Warning**
>
> ⚠ The vehicle must be raised and supported in a safe manner. Always use approved lifts or jacks and jack stands.

☐ 5. Install one end of a tube on the specified bleeder screw and immerse the other end in a jar or bottle one-quarter filled with clean brake fluid.

> **Note**
>
> Most manufacturers recommend beginning the bleeding process at the wheel farthest from the master cylinder, usually the right rear.

☐ 6. Have your assistant pump the brake pedal slowly several times and then hold the pedal in the applied position.

☐ 7. Loosen the bleeder screw and allow air and fluid to exit, **Figure 45-1**.

☐ 8. When no more air or fluid exits, close the bleeder. Then, have your assistant release the brake pedal.

☐ 9. Repeat steps 5 through 8 for all the wheels until only fluid exits from every bleeder.

Figure 45-1. When manually bleeding a brake system, place a hose in a jar that contains clean brake fluid.

Goodheart-Willcox Publisher

Caution

Frequently check and refill the master cylinder reservoir during the bleeding process. If the master cylinder reservoir is allowed to empty, air will be drawn into the system and the bleeding process must be started over from the beginning.

☐ 10. Ask your assistant to frequently report on pedal height and firmness.

Is pedal height and firmness acceptable after all wheels have been bled?
Yes ___ No ___
If No, go to step 11.
If Yes, go to step 12.

☐ 11. Repeat steps 5 through 8 until pedal height and firmness are acceptable.

☐ 12. When bleeding is complete, lower the vehicle and perform a road test.

Bleed Brakes Using Pressure Bleeder

☐ 1. Check that the pressure bleeder is in operating condition and contains enough fluid for the bleeding operation.

Is the bleeder in proper operating condition? Yes ___ No ___
Is the bleeder fluid level acceptable? Yes ___ No ___

☐ 2. Add fluid to the bleeder if necessary.

☐ 3. Install the pressure bleeder adapter on the brake fluid reservoir.

☐ 4. If necessary, attach an air hose to the pressure bleeder; then adjust the bleeder pressure.

Pressure was set to _____ psi/kPa.

Job 45—Bleed a Brake System (continued)

> **Caution**
>
> Do not set the pressure higher than recommended. Pressures above 10 psi (69 kPa) can damage brake fluid reservoirs.

☐ 5. Raise the vehicle to gain access to the brake bleeder screws.

> **Warning**
>
> The vehicle must be raised and supported in a safe manner. Always use approved lifts or jacks and jack stands.

☐ 6. Install a tube on the bleeder screw and immerse the other end of the tube in a jar or bottle partially filled with clean brake fluid.

> **Note**
>
> Most manufacturers recommend beginning the bleeding process at the wheel farthest from the master cylinder, usually the right rear.

☐ 7. Loosen the bleeder screw and allow air and fluid to exit.

☐ 8. When there is no evidence of air flowing from the hose, close the bleeder.

☐ 9. Repeat steps 6 through 8 for the remaining wheels.

☐ 10. Check pedal height and firmness.

   Is pedal height and firmness acceptable? Yes ___ No ___
   If No, go to step 11.
   If Yes, go to step 12.

☐ 11. If the pedal is soft or low, repeat steps 6 through 9 until height and firmness are acceptable.

☐ 12. When all bleeding is complete, lower the vehicle and perform a road test.

Bleed Brakes Using a Vacuum Bleeder

☐ 1. Raise the vehicle to gain access to the brake bleeder screws.

> **Warning**
>
> The vehicle must be raised and supported in a safe manner. Always use approved lifts or jacks and jack stands.

☐ 2. Attach the vacuum bleeder to the bleeder screw farthest from the master cylinder.

☐ 3. Open the bleeder screw.

☐ 4. Operate the vacuum pump to draw air from the hydraulic system.

☐ 5. Repeat steps 2 through 4 for all wheels until only fluid exits from each bleeder.

> **Caution**
>
> Frequently check and refill the master cylinder reservoir during the bleeding process.

☐ 6. Check pedal height and firmness.

Is pedal height and firmness acceptable? Yes ___ No ___

If No, go to step 7.

If Yes, go to step 8.

☐ 7. If the pedal is soft or low, repeat steps 2 through 6 until height and firmness are acceptable.

☐ 8. When all bleeding is complete, lower the vehicle and perform a road test.

Flush a Brake System

☐ 1. Check the level of brake fluid in the reservoir.

Is the fluid level low? Yes ___ No ___

☐ 2. Add fluid if necessary and replace the reservoir cover.

Type of brake fluid added:_____

Amount of brake fluid added: _____

> **Note**
>
> A pressure bleeder can be used to perform this job. Attach the bleeder as explained in the previous pressure bleeding section.

☐ 3. Raise the vehicle to gain access to the brake bleeder screws.

> **Warning**
>
> The vehicle must be raised and supported in a safe manner. Always use approved lifts or jacks and jack stands.

☐ 4. Install one end of a tube on the bleeder screw and place the other end in a jar or bottle.

☐ 5. Have the assistant pump the brake pedal slowly several times, then hold the pedal in the applied position.

☐ 6. Loosen the bleeder screw and allow fluid to exit into the jar or bottle.

> **Note**
>
> Pour fluid out of the jar or bottle as needed to keep it from overflowing.

☐ 7. Repeat steps 4 through 6 on the remaining wheels until clean fluid exits from all bleeders.

Job 45—Bleed a Brake System (continued)

> **Caution**
>
> Frequently check and refill the master cylinder reservoir during the flushing process.

☐ 8. When the lines to all the wheels have been flushed, lower the vehicle and perform a road test.

Job Wrap Up

☐ 1. Return all tools and equipment to storage.

☐ 2. Clean the work area.

☐ 3. Did you encounter any problems during this procedure? Yes ___ No ___

If Yes, describe the problems: _____

_____

_____

What did you do to correct the problems?_____

_____

_____

☐ 4. Have your instructor check your work and sign this job sheet.

Performance Evaluation—Instructor Use Only

Did the student complete the job in the time allotted? Yes ___ No ___

If No, which steps were not completed?_____

How would you rate this student's overall performance on this job?____

5–Excellent, 4–Good, 3–Satisfactory, 2–Unsatisfactory, 1–Poor

Comments: _____

_____

_____

INSTRUCTOR'S SIGNATURE _____

Notes

Job

Identify Brake Warning Light Components and Diagnose Problems

After completing this job, you will be able to identify components of the brake warning light system and diagnose warning light system defects.

Instructions

As you read the job instructions, answer the questions and perform the tasks. Print your answers neatly and use complete sentences. Consult the proper service literature and ask your instructor for help as needed.

Note

This job addresses the instrument panel brake warning light only. This light is red and is operated by on-off switches on the components being monitored. Amber or blue colored anti-lock braking system (ABS) and traction control system (TCS) lights are computer-controlled and are not connected to the red warning light system.

Warning

Before performing this job, review all pertinent safety information in the text and discuss safety procedures with your instructor.

Questions

_____ 1. True or False? The brake warning light is always grounded and illuminates when a circuit is energized from a positive connection through the bulb.

_____ 2. True or False? Brake warning light switches are simple on-off types.

_____ 3. When the circuit of a correctly operating brake warning light is complete, the light will be _____.
   A. on (illuminated)
   B. off

4. List the two major classes of brake warning light problems:

_____

_____ 5. A misadjusted parking brake switch could cause the warning
   light to be _____.
   A. on when the parking brake is not applied
   B. off when the parking brake is applied
   C. Either A or B.

6. What two steps should the technician take when the brake warning light is
   illuminated because of a low brake fluid reservoir level?

_____

_____ 7. The brake warning light is illuminated because of an out
   of position pressure differential switch. What should the
   technician do to reposition the switch?

_____

_____ 8. True or False? When the brake pads are worn out, the brake
   warning light may come on when the brakes are not applied.

9. What is the most common reason disc brake pad wear sensors cause the warning
   light to come on?

_____

_____ 10. True or False? A blown brake warning light system fuse will
   cause the light to be on at all times.

Optional Job: Diagnose Brake Warning Light

Note

Most warning light problems can be diagnosed by visual inspection or
with a non-powered test light.

Procedures

☐ 1. Obtain a vehicle to be used in this job. Your instructor may direct you to perform
   this job on a shop vehicle.

☐ 2. Gather the tools needed to perform the following job.

Diagnose a Warning Light That Does Not Light at Any Time

☐ 1. Determine which fuse controls the warning light system and check the fuse.
   Is the fuse good? Yes ___ No ___
   If Yes, go to step 3.

☐ 2. If the fuse is blown, check for short circuits caused by pinched wiring, high
   resistance switches or connectors, and grounded wires.
   Problems found: _____

_____

Job 46—Identify Brake Warning Light Components and Diagnose Problems (continued)

☐ 3. If the fuse is good, check the parking brake electrical switch using a non-powered test light. The switch may be out of adjustment or defective, or the electrical connector may be disconnected or overheated.

Problems found: _____

_____

☐ 4. Adjust or repair components as necessary.

☐ 5. If the fuse and switch are ok, check the warning light bulb. The bulb may be burned out, or may have fallen out of its socket. In some cases, someone has removed the bulb because it was on at all times.

> **Note**
> To remove the bulb, it may be necessary to remove the instrument cluster, air conditioner ducts, or partially disassemble the dashboard. Consult the proper service manual for these procedures.

Problems found: _____

_____

☐ 6. Replace bulb as necessary. If the light is now on at all times, refer to the next section.

Diagnose a Warning Light That Is On at All Times

> **Note**
> The light is usually illuminated during cranking to ensure that the bulb is not burned out. Illumination during cranking is a normal condition.

☐ 1. If the warning light is on at all times, first determine which vehicle systems operate the light and unplug their related switches or sensors as applicable:

- Parking brake.

  Light goes out: Yes ___ No ___ Not applicable ___

- Brake fluid reservoir level sensor.

  Light goes out: Yes ___ No ___ Not applicable ___

- Pressure differential switch.

  Light goes out: Yes ___ No ___ Not applicable ___

- Disc brake pad wear sensors.

  Light goes out: Yes ___ No ___ Not applicable ___

☐ 2. Replace any worn brake parts, and otherwise service the brakes as necessary. If the light remains on when all switches have been disconnected, look for a wire that has grounded against the vehicle body.

☐ 3. When all repairs are completed, recheck brake warning light operation.

Job Wrap Up

☐ 1. Return all tools and equipment to storage.

☐ 2. Clean the work area.

☐ 3. Did you encounter any problems during this procedure? Yes ___ No ___

If Yes, describe the problems: _____

_____

_____

What did you do to correct the problems?_____

_____

_____

☐ 4. Have your instructor check your work and sign this job sheet.

Performance Evaluation—Instructor Use Only

Did the student complete the job in the time allotted? Yes ___ No ___

If No, which steps were not completed?_____

How would you rate this student's overall performance on this job?_____

5–Excellent, 4–Good, 3–Satisfactory, 2–Unsatisfactory, 1–Poor

Comments: _____

_____

INSTRUCTOR'S SIGNATURE _____

After completing this job, you will be able to diagnose and service drum brake systems.

Instructions

As you read the job instructions, answer the questions and perform the tasks. Print your answers neatly and use complete sentences. Consult the proper service literature and ask your instructor for help as needed.

> **Warning**
> ⚠ Before performing this job, review all pertinent safety information in the text and discuss safety procedures with your instructor.

Procedures

☐ 1. Obtain a vehicle to be used in this job. Your instructor may direct you to perform this job on a shop vehicle.

☐ 2. Gather the tools needed to perform this job.

☐ 3. Raise the vehicle.

> **Warning**
> ⚠ The vehicle must be raised and supported in a safe manner. Always use approved lifts or jacks and jack stands.

☐ 4. Remove the wheels from the axle to be serviced.

☐ 5. Put on the respirator and remove the brake drums.

What did you have to do to remove the drums?_____

_____

> **Warning**
>
> ⚠ Brake dust may contain asbestos. Wear a respirator whenever you are working on any brake friction materials.

☐ 6. Clean both brake assemblies using a closed cleaning system (liquid or HEPA vacuum).

> **Note**
>
> 📄 If you are unsure about the placement of brake parts, disassemble one side at a time. Refer to the other side as needed.

Disassemble Brakes

☐ 1. Remove the brake return springs, **Figure 47-1**.

☐ 2. Remove the brake hold-down spring or springs and any related cables or linkage. See **Figure 47-2**.

☐ 3. Remove the parking brake linkage.

☐ 4. Remove the brake shoes from the vehicle.

☐ 5. Remove the parking brake link from the backing plate. Identify the shoe type.

    ☐ Servo.

    ☐ Non-servo.

☐ 6. Place the brake shoes on a clean workbench.

☐ 7. If necessary, remove the spring holding the shoes and star wheel adjuster together and disassemble the brakes.

Figure 47-1. A special tool is needed to remove most return springs.

Goodheart-Willcox Publisher

Job 47—Service Drum Brakes (continued)

Figure 47-2. These brake shoes are held in position by a single large hold-down wire. Other shoes are held in place by small coil springs.

Goodheart-Willcox Publisher

Inspect Brakes

☐ 1. Inspect the brake shoes for wear, cracks, and evidence of oil or brake-fluid soaking.
Was any damage found? Yes ___ No ___
If Yes, explain:_____
_____

☐ 2. Clean all springs and other hardware, and check them for bends, breaks, and signs of overheating.
Was any damage found? Yes ___ No ___
If Yes, explain:_____
_____

☐ 3. Return to the vehicle and pull the dust boots away from the wheel cylinder. A slightly damp appearance is acceptable, but any liquid is grounds for overhaul or replacement. See **Figure 47-3.**
Is brake fluid present? Yes ___ No ___
If Yes, consult your instructor about rebuilding or replacing the wheel cylinder.

☐ 4. Inspect the backing plate and attaching hardware.
Is the backing plate bent or damaged? Yes ___ No ___
Is the attaching hardware loose or damaged? Yes ___ No ___

Figure 47-3. Gently pull back the wheel cylinder dust boots to check for fluid leaks.

Goodheart-Willcox Publisher

5. Check the brake drums for wear, glazing, scoring, and overheating.

Visual Inspection of Drums				
Drum Condition	Front-Left	Front-Right	Rear-Left	Rear-Right
Worn				
Glazed				
Scored				
Overheated				

Micrometer Readings				
	Front-Left	Front-Right	Rear-Left	Rear-Right
Maximum diameter				
Out-of-round				
Taper				

Can the drum(s) be turned and reused? Yes ___ No ___
If No, explain why? _____

_____

6. Determine which parts are needed to successfully repair the brakes. List them here.

_____

_____

> **Note**
>
> See Job 48 for brake drum turning procedures.

Job 47—Service Drum Brakes (continued)

Reassemble Brakes

☐ 1. Obtain new shoes and other parts as necessary.

☐ 2. Reinstall the wheel cylinder if it was removed.

Fastener torque (if applicable):_____

☐ 3. Apply a small amount of high-temperature lube to the shoe contact pads.

> **Warning**
> ⚠ Be careful not to apply too much lube to the contact pads. Excessive lube may get on the brake shoe's friction material and cause brake failure.

☐ 4. Reassemble the shoes and star wheel on the bench if necessary.

☐ 5. Replace the brake link or self-adjuster on the backing plate if needed.

☐ 6. Place the shoe assembly on the backing plate and install the hold-down spring or springs.

> **Note**
> 📄 If any of the self-adjuster or parking brake parts are located under the hold-down springs, install them before installing the springs.

☐ 7. Reattach the parking brake linkage (rear brakes).

☐ 8. Make sure the shoes engage the wheel cylinder pistons or apply pins.

☐ 9. Install the shoe retractor springs and any related cables or links.

☐ 10. Make sure the self-adjuster operates properly.

☐ 11. Using a shoe-to-drum gauge, adjust the brake shoe clearance.

☐ 12. Reinstall the drum.

☐ 13. Repeat steps 1 through 12 for the other brake assembly.

☐ 14. Bleed the brakes if the wheel cylinders were removed. Refer to Job 45.

☐ 15. Reinstall the wheels and torque the fasteners to the proper values.

Fastener torque:_____

☐ 16. Road test the vehicle.

☐ 17. Readjust the brake shoe clearance if necessary.

a. Locate and remove the adjuster plug.

b. Insert a small screwdriver or awl through the adjuster opening to disengage the self-adjuster lever.

c. Insert an adjusting spoon into the adjuster opening and turn the star wheel.

d. Adjust the star wheel until there is a small amount of drag when the wheel is turned.

e. Remove the screwdriver and adjusting spoon and replace the plug.

f. Repeat as necessary on other wheels.

Job Wrap Up

☐ 1. Return all tools and equipment to storage.

☐ 2. Clean the work area.

☐ 3. Did you encounter any problems during this procedure? Yes ___ No ___

If Yes, describe the problems: _____

_____

_____

What did you do to correct the problems?_____

_____

_____

☐ 4. Have your instructor check your work and sign this job sheet.

Performance Evaluation—Instructor Use Only

Did the student complete the job in the time allotted? Yes ___ No ___

If No, which steps were not completed?_____

How would you rate this student's overall performance on this job?_____

5–Excellent, 4–Good, 3–Satisfactory, 2–Unsatisfactory, 1–Poor

Comments: _____

_____

_____

INSTRUCTOR'S SIGNATURE _____

After completing this job, you will be able to machine (turn) brake drums.

Instructions

As you read the job instructions, answer the questions and perform the tasks. Print your answers neatly and use complete sentences. Consult the proper service literature and ask your instructor for help as needed.

> **Warning**
>
> Before performing this job, review all pertinent safety information in the text and discuss safety procedures with your instructor.

Procedures

☐ 1. Put on your safety glasses and respirator.

> **Warning**
>
> Rotor or drum machining produces metal chips and brake dust. Wear safety glasses and a respirator at all times while performing this job.

> **Note**
>
> Actual machining procedures vary between lathe manufacturers. If there are any differences between the procedures given below and the manufacturer's procedures, follow the manufacturer's procedures.

☐ 2. Clean the drum interior.

> **Warning**
>
> Use a vacuum or wet cleaner to remove brake dust. Do not remove dust with compressed air.

☐ 3. Remove all grease, dust, and metal debris from the brake lathe arbor.

☐ 4. Check the condition of the cutting bits and make sure the boring bar is tightly installed.

☐ 5. Select the proper adapters and mount the drum on the arbor.

☐ 6. Install the silencer band around the drum.

☐ 7. Make sure the lathe's automatic feed mechanism is disengaged.

☐ 8. Start the lathe and ensure the drum revolves evenly, without excessive wobbling. If the drum wobbles, reposition the drum and adapters as necessary.

☐ 9. Loosen the locknut on the cutting depth adjuster knob and turn the depth adjuster to a position that ensures the cutting bit does not contact the inside of the drum.

☐ 10. Turn the automatic feed mechanism wheel to move the bit to the inside of the drum. Make sure the cutting tip does not contact the rotating drum.

☐ 11. Use the depth adjuster knob to move the cutting bit into slight contact with the inner surface of the drum.

☐ 12. Tighten the lock on the cutting depth adjuster knob.

☐ 13. Turn the movable collar on the cutting bit adjuster to zero.

☐ 14. Use the manual feed to position the cutting bit at the rear of the drum, **Figure 48-1**.

☐ 15. Loosen the locknut and turn the cutting depth adjuster knob to the desired cut.

First cut depth: _____

☐ 16. Set the speed of the automatic feed.

Speed: _____

Is this a rough cut or a finish cut? _____

☐ 17. Engage the automatic feed.

☐ 18. Observe the drum as it is being cut.

☐ 19. When the cutting bit exits the drum, turn off the automatic feed.

Figure 48-1. A brake drum is being machined in this image. The drum should machine evenly, with no wobble or chattering.

Hunter Engineering

Job 48—Machine a Brake Drum (continued)

☐ 20. If necessary, repeat steps 15 through 20 until the entire drum surface is cut, with no grooves or shiny spots on the surface.

How many cuts were needed to clean up the drum? _____

What was the total cut depth? _____

> **Note**
> Be sure to make the final cut at a low speed to produce a smooth finished surface.

☐ 21. Turn off the lathe.

☐ 22. Check the drum diameter using a drum micrometer.

Micrometer reading: _____

Minimum thickness specification: _____

Can the drum be reused? Yes ___ No ___

☐ 23. Remove the silencer band from the drum.

☐ 24. Remove the drum from the lathe arbor.

☐ 25. Repeat steps 2 through 24 for the other drum(s).

Job Wrap Up

☐ 1. Return all tools and equipment to storage.

☐ 2. Clean the work area.

☐ 3. Did you encounter any problems during this procedure? Yes ___ No ___

If Yes, describe the problems: _____

_____

What did you do to correct the problems?_____

_____

☐ 4. Have your instructor check your work and sign this job sheet.

Performance Evaluation—Instructor Use Only

Did the student complete the job in the time allotted? Yes ___ No ___

If No, which steps were not completed?_____

How would you rate this student's overall performance on this job?_____

5–Excellent, 4–Good, 3–Satisfactory, 2–Unsatisfactory, 1–Poor

Comments: _____

_____

INSTRUCTOR'S SIGNATURE _____

Notes

Job

Service Disc Brakes

After completing this job, you will be able to inspect and replace disc brake components.

Instructions

As you read the job instructions, answer the questions and perform the tasks. Print your answers neatly and use complete sentences. Consult the proper service literature and ask your instructor for help as needed.

> **Warning**
>
> ⚠ Before performing this job, review all pertinent safety information in the text and discuss safety procedures with your instructor.

Procedures

☐ 1. Obtain a vehicle to be used in this job. Your instructor may direct you to perform this job on a shop vehicle.

☐ 2. Gather the tools needed to perform this job.

Disassemble Disc Brakes

☐ 1. Raise the vehicle.

> **Warning**
>
> ⚠ Raise and support the vehicle in a safe manner. Always use approved lifts or jacks and jack stands.

 2. Remove wheels as needed to access the brakes to be serviced.

> **Warning**
>
> ⚠ Brake pads may contain asbestos. Clean the brake assembly using a closed liquid cleaning system or HEPA vacuum.

☐   3.   Place a drip pan under the brake caliper to be serviced.

☐   4.   Open the caliper's bleeder valve.

☐   5.   Push the caliper piston(s) away from the rotor and into the caliper body.

☐   6.   Close the bleeder valve.

☐   7.   Repeat steps 3 through 6 on the other wheel.

☐   8.   Remove the caliper fasteners.

☐   9.   Remove the calipers from the rotors.

Caution

⚠   To avoid damaging the brake hoses, hang the calipers on wire hooks. Do not allow them to hang freely by their hoses.

☐ 10.   Remove the pads from the calipers or caliper brackets.

☐ 11.   Remove the rotor from the hub.

Note

📄   Most rotors can be pulled from the wheel studs once the wheel and caliper are removed. If the rotor is pressed onto the hub, it must be removed with a special puller. Follow the manufacturer's instructions to remove a pressed-on rotor. Do not attempt to hammer the rotor free. Some rotors can be serviced with an on-vehicle lathe, eliminating the need to remove them.

Inspect Disc Brake Components

☐   1.   Inspect the pads. Indicate any obvious pad defects. Place a check mark next to all that apply.

      ☐ Worn/thin.

      ☐ Cracked.

      ☐ Loose on backing plate.

      ☐ Other (describe):_____

☐   2.   Inspect the pad wear indicator.

Mechanical Type

• Locate the pad wear indicator.

• Note whether the indicator is recessed at least 1/8″ (3 mm) away from the surface of the pad.

• If the indicator is not 1/8″ (3 mm) away from the pad, discard the pad.

Note

📄   If the instrument panel pad wear indicator light is on, the pad can be assumed to be worn to the indicator button.

Electrical or Electronic Type

• Observe the center of the brake pad.

• Note whether the wear indicator button in the pad is visible.

• If the wear indicator button is visible, replace the pads.

Job 49—Service Disc Brakes (continued)

☐ 3. Check the backing plate and attaching hardware. Place a check mark next to all that apply.

    ☐ Backing plate bent or damaged.

    ☐ Attaching hardware loose, stripped, or damaged.

    ☐ Caliper mounting and sliding surfaces or slide pins worn, burred, or dented.

☐ 4. Check the rotor for visible signs of damage. Place check marks in the appropriate columns.

Visual Inspection of Rotors				
Rotor Condition	Front-Left	Front-Right	Rear-Left	Rear-Right
Worn				
Glazed				
Scored				
Overheated				
Bearing damage (if applicable)				

Was any damage found? Yes ___ No ___

If Yes, explain:_____

☐ 5. Attach a dial indicator to the rotor as shown in **Figure 49-1**. Check the rotor for warping (runout) by slowly turning the rotor through several revolutions. It may be necessary to reinstall the wheel nut temporarily to perform this test.

Maximum variation on the front-left rotor:_____

Maximum variation on the front-right rotor:_____

Maximum variation on the rear-left rotor:_____

Maximum variation on the rear-right rotor:_____

☐ 6. Use an outside micrometer to measure the rotor thicknesses at various points around the discs. Enter the values in the following table.

Micrometer Readings of Rotors				
Measurements	Front-Left	Front-Right	Rear-Left	Rear-Right
Maximum thickness				
Minimum thickness				
Thickness variation				
Taper				

Can the rotor(s) be turned and reused? Yes ___ No ___

If No, what is the reason?_____

_____

Figure 49-1. A dial indicator is used to check a rotor for warping. Adjust the wheel bearings before making this test.

Goodheart-Willcox Publisher

> **Note**
>
> To remove and turn rotors, see Job 50.

7. If applicable, check the wheel bearings and seals:

Bear and Seal Condition				
	Front-Left	**Front-Right**	**Rear-Left**	**Rear-Right**
Lubricant dirty/ missing				
Bearings worn/ damaged				
Seal leaking				

> **Note**
>
> See Job 52 for wheel bearing service procedures.

8. Determine which parts are needed to successfully repair the brakes. List them in the space provided.

_____

_____

_____

_____

Job 49—Service Disc Brakes (continued)

Reassemble Disc Brakes

☐ 1. If necessary, reinstall the bearings in the rotor hub. See Job 52.

☐ 2. Reinstall the rotors if they were removed for turning. Also, reattach the caliper brackets if they were removed.

☐ 3. Apply anti-squeal compound or insulation material to the backs of the pads. Consult the service manual for the exact materials and methods for this step.

☐ 4. Lightly lubricate the caliper sliding surfaces with the correct type of high-temperature lubricant.

☐ 5. Place the new pads in the calipers or brackets as necessary.

☐ 6. Reinstall the calipers over the rotors.

☐ 7. Bleed the brake system at the calipers.

> **Caution**
> ⚠ Check the fluid level in the reservoir before bleeding and add fluid as necessary.

☐ 8. Reinstall the wheels and torque the fasteners to the proper values.
Fastener torque:_____

☐ 9. Road test the vehicle.

> **Caution**
> ⚠ Before beginning the road test, ensure that you have a firm pedal. Follow the manufacturer's recommendations for seating and burnishing the new brake pads. The burnishing process removes roughness and unevenness between the brake mating surfaces, thermally changes the composition of the pad material, and heat cycles the pad. The seating and burnishing procedure is necessary to ensure proper operation and longevity of the brake pads.

Job Wrap Up

☐ 1. Return all tools and equipment to storage.

☐ 2. Clean the work area.

☐ 3. Did you encounter any problems during this procedure? Yes ___ No ___
If Yes, describe the problems: _____
_____

What did you do to correct the problems?_____
_____

☐ 4. Have your instructor check your work and sign this job sheet.

Performance Evaluation—Instructor Use Only

Did the student complete the job in the time allotted? Yes ___ No ___
If No, which steps were not completed?_____
How would you rate this student's overall performance on this job?_____
5–Excellent, 4–Good, 3–Satisfactory, 2–Unsatisfactory, 1–Poor
Comments: _____
_____
_____

INSTRUCTOR'S SIGNATURE _____

Job

Machine a Brake Rotor

50

After completing this job, you will be able to machine a brake rotor.

Instructions

As you read the job instructions, answer the questions and perform the tasks. Print your answers neatly and use complete sentences. Consult the proper service literature and ask your instructor for help as needed.

> **Warning**
>
> Before performing this job, review all pertinent safety information in the text and discuss safety procedures with your instructor.

Procedures

☐ 1. Obtain a vehicle to be used in this job. Your instructor may direct you to perform this job on a shop vehicle.

☐ 2. Gather the tools needed to perform this job.

> **Note**
>
> This portion of the job can be performed with either a bench lathe or an on-car lathe. Be sure to use the same lathe to cut both rotors. Do not use a different type of lathe on each rotor or only cut one rotor. If you are using a bench lathe, proceed with the next step. If you are using an on-car lathe, go to the *Prepare to Use an On-Vehicle Lathe* section of this job.

Prepare to Use a Bench Lathe

☐ 1. Remove the rotors following the procedure in Job 49. If the rotors use serviceable wheel bearings, clean the wheel bearings and set them aside.

List the steps needed to remove the rotor:_____

> **Warning**
>
> ⚠ Use a closed HEPA vacuum or wet cleaner to remove brake dust from the brake assembly. Do not remove dust with compressed air.

☐ 2. Remove all grease, dust, and metal debris from the brake lathe arbor.

☐ 3. Check the condition of the cutting bits and ensure the boring bar is tightly installed.

☐ 4. Select the proper adapters and mount the first rotor on the arbor.

☐ 5. Install the silencer band around the rotor.

☐ 6. Start the lathe and make sure the rotor revolves evenly, without excessive wobbling.

   If the rotor wobbles, reposition the rotor and adapters as necessary. See **Figure 50-1**.

Prepare to Use an On-Vehicle Lathe

☐ 1. Check for play in the wheel bearings. If play is excessive, correct it before proceeding.

☐ 2. If the rotors are on the driving axle, place the vehicle's transmission or transaxle in neutral.

☐ 3. Remove all dust and metal debris from the brake lathe attaching fixtures.

☐ 4. Check the condition of the cutting bits and make sure they are tightly installed on the fixture.

☐ 5. Select the proper adapters and mount the lathe to the hub and rotor.

☐ 6. Compensate for rotor runout or shaft wobble as necessary.

☐ 7. Install the silencer band around the rotor. Not all on-vehicle lathes require this step.

☐ 8. Start the lathe and make sure it does not vibrate or wobble excessively as the rotor turns.

   If the lathe vibrates or wobbles excessively, readjust the lathe as necessary.

Figure 50-1. This rotor is being turned on a bench-type lathe. Check the service manual and the lathe operation manual if needed.

Hunter Engineering

Job 50—Machine a Brake Rotor (continued)

Cut Rotors

> **Note**
>
> This section applies to both on-vehicle lathes and bench lathes.

☐ 1. Loosen the locknut on both cutting depth adjuster knobs and turn the knobs to move the cutting bits into light contact with each side of the rotor.

☐ 2. Tighten the locks on each cutting depth adjuster knob.

☐ 3. Turn the movable collars on each cutting depth adjuster to zero.

☐ 4. Use the manual feed to position the cutting bits at the inside of the rotor.

☐ 5. Loosen the locks and turn each cutting depth adjuster knob to the desired cut.

First-cut depth, outboard rotor surface:_____

First-cut depth, inboard rotor surface:_____

☐ 6. Set the speed of the automatic feed.

Speed:_____

Is this a rough cut or a finish cut?_____

☐ 7. Engage the automatic feed.

☐ 8. Observe each side of the rotor as it is being cut.

☐ 9. When the cutting bit exits both sides of the rotor, turn off the automatic feed.

☐ 10. If necessary, repeat steps 5 through 9 until both rotor surfaces are smooth, with no grooves or shiny spots on either surface.

Cuts needed to clean up the rotor:_____

Total cut on inner surface:_____

Total cut on outer surface:_____

☐ 11. Turn off the lathe.

☐ 12. Check the rotor thickness using a micrometer.

Micrometer reading:_____

Minimum thickness specification:_____

Can the rotor be reused? Yes ___ No ___

☐ 13. Using a lathe-mounted or handheld grinder, swirl grind the rotor to produce a nondirectional finish.

> **Note**
>
> Some manufacturers do not recommend swirl grinding the rotor after machining.

☐ 14. Remove the silencer band from the rotor if necessary.

☐ 15. Remove the rotor from the lathe (bench lathe) or the lathe from the rotor (on-vehicle lathe).

☐ 16. Remove all metal chips from the rotor.

☐ 17. Repack the wheel bearings if applicable.

☐ 18. Repeat the cutting procedure on the other rotor.

☐ 19. Check the rotor thickness using a micrometer.

Micrometer reading: _____

Minimum thickness specification: _____

Can the rotor be reused? Yes ___ No ___

Job Wrap Up

☐ 1. Return all tools and equipment to storage.

☐ 2. Clean the work area.

☐ 3. Did you encounter any problems during this procedure? Yes ___ No ___

If Yes, describe the problems: _____

_____

_____

What did you do to correct the problems?_____

_____

_____

☐ 4. Have your instructor check your work and sign this job sheet.

Performance Evaluation—Instructor Use Only

Did the student complete the job in the time allotted? Yes ___ No ___

If No, which steps were not completed?_____

How would you rate this student's overall performance on this job?_____

5–Excellent, 4–Good, 3–Satisfactory, 2–Unsatisfactory, 1–Poor

Comments: _____

_____

_____

INSTRUCTOR'S SIGNATURE _____

Job

Diagnosing a Power Assist System

5 1

After completing this job, you will be able to diagnose problems in a power assist system.

Instructions

As you read the job instructions, answer the questions and perform the tasks. Print your answers neatly and use complete sentences. Consult the proper service literature and ask your instructor for help as needed.

> **Warning**
>
> ⚠ Before performing this job, review all pertinent safety information in the text and discuss safety procedures with your instructor.

Procedures

☐ 1. Obtain a vehicle to be used in this job. Your instructor may direct you to perform this job on a shop vehicle.

☐ 2. Gather the tools needed to perform this job.

Check Power Booster: Pedal Travel Test

☐ 1. With the engine off, pump the brake pedal 10 times if the vehicle has a vacuum power booster and 20 times if the vehicle uses a Hydro-Boost system.

☐ 2. Firmly apply the brake pedal.

☐ 3. Start the engine.

> **Note**
> If the vehicle uses an auxiliary vacuum pump, simply turn the ignition switch to the *On* position. It is not necessary to start the engine.

Does the brake pedal drop an additional amount when the engine starts?
Yes ___ No ___
If Yes, the system is operating properly.
If No, check the following:

Vacuum Power Booster
- Engine condition.
Describe any problems found: _____

_____

- Vacuum hose, **Figure 51-1**.
Describe any problems found: _____

_____

- Booster assembly.
Describe any problems found: _____

_____

- Auxiliary vacuum pump (if used).
Describe any problems found: _____

_____

Hydro-Boost System
- Power steering pump and belt.
Describe any problems found: _____

_____

- Pump-to-booster hoses.
Describe any problems found: _____

_____

- Control valve assembly.
Describe any problems found: _____

_____

- Accumulator.
Describe any problems found: _____

_____

Measure and Adjust Booster Push Rod Length

☐ 1. Obtain needed push rod measuring gauge.
☐ 2. Remove the master cylinder from the vacuum or hydraulic booster.
☐ 3. Place the gauge over push rod.
Does the gauge indicate the proper push rod length? Yes ___ No ___
If Yes, skip to step 6.

Job 51—Diagnosing a Power Assist System (continued)

Figure 51-1. When troubleshooting a vacuum booster, be sure to check the condition of the vacuum lines.

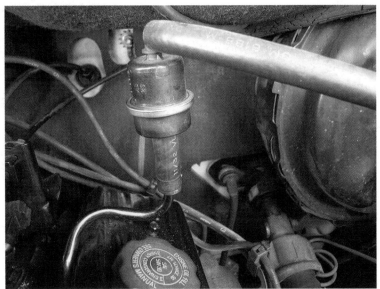

Goodheart-Willcox Publisher

- [ ] 4. Use the proper wrenches to adjust push rod length.
- [ ] 5. Use the gauge to recheck push rod length.
  Is the push rod length now correct? Yes ___ No ___
  If No, repeat step 4 as necessary until reading is correct.
- [ ] 6. Reinstall the master cylinder and check brake operation.

Diagnose a Vacuum Power Booster

- [ ] 1. Start the engine if it is not already running.
- [ ] 2. Remove the vacuum line and check valve from the booster.
- [ ] 3. Place your thumb over the check valve.
  Is vacuum present? Yes ___ No ___
- [ ] 4. Remove the check valve from the vacuum line.
- [ ] 5. Attach a vacuum gauge to the inlet hose of the vacuum booster and measure the engine vacuum at idle.
  Engine vacuum at idle:_____
- [ ] 6. Reinstall the check valve in the vacuum line and reinstall the valve in the booster.
- [ ] 7. Stop the engine after allowing it to run for about 60 seconds to establish a vacuum in the booster.
- [ ] 8. Allow the vehicle to sit for about 5 minutes.
- [ ] 9. Apply the brake.
  Is there the sound of escaping air when the pedal is depressed? Yes ___ No ___
  If Yes, the power booster is holding vacuum. Go to step 10.
  If No, go to step 11.

> **Note**
>
> As part of step 9, you should also feel power assist for at least three brake pedal applications. If the pedal is hard (no power assist), this also indicates that the booster is leaking.

☐ 10. Remove the check valve and attempt to blow through it from the hose side.

Does the check valve allow air to pass through? Yes ___ No ___

If Yes, the valve is defective and should be replaced.

☐ 11. With the check valve removed, use a hand vacuum pump to apply vacuum to the booster vacuum inlet. Use fittings and adapters that allow a tight seal at the check valve inlet. See **Figure 51-2**.

☐ 12. Wait about 2 minutes and then check vacuum.

Does vacuum drop? Yes ___ No ___

If Yes, the booster is leaking and should be replaced.

Diagnose a Hydro-Boost Power Booster System

☐ 1. Check the power steering fluid level.

Is the level within normal range? Yes ___ No ___

☐ 2. Check for leaks at the Hydro-Boost control valve and accumulator.

Were any leaks noted? Yes ___ No ___

If Yes, give the location(s): _____

_____

☐ 3. Check belt tension and condition:

Is the belt properly tensioned? Yes ___ No ___

Is the belt in good condition? Yes ___ No ___

Figure 51-2. When installing a vacuum pump to the booster, adapters may be needed to form a proper seal between the booster inlet and the vacuum pump hose.

Goodheart-Willcox Publisher

Job 51—Diagnosing a Power Assist System (continued)

☐ 4. Test the accumulator:

a. Start the engine.

b. Turn the steering wheel in one direction for five seconds.

c. Without moving the steering wheel, stop the engine.

d. Wait about 30 minutes.

e. Apply the brake. You should feel power assist for two to three brake pedal applications.

Results of test: _____

☐ 5. Based on the results of steps 1 through 4, determine needed service.

Service needed: _____

_____

☐ 6. With your instructor's approval, make needed repairs.

> **Warning**
>
> ⚠ Pump the brake pedal 20 times to remove all pressure before making repairs.

☐ 7. Recheck system operation.

Do any brake booster problems exist? Yes ___ No ___

If Yes, return to the beginning of this job and recheck the system.

Job Wrap Up

☐ 1. Return all tools and equipment to storage.

☐ 2. Clean the work area.

☐ 3. Did you encounter any problems during this procedure? Yes ___ No ___

If Yes, describe the problems: _____

_____

_____

What did you do to correct the problems?_____

_____

_____

☐ 4. Have your instructor check your work and sign this job sheet.

Performance Evaluation—Instructor Use Only

Did the student complete the job in the time allotted? Yes ___ No ___

If No, which steps were not completed?_____

How would you rate this student's overall performance on this job?_____

5–Excellent, 4–Good, 3–Satisfactory, 2–Unsatisfactory, 1–Poor

Comments: _____

_____

_____

INSTRUCTOR'S SIGNATURE _____

Job

Service Wheel Bearings

52

After completing this job, you will be able to service tapered roller and sealed wheel bearings.

Instructions

As you read the job instructions, answer the questions and perform the tasks. Print your answers neatly and use complete sentences. Consult the proper service literature and ask your instructor for help as needed.

> **Warning**
>
> ⚠ Before performing this job, review all pertinent safety information in the text and discuss safety procedures with your instructor.

Procedures

 1. Obtain a vehicle to be used in this job. Your instructor may direct you to perform this job on a shop vehicle.

☐ 2. Gather the tools needed to perform this job.

Diagnose Wheel Bearing Problems

 1. Raise the vehicle.

> **Warning**
>
> ⚠ The vehicle must be raised and supported in a safe manner. Always use approved lifts or jacks and jack stands.

☐ 2. Shake the suspect wheel from side to side and from top to bottom and note any excessive movement. If the wheel moves excessively in one direction only, the problem is in the suspension or steering systems. If the wheel moves excessively in all directions, the wheel bearing is loose or worn.

Was any looseness detected? Yes ___ No ___

If Yes, describe:_____

_____

☐ 3. Rotate each wheel while listening for noises and checking for roughness. Grinding or scraping noises indicate a dry or damaged bearing. Roughness or binding as the wheel is turned indicates that at least one roller or ball bearing has been damaged.

Was roughness or noise detected? Yes ___ No ___

If Yes, describe:_____

_____

☐ 4. Inform your instructor of your findings. Your instructor may direct you to perform the steps below to further inspect, adjust, or replace the bearings.

Service Tapered Roller Wheel Bearings

☐ 1. Safely raise the vehicle.

☐ 2. Remove the wheel from the vehicle.

☐ 3. On a disc brake system, remove the brake caliper.

☐ 4. Remove the dust cap and then remove the cotter key from the spindle nut.

☐ 5. Remove the spindle nut and washer.

☐ 6. Remove the brake drum or rotor and hub.

☐ 7. If necessary, separate the hub from the drum or rotor.

☐ 8. Remove the outer bearing from the hub.

☐ 9. Remove the grease seal from the inner hub and discard it.

☐ 10. Remove the inner bearing from the hub.

☐ 11. Clean the bearings thoroughly and blow dry.

> ### Warning
> ⚠ Do not spin the bearings with air pressure.

☐ 12. Inspect the bearings for wear or damage.

List any signs of bearing damage:_____

_____

Can this bearing be reused? Yes ___ No ___

If No, consult your instructor before proceeding.

☐ 13. Clean the bearing races and the hub interior.

☐ 14. Check the races for wear and damage.

List any signs of race damage: _____

_____

Can this race be reused? Yes ___ No ___

If No, consult your instructor before proceeding.

Job 52—Service Wheel Bearings (continued)

☐ 15. If a bearing race must be replaced, drive out the old race and install the new race. See **Figure 52-1**.

☐ 16. Place a small amount of grease in the hub cavity.

☐ 17. Grease the bearings by hand or with a packing tool.

☐ 18. Place the inner bearing in the hub and install the new seal.

☐ 19. Clean the spindle.

☐ 20. Reinstall the hub on the spindle.

☐ 21. Reinstall the outer bearing.

☐ 22. Install the washer and spindle nut.

☐ 23. Adjust bearing preload:

    a. Tighten the nut to about 100 ft lb to seat all the components.

    b. Back off the nut until it is only finger tight.

    c. Tighten the nut until the proper preload is obtained. Depending on the manufacturer, preload is measured by determining the endplay of the hub or by measuring the amount of force needed to turn the hub.

☐ 24. Install a new cotter pin.

☐ 25. Reinstall the caliper, if necessary.

☐ 25. Reinstall the wheel.

_____

Figure 52-1. Note that the rear of the bearing race is visible through the notches in the rear of the hub. Place the punch or other removal tool on the bearing at the notch and drive it out. Alternate between sides to avoid cocking the race on the hub.

Goodheart-Willcox Publisher

Remove and Replace a Sealed Wheel Bearing Assembly

☐   1.   Raise the vehicle and support it in a safe manner.

> **Warning**
>
> ⚠   The vehicle must be raised and supported in a safe manner. Always use approved lifts or jacks and jack stands.

☐   2.   Remove the wheel at the bearing assembly to be replaced.

☐   3.   If the vehicle has disc brakes, remove the caliper and rotor.

       or

       If the vehicle has drum brakes, remove the wheel bearing nut and remove the drum.

> **Note**
>
> 📄   If the vehicle has a wheel speed sensor, remove it now to prevent damage. Some speed sensors are attached to the bearing assembly and cannot be removed.

☐   4.   If the speed sensor is attached to the bearing assembly, remove the electrical connector.

☐   5.   Remove the fasteners holding the bearing assembly to the axle and remove the bearing.

☐   6.   Compare the old and new bearing assemblies to ensure that the new bearing is the correct replacement.

☐   7.   Place the new bearing in position on the axle and install the fasteners. See **Figure 52-2**.

☐   8.   If necessary, reinstall the speed sensor and/or attach the speed sensor electrical connector.

Figure 52-2. The new sealed wheel bearing is positioned on the vehicle before the fasteners are installed.

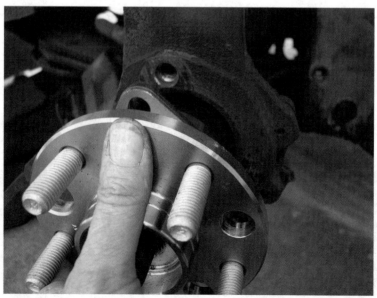

Goodheart-Willcox Publisher

Job 52—Service Wheel Bearings (continued)

☐ 9. Reinstall the drum or rotor and caliper as applicable.

> **Caution**
>
> ⚠ Use a new retaining nut if required by the manufacturer.

☐ 10. Reinstall the wheel.

☐ 11. Road test the vehicle to ensure that the bearing assembly replacement has been successful.

Job Wrap Up

☐ 1. Return all tools and equipment to storage.

☐ 2. Clean the work area.

☐ 3. Did you encounter any problems during this procedure? Yes ___ No ___

If Yes, describe the problems: _____

_____

What did you do to correct the problems?_____

_____

☐ 4. Have your instructor check your work and sign this job sheet.

Performance Evaluation—Instructor Use Only

Did the student complete the job in the time allotted? Yes ___ No ___

If No, which steps were not completed?_____

How would you rate this student's overall performance on this job?_____

5–Excellent, 4–Good, 3–Satisfactory, 2–Unsatisfactory, 1–Poor

Comments: _____

_____

_____

INSTRUCTOR'S SIGNATURE _____

Notes

After completing this job, you will be able to service parking brakes.

Instructions

As you read the job instructions, answer the questions and perform the tasks. Print your answers neatly and use complete sentences. Consult the proper service literature and ask your instructor for help as needed.

> **Warning**
>
> Before performing this job, review all pertinent safety information in the text and discuss safety procedures with your instructor.

Procedures

☐ 1. Obtain a vehicle to be used in this job. Your instructor may direct you to perform this job on a shop vehicle.

☐ 2. Gather the tools needed to perform this job.

Test Parking Brake Operation

☐ 1. Start the vehicle and move it to a flat area with enough room to allow it to move forward.

☐ 2. If the vehicle has an automatic transmission, place it in *Park*. If the vehicle has a manual transmission, place it in neutral.

☐ 3. Apply the parking brake.

☐ 4. Remove your hand or foot from the parking brake lever and observe whether the lever remains in the applied position.

Does the lever remain applied? Yes ___ No ___

If Yes, proceed to the next step.

If No, inspect and repair the lever before moving to the next step.

☐ 5. Observe the parking brake warning light.

Is the warning light on? Yes ___ No ___

☐ 6. Place the transmission in drive (automatic) or place the shift lever in first gear and slowly release the clutch (manual). Do not apply the service brake pedal.

> **Note**
>
> If the vehicle has an automatic parking brake release, hold the parking brake in the applied position with your foot.

☐ 7. Observe vehicle movement.

Automatic Transmission

Does the vehicle move? Yes ___ No ___

Manual Transmission

Does the engine die when the clutch is released ? Yes ___ No ___

☐ 8. Release the parking brake and observe vehicle movement.

Automatic transmission: Does the vehicle move? Yes ___ No ___

Manual transmission: Does the engine die when the clutch is released?
Yes ___ No ___

☐ 9. Observe the warning light.

Is the warning light on? Yes ___ No ___

Based on the above tests, does the parking brake require service? Yes ___ No ___

Inspect Parking Brake Components

> **Note**
>
> This procedure assumes the service brakes have been checked or are known to be in good condition and properly adjusted. See Jobs 43, 44, 47, and 49 for service brake inspection and adjustment procedures.

☐ 1. In the passenger compartment, observe the condition of the parking brake lever components:

Component	Worn	Broken	Sticking	Other (Describe)
Lever assembly				
Release mechanism				
Cable end and fastener				

☐ 2. Raise the vehicle.

> **Warning**
>
> The vehicle must be raised and supported in a safe manner. Always use approved lifts or jacks and jack stands.

Job 53—Service a Parking Brake (continued)

☐ 3. Check the condition of the parking brake linkage:

Component	Worn	Broken	Sticking	Other (Describe)
Equalizer/ multiplier levers				
Cables/sheaths				
Adjuster				

Adjust Parking Brake Linkage

Manually Adjusted Linkage

☐ 1. Engage the hand or foot lever two or three notches.

☐ 2. Safely raise the vehicle.

> **Warning**
>
> ⚠ The vehicle must be raised and supported in a safe manner. Always use approved lifts or jacks and jack stands.

☐ 3. If a locknut is used to hold the equalizer adjuster, loosen it now.

☐ 4. Turn the adjusting nut until there is a slight drag at the rear wheels.
Number of turns needed: _____

☐ 5. Loosen the nut until the wheels turn freely. See **Figure 53-1**.

☐ 6. Tighten the locknut if applicable.

☐ 7. Firmly apply the parking brake and release.

☐ 8. Repeat steps 3 through 9 in the *Test Parking Brake Operation* section to ensure that the parking brake operates properly.

Self-Adjusting Linkage

☐ 1. Make sure the parking brake is fully released.

☐ 2. Release the parking brake adjuster lock clip. Most lock clips are pulled away from the cable to release them. The tensioner spring will take up any slack in the cable.

☐ 3. Reinstall the brake adjuster lock clip. If the clip does not line up with the nearest groove in the cable, move the cable slightly so the clip aligns with the nearest groove.

☐ 4. Apply and release the parking brake.

☐ 5. Test the parking brakes to ensure they operate properly.

Figure 53-1. To adjust the parking brake, turn the adjusting nut until there is a slight drag at the rear wheels and then loosen the nut until the wheels turn freely.

Goodheart-Willcox Publisher

Adjust Separate Drum-Type Parking Brakes

> **Note**
> This procedure assumes the brakes are in good condition, with sufficient lining.

- [ ] 1. Remove the wheels from the rear axle.
- [ ] 2. Remove the calipers and rotors from the rear axle.
- [ ] 3. Using a shoe-to-drum gauge, measure the drum diameter of one rotor.
       Drum diameter: _____
- [ ] 4. Measure the shoe diameter and adjust the shoes to the proper clearance.
- [ ] 5. Reinstall the drum and recheck the adjustment. You should feel a slight drag when the drum is rotated through one revolution.
- [ ] 6. Repeat steps 3 through 5 on the other drum and shoes.
- [ ] 7. Apply and release the parking brake.
- [ ] 8. Test the parking brakes to ensure they operate properly.

Adjust a Parking Brake in a Rear Disc Brake Assembly

> **Note**
> This procedure assumes the brakes are in good condition, with sufficient lining and no caliper leaks.

- [ ] 1. Safely raise the vehicle.

Job 53—Service a Parking Brake (continued)

> **Warning**
>
> ⚠ The vehicle must be raised and supported in a safe manner. Always use approved lifts or jacks and jack stands.

☐ 2. Note the amount of drag present on the brakes.

☐ 3. Remove the rear wheels.

☐ 4. Check the clearance between the inner brake pad and the rotor on one brake assembly.

   Is there a noticeable space between the inner pad and the rotor? Yes ___ No ___

☐ 5. If needed, adjust the inner pad-to-rotor clearance. Consult the proper service literature for exact adjustment procedures.

☐ 6. Repeat steps 4 and 5 for the other brake assembly.

☐ 7. Apply and release the parking brake.

☐ 8. Test the parking brakes to ensure they operate properly.

Retract an Integrated Parking Brake Caliper Piston

> **Caution**
>
> ◇ Special tools may be needed to perform this job.

> **Note**
>
> ▤ Turning the disc brake apply piston retracts most disc-type parking brakes. Consult the service information to determine the exact retraction procedure.

☐ 1. If necessary, remove the caliper.

☐ 2. Remove the disc brake pads from the caliper and remove the brake pads.

☐ 3. Put firm pressure on the piston face. This is accomplished with a C-clamp or by prying on the piston face with a pry bar.

☐ 4. Rotate the piston into the caliper body. This can be done by using a special tool, operating the use apply lever at the back of the caliper assembly, or turning the piston with a large pair of pliers. Maintain pressure on the piston face as the piston is rotated.

> **Note**
>
> ▤ Most pistons are rotated clockwise to move them back into the caliper body. A few pistons rotate counterclockwise. Always consult the proper service literature for the proper turning direction. Tighten the C-clamp after every rotation of the piston in order to maintain pressure on the piston.

> **Caution**
>
> ⚠ Do not twist or cut the rubber piston boot.

☐ 5. Once the piston is fully retracted, reinstall the disc brake pads if necessary.

☐ 6. Reinstall the caliper if necessary.

Clean, Lubricate, and Replace Parking Brake Linkage

Clean and Lubricate Linkage

☐ 1. Safely raise the vehicle.

> **Warning**
>
> ⚠ The vehicle must be raised and supported in a safe manner. Always use approved lifts or jacks and jack stands.

☐ 2. Remove the cable ends if possible.

☐ 3. Spray penetrating oil on both ends of the cable where it enters the sheath.

☐ 4. Allow the penetrating oil to soak for 5 to 10 minutes.

☐ 5. Clean dirt and corrosion from the cable.

☐ 6. Work the cable back and forth in the sheath, applying more penetrating oil as needed.

☐ 7. Check cable operation. If the cable cannot be freed up, it must be replaced.

☐ 8. Apply and release the parking brake.

☐ 9. Test the parking brakes to ensure they operate properly. Readjust the parking brake if necessary.

Replace a Parking Brake Cable

☐ 1. Safely raise the vehicle.

> **Warning**
>
> ⚠ The vehicle must be raised and supported in a safe manner. Always use approved lifts or jacks and jack stands.

☐ 2. Back off the cable adjuster to remove tension from the linkage.

☐ 3. Remove the cable ends.

☐ 4. Loosen and remove any clips or brackets holding the cable to the vehicle.

☐ 5. Compare the old and new cable. Make sure the cable ends and any clips on the new cable exactly match the original cable.

☐ 6. Install the new cable, routing it exactly as the old cable was routed. Be sure the new cable does not contact any moving parts or the exhaust system.

☐ 7. Install the cable ends.

☐ 8. Readjust the parking brake.

☐ 9. Apply and release the parking brake.

☐ 10. Test the parking brakes to ensure they operate properly.

Job 53—Service a Parking Brake (continued)

Replace a Parking Brake Lever

☐ 1. Safely raise the vehicle.

> **Warning**
>
> ⚠ The vehicle must be raised and supported in a safe manner. Always use approved lifts or jacks and jack stands.

☐ 2. Back off the cable adjuster to remove tension from the lever.

☐ 3. Remove the cable end(s) from the lever.

☐ 4. Remove any fasteners and remove the lever from the vehicle.

☐ 5. Compare the old and new levers. Make sure they match exactly.

☐ 6. Install the cable(s) on the lever.

☐ 7. Readjust the parking brake.

☐ 8. Apply and release the parking brake.

☐ 9. Test the parking brakes to ensure they operate properly.

Job Wrap Up

☐ 1. Return all tools and equipment to storage.

☐ 2. Clean the work area.

☐ 3. Did you encounter any problems during this procedure? Yes ___ No ___
If Yes, describe the problems: _____

_____

What did you do to correct the problems?_____

_____

☐ 4. Have your instructor check your work and sign this job sheet.

Performance Evaluation—Instructor Use Only

Did the student complete the job in the time allotted? Yes ___ No ___
If No, which steps were not completed?_____
How would you rate this student's overall performance on this job?_____
5–Excellent, 4–Good, 3–Satisfactory, 2–Unsatisfactory, 1–Poor
Comments: _____

_____

INSTRUCTOR'S SIGNATURE _____

Notes

Job
Identify and Inspect ABS and TCS Components

54

After completing this job, you will be able to inspect anti-lock brake and/or traction control systems for proper operation. You will also be able to identify ABS and TCS problems resulting from component failures due to wear or damage.

Instructions

As you read the job instructions, answer the questions and perform the tasks. Print your answers neatly and use complete sentences. Consult the proper service literature and ask your instructor for help as needed.

> **Warning**
> ⚠ Before performing this job, review all pertinent safety information in the text and discuss safety procedures with your instructor.

Procedures

☐ 1. Obtain a vehicle to be used in this job. Your instructor may direct you to perform this job on a shop vehicle.

☐ 2. Gather the tools needed to perform this job.

☐ 3. Obtain the correct service literature for the vehicle being serviced and fill in the following information about the ABS/TCS system being serviced.

System type: ABS only ___ ABS/TCS ___ 2-wheel system ___ 4-wheel system ___

Is this an integral system (no separate master cylinder)? Yes ___ No ___

System manufacturer: _____

☐ 4. Check the brake fluid level in the reservoir.

> **Warning**
> ⚠ Depressurize integral systems by depressing the brake pedal 40–50 times. Do not turn the ignition on while checking the system fluid.

5. Add fluid to the reservoir as necessary.
   Type of fluid added:_____

> **Warning**
>
> ⚠ Do not use silicone fluid (DOT# 5) in any ABS/TCS system.

6. Start the engine and compare the operation of the dashboard brake, ABS, and TCS warning lights with normal operation as defined in the service literature.
   Did the warning lights come on and then go off after the normal start-up sequence?
   Yes ___ No ___
   If Yes, proceed to step 7.
   If No, consult your instructor for additional directions.

7. Raise the vehicle.

> **Warning**
>
> ⚠ The vehicle must be raised and supported in a safe manner. Always use approved lifts or jacks and jack stands.

> **Note**
>
> 📄 If the base brakes are known to be in good condition, or if told to do so by your instructor, skip steps 8 and 9.

8. Remove all wheels from the vehicle.

9. Inspect the base brake system and summarize the condition of the hydraulic and friction components (refer to other jobs as necessary).
   Describe any defects found in the base-brake hydraulic system: _____

   _____

   Describe any service needed for the base-brake hydraulic system: _____

   _____

   Describe any defects found in the base-brake friction system:_____

   _____

   Describe any service needed for the base-brake friction system:_____

   _____

10. Inspect the wheel speed sensors and rotors (trigger wheels). Look for the following problems:
    • Damaged or disconnected sensor.
    • Metal shavings on sensor tip. See **Figure 54-1**.
    • Debris on rotors. See **Figure 54-2**.
    • Damaged rotor.
    • Improper sensor-to-rotor clearance.

Job 54—Identify and Inspect ABS and TCS Components (continued)

Figure 54-1. Excessive metal shavings on this wheel speed sensor make it unusable. In many cases, the sensor can be cleaned.

Goodheart-Willcox Publisher

Figure 54-2. Debris on this rotor will affect the signal generated by the sensor.

Goodheart-Willcox Publisher

☐ 11. Describe the condition of each sensor and rotor at the locations listed below. If the ABS/TCS system being inspected does not have the sensor listed, write N/A in the space.

Left-front wheel: _____

Right-front wheel: _____

Left-rear wheel: _____

Right-rear wheel: _____

Transmission-mounted sensor: _____

Differential-mounted sensor: _____

☐ 12. Reinstall the wheels if they were removed. Torque lug nuts to the correct values.

☐ 13. Lower the vehicle.

☐ 14. Locate and note the condition of the following ABS/TCS components. Look for leaks, disconnected or corroded wires, damage, or other defects. If the listed component is not used on the vehicle being serviced, write N/A in the blank.

- Control module: _____

- ABS hydraulic actuator: _____

- Relays: _____

- G-force sensor: _____

- Lateral acceleration sensor: _____

- TCS hydraulic actuator, if used. Put "integral" if the TCS hydraulic actuator is part of the ABS actuator: _____

- TCS disable switch: _____

- Engine torque management control: _____

☐ 15. Take the vehicle to a road with little or no traffic and test ABS and/or TCS system operation using the procedures outlined in the service literature.

Warning

⚠ Be sure to select an empty section of road for these tests. Wait until all other traffic has cleared before beginning the tests. Be sure you have read and understand all the manufacturer's safety instructions before beginning any test.

☐ 16. Consult with your instructor and determine whether further inspection of the ABS/TCS is needed.

Is further testing needed? Yes ___ No ___

Job 54—Identify and Inspect ABS and TCS Components (continued)

Job Wrap Up

☐ 1. Return all tools and equipment to storage.

☐ 2. Clean the work area.

☐ 3. Did you encounter any problems during this procedure? Yes ___ No ___

If Yes, describe the problems: _____

_____

_____

What did you do to correct the problems?_____

_____

_____

☐ 4. Have your instructor check your work and sign this job sheet.

Performance Evaluation—Instructor Use Only

Did the student complete the job in the time allotted? Yes ___ No ___

If No, which steps were not completed?_____

How would you rate this student's overall performance on this job?____

5–Excellent, 4–Good, 3–Satisfactory, 2–Unsatisfactory, 1–Poor

Comments: _____

_____

_____

INSTRUCTOR'S SIGNATURE _____

Notes

Job

Perform General Electrical Tests and Services

55

After completing this job, you will be able to demonstrate basic knowledge of electrical and electronic systems. You will also be able to perform various electrical tasks involving knowledge of electrical circuits and Ohm's law.

Instructions

As you read the job instructions, answer the questions and perform the tasks. Print your answers neatly and use complete sentences. Consult the proper service literature and ask your instructor for help as needed.

> **Warning**
> ⚠ Before performing this job, review all pertinent safety information in the text and discuss safety procedures with your instructor.

Procedures

1. Obtain a vehicle to be used in this job. Your instructor may direct you to perform this job on a shop vehicle.
2. Gather the tools needed to perform the following job.

Use a Multimeter to Calculate/Read Amperage

1. Obtain a multimeter capable of reading volts, amps, and ohms. Ensure that the multimeter has the needed electrical leads.
2. Obtain a vehicle to be used for this job.
3. Locate a vehicle circuit that can be disconnected from the electrical system without causing disruptions to other vehicle systems.

> **Note**
> Use a resistive circuit such as a light or heater. Motors and coils use extra current for the creation of magnetic fields. Circuits containing these devices, therefore, are not suitable for this job. Check with your instructor about what circuit to use.

☐   4.   Turn on the multimeter, attach leads as necessary, and set the meter to read voltage.

☐   5.   Read the voltage as displayed on the multimeter between the positive connection and ground.

        Voltage reading:_____

☐   6.   Disconnect all power from the circuit.

☐   7.   Use the multimeter to read resistance in the circuit between the positive and negative connections.

        Resistance in ohms:_____

☐   8.   Use Ohm's law to calculate amperage flow using voltage and resistance values.

> **Note**
>
> Remember that calculating values for multiple resistors in a circuit, and/or for resistors in parallel in the circuit, are more complex than calculating for a single resistor. Refer to your textbook or your instructor for more information.

        Calculated value in amps:_____

☐   9.   Reconnect the circuit and energize it by turning the control switch on.

☐ 10.   Use the multimeter and appropriate leads to read amperage.

        Does the amperage reading match calculated amperage? Yes ___ No ___
        If No, what could be the explanation?_____

Optional Job—Use a Multimeter to Calculate/Read Resistance

☐   1.   Obtain a multimeter and related electrical leads. The multimeter should be capable of reading volts, amps, and ohms.

☐   2.   Obtain a vehicle to be used for this job.

☐   3.   Locate a vehicle circuit capable of being disconnected from the vehicle.

> **Note**
>
> Use a resistive circuit such as a light or heater. Circuits using motors or coils often use extra current to create magnetic fields and are not suitable for this job.

☐   4.   Set the multimeter to read voltage and attach leads as necessary.

☐   5.   Use the multimeter to read voltage between the positive connection and ground.

        Voltage:_____

☐   6.   Set the multimeter to read amperage and attach leads as necessary.

☐   7.   Turn the circuit on and read amperage. _____ amps

☐   8.   Use Ohm's law to calculate resistance using voltage and amperage values.

Job 55—Perform General Electrical Tests and Services (continued)

> **Note**
>
> Remember that calculating values for multiple resistors in a circuit, and/or for resistors in parallel in the circuit, are more complex than calculating for a single resistor. Refer to your textbook material or your instructor for more information.

Calculated resistance in ohms:_____

☐ 9. Disconnect all power from the circuit.

☐ 10. Use the multimeter to read resistance in the circuit between the positive and negative connections.

Resistance in ohms:_____

Does the resistance reading match calculated resistance? Yes ___ No ___

If No, what could be the explanation?_____

_____

_____

☐ 11. Reconnect the power to the circuit and check circuit operation.

Identify Series, Parallel, and Series-Parallel Circuits

☐ 1. Using a vehicle schematic, determine whether the following circuits are series, parallel, or series-parallel types. The schematic can be obtained from your instructor, from approved service literature in the shop or accessed on the Internet. Write your answer in the blank provided.

Circuit from battery through starter relay to starter: _____

Circuit through headlight switch to headlights: _____

Circuit through brake pedal switch to brake lights: _____

Circuit through doorjamb switch to single dome light: _____

Circuit through doorjamb switch to multiple interior lights: _____

Circuit through rear harness connector to taillights: _____

Optional Circuits (Assigned by Instructor)

a. What does the circuit control? _____

Is the circuit series, parallel, or series-parallel? _____

b. What does the circuit control? _____

Is the circuit series, parallel, or series-parallel? _____

c. What does the circuit control? _____

Is the circuit series, parallel, or series-parallel? _____

d. What does the circuit control? _____

Is the circuit series, parallel, or series-parallel? _____

Check Circuit Protection Devices

> **Note**
>
> Removing an undamaged fuse or fusible link will remove power from the circuit that the fuse/fusible link controls. This may cause loss of memory in electronic modules controlling various vehicle systems.

Inspect a Fuse

☐ 1. Remove the fuse and visually inspect it.

Is the fuse undamaged? Refer to **Figure 55-1**. Yes ___ No ___

If No, describe the condition: _____

_____

Check Fuse Condition with a Test Light

☐ 1. Obtain a non-powered test light.

☐ 2. Turn the ignition switch to the *On* position.

☐ 3. Use the test light to check fuse operation. Note your conclusions below.

Is there power at both sides of the fuse? Yes ___ No ___

Is there power at only one side of the fuse? Yes ___ No ___

Is there no power to both sides of the fuse? Yes ___ No ___

Using your own words, what conclusion can you draw from the readings? _____

_____

☐ 4. Turn the ignition switch to the *Off* position.

Inspect a Fusible Link

☐ 1. Examine the insulation on the fusible link.

Does the insulation appear to be discolored or melted, or show other signs of overheating? Yes ___ No ___

If Yes, describe the condition of the insulation. _____

_____

Figure 55-1. The fuse on the left is in good condition. The fuse on the right is blown.

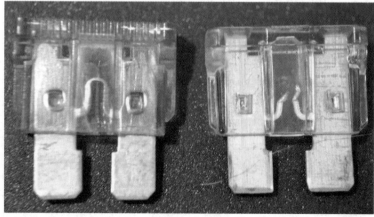

Goodheart-Willcox Publisher

Job 55—Perform General Electrical Tests and Services (continued)

☐ 2. Grasp each side of the fusible link and tug on it.

Does it show any signs of stretching, indicating broken internal wires?

Yes ___ No ___

If Yes, describe the results of your tests: _____

_____

_____

Check Circuit Breaker Condition

☐ 1. Obtain a non-powered test light.

☐ 2. Turn the ignition switch to the *On* position.

☐ 3. Check for power at one side of the circuit breaker using the test light.

Does the test light illuminate? Yes ___ No ___

☐ 4. Check for power at the other side of the circuit breaker using the test light.

Does the test light illuminate? Yes ___ No ___

☐ 5. Turn the ignition switch to the *Off* position.

☐ 6. Remove the circuit breaker and test for resistance using an ohmmeter.

Reading in ohms:_____

> **Note**
> Removing a working circuit breaker will remove power from the circuit that the breaker controls. This may cause loss of memory in electronic modules controlling various vehicle systems.

☐ 7. Describe, in your own words, what these tests indicate.

_____

_____

Check for Parasitic Battery Load

☐ 1. Ensure that the vehicle's ignition switch is in the off position and that all electrical equipment is turned off.

> **Note**
> Some manufacturers recommend waiting a specified time after stopping the engine to ensure that all electronic devices have powered down.

☐ 2. Remove the battery negative cable.

☐ 3. Install a fused jumper wire in series between the battery negative terminal and battery negative cable.

Does the fuse blow? Yes ___ No ___

If No, proceed to step 4.

If Yes, there is a heavy current draw which must be located before proceeding.

☐ 4. Obtain a multimeter and set it to read amperage. Adjust the scale as needed.

☐ 5. Remove the fused jumper wire and install the multimeter leads in series between the battery negative terminal and battery negative cable.

☐ 6. Observe the multimeter reading. Check the manufacturer's service literature for the exact reading. The reading generally should be around 25 milliamps.

Is the amperage reading within specifications? Yes ___ No ___

If Yes, the parasitic draw is not excessive.

If No, one of the vehicle's electrical circuits is causing parasitic draw.

Questions

Demonstrate knowledge of causes and effects of short circuits by answering the following questions:

_____ 1. True or False? A short circuit bypasses at least part of the original circuit.

_____ 2. A short circuit can damage wiring due to excess _____ flow.

3. Most short circuits are prevented from causing major damage by the presence of protective devices in the circuit. List the three types of protective devices.

_____

_____

_____

Demonstrate your knowledge of causes and effects of grounded circuits by answering the following questions.

_____ 4. A grounded circuit is a wire on the _____ side of a circuit that contacts the vehicle body or frame.

_____ 5. True or False? A grounded circuit can be thought of as a type of short circuit through the vehicle body or frame.

Demonstrate your knowledge of causes and effects of open circuits by answering the following questions.

_____ 6. Does more or less current flow in an open circuit compared to a normally operating circuit?

_____ 7. True or False? A blower motor circuit with a detached connector at the blower is a type of open circuit.

Demonstrate your knowledge of causes and effects of high resistance in circuits by answering the following questions.

_____ 8. Does more or less current flow in a circuit with high resistance compared to a normally operating circuit?

_____ 9. True or False? A light circuit with a burned out bulb filament is a type of high resistance circuit.

Job 55—Perform General Electrical Tests and Services (continued)

10. Identify the following circuits as complete, open, shorted, or grounded.

    A. _____
    B. _____
    C. _____
    D. _____

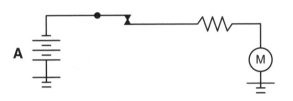
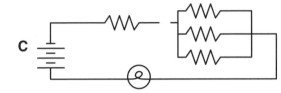
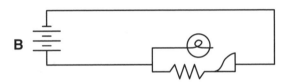

Goodheart-Willcox Publisher

Job Wrap Up

☐ 1. Return all tools and equipment to storage.

☐ 2. Clean the work area.

☐ 3. Did you encounter any problems during this procedure? Yes ___ No ___
   If Yes, describe the problems: _____
   _____
   _____
   What did you do to correct the problems?_____
   _____
   _____

☐ 4. Have your instructor check your work and sign this job sheet.

Performance Evaluation—Instructor Use Only

Did the student complete the job in the time allotted? Yes ___ No ___
If No, which steps were not completed?_____
How would you rate this student's overall performance on this job?____
5–Excellent, 4–Good, 3–Satisfactory, 2–Unsatisfactory, 1–Poor
Comments: _____
_____
_____

INSTRUCTOR'S SIGNATURE _____

Notes

Job

Service Wiring and Wiring Connectors

56

After completing this job, you will be able to repair wiring and service wire connectors.

Instructions

As you read the job instructions, answer the questions and perform the tasks. Print your answers neatly and use complete sentences. Consult the proper service literature and ask your instructor for help as needed.

Note

 Fiber optic cables are used on many newer vehicles to connect data buses, controller area networks (CANs), sound and video systems, and remote communication and security systems. Although, in theory, fiber optic cables can be repaired, most vehicle manufacturers recommend that the entire cable be replaced.

Warning

⚠ Before performing this job, review all pertinent safety information in the text and discuss safety procedures with your instructor.

Procedures

☐ 1. Obtain a primary wire in need of repair. The wire may be installed on a vehicle, or it may be a length of wire supplied by your instructor.

Describe the wire you will be using: _____

_____

☐ 2. Gather the tools needed to perform this job.

Identify Hybrid Vehicle High-Voltage Circuits

> **Warning**
>
> ⚠ Do not try to repair hybrid high-voltage (orange covered) wiring. Always replace a hybrid vehicle wiring harness.

☐ 1. Obtain a hybrid vehicle.

☐ 2. Put on insulated safety gloves.

☐ 3. Open the vehicle hood and locate any wires having orange insulation and any high-voltage warning labels.

Describe the location of any wires with orange insulation, and any warning labels:

_____

_____

Install a Crimp Connector

☐ 1. Remove about 1/2" (12 mm) of insulation from one end of the wire. If possible, use a wire stripper to remove the insulation.

> **Caution**
>
> The outer insulation of some wires is covered with braided wire or metallic tape. This covering is an electrical interference shield. Repair the shielding according to manufacturer's instructions after repairs are made to the internal wire.

☐ 2. Slide the stripped end of the wire into the connector.

☐ 3. Use a crimping tool to compress the connector around the wire. See **Figure 56-1**.

Figure 56-1. This crimping tool is set up to crimp a connector around a wire. Make sure the crimp is made at the proper place on the connector.

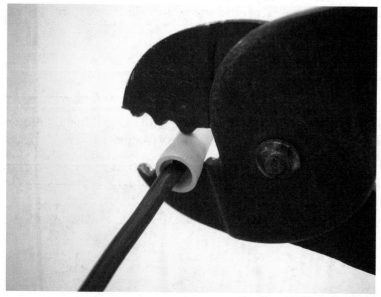

Goodheart-Willcox Publisher

Job 56—Service Wiring and Wiring Connectors (continued)

☐ 4. Pull on the wire and terminal lightly to ensure that the connection will not come apart.

☐ 5. If you are installing a butt connector, repeat steps 1 through 4 for the other wire end.

Solder Two Wires

☐ 1. If necessary, move to a work surface that will not be affected by heat.

☐ 2. Make sure the wires to be soldered are clean and that at least 1/2″ (12 mm) of insulation has been removed from the end of each wire.

☐ 3. Connect the wires to be soldered by twisting them together. An elaborate splice is usually not necessary, but the wires should be secure enough to resist being pulled apart by light pressure.

☐ 4. Check the condition of the soldering gun (or iron). Ensure that the tip is clean and lightly tinned (coated with melted solder).

Is the soldering iron/gun tip clean and tinned? Yes ___ No ___

☐ 5. Turn on the soldering gun and allow it to reach operating temperature. Clean and tin the tip if necessary.

> **Warning**
>
> ⚠ Be careful while performing the following steps. The soldering gun or melted solder can cause severe burns.

☐ 6. Touch the soldering gun tip to the connection and allow it to preheat the wires.

☐ 7. Touch the solder to the connection while continuing to apply heat, **Figure 56-2**. Wait until the solder melts and flows into the wires.

Figure 56-2. Once the connection is hot, apply the solder to the wires while continuing to apply heat.

Goodheart-Willcox Publisher

☐ 8. Remove the soldering gun tip from the connection and allow the soldered joint to cool for a few seconds before moving the joint.

☐ 9. After allowing the joint to cool, lightly pull on it to ensure that it is solid.

Install a Terminal End in a Connector

☐ 1. Determine which connector terminal is defective, then make a sketch of the connector end and indicate the defective terminal(s).

☐ 2. Using a special tool or a small screwdriver, depress the terminal locking tang and pull the terminal from the connector.

☐ 3. Install the new terminal by pushing it into place in the connector. After installation, lightly pull on the connector wire to ensure the tang is holding the terminal in place.

☐ 4. Connect the terminal wire to the existing wire in the harness by crimping or soldering, as explained previously.

☐ 5. Reattach the connector and check component operation.

Job Wrap Up

☐ 1. Return all tools and equipment to storage.

☐ 2. Clean the work area.

☐ 3. Did you encounter any problems during this procedure? Yes ___ No ___

If Yes, describe the problems: _____

_____

_____

What did you do to correct the problems?_____

_____

_____

☐ 4. Have your instructor check your work and sign this job sheet.

Performance Evaluation—Instructor Use Only

Did the student complete the job in the time allotted? Yes ___ No ___

If No, which steps were not completed?_____

How would you rate this student's overall performance on this job?_____

5–Excellent, 4–Good, 3–Satisfactory, 2–Unsatisfactory, 1–Poor

Comments: _____

_____

INSTRUCTOR'S SIGNATURE _____

Job

Inspect and Test
a Battery

57

After completing this job, you will be able to inspect a battery and perform a variety of tests on it.

Instructions

As you read the job instructions, answer the questions and perform the tasks. Print your answers neatly and use complete sentences. Consult the proper service literature and ask your instructor for help as needed.

> **Warning**
>
> ⚠ Before performing this job, review all pertinent safety information in the text and discuss safety procedures with your instructor.

Procedures

 1. Obtain a vehicle with a battery in need of service.

 2. Gather the tools needed to perform this job.

> **Warning**
>
> ⚠ Before performing service on a 12-volt battery installed in a hybrid vehicle, disconnect the high-voltage system according to manufacturer's instructions. Then wait at least five minutes to ensure that any high-voltage capacitors have discharged.

Perform Basic Battery Tests

☐ 1. Perform a visual inspection of the battery and answer the following questions:

- Is the battery top clean and dry? Yes ___ No ___

If No, clean and dry the top of the battery before proceeding.

- Are the terminals and clamps clean, tight, and free from corrosion? Yes ___ No ___

If No, clean the battery terminals and clamps before proceeding.

- Are the battery hold-down and its hardware tight and free from corrosion? Yes ___ No ___

If No, replace hardware as needed and tighten the battery hold-down before proceeding.

- Is the battery case cracked or damaged? Yes ___ No ___

If Yes, consult with your instructor before proceeding.

- If the battery has removable vent caps, is the battery filled to the proper level? Yes ___ No ___

If No, fill the battery to the proper level with distilled water.

☐ 2. Confirm that the battery is powerful enough to start the engine by comparing its cold cranking amps (CCA) with the published specifications for the engine in the vehicle. The CCA is usually found on the top of the battery, as in **Figure 57-1**.

CCA of battery:_____

CCA specified in the service literature:_____

Is this battery powerful enough to start this engine? Yes ___ No ___

If No, replace the battery with a battery having the correct capacity.

Figure 57-1. Modern batteries have a top-mounted label containing information on battery size and electrical capacity.

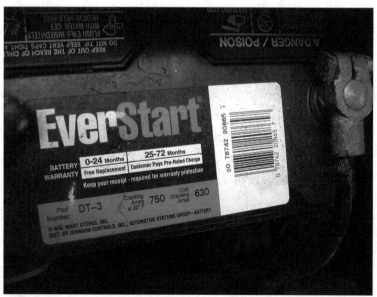

Goodheart-Willcox Publisher

Job 57—Inspect and Test a Battery (continued)

☐ 3. If possible, and if your instructor directs you to, check each battery cell with a hydrometer. Remove the cell caps and insert the hydrometer hose. Draw in only enough electrolyte to float the bulb and do not allow the bulb to contact the sides of the cylinder. Record the readings in the blanks provided.

Cell 1:_____   Cell 2:_____   Cell 3:_____

Cell 4:_____   Cell 5:_____   Cell 6:_____

Based on these readings, what is the state of charge of the battery: fully charged, 3/4 charged, 1/2 charged, 1/4 charged, or discharged?_____

Does any cell reading differ significantly from the others? Yes ___ No ___

If Yes, what is the cause? _____

_____

☐ 4. Attach an electrical system tester to the battery, **Figure 57-2**.

> ### Warning
> ⚠ Do not attempt to make electrical tests to a frozen battery. Freezing may cause the battery plates to buckle, making the battery unsafe and/or unusable. A frozen battery should be replaced.

☐ 5. Measure and record the no-load voltage.

No-load voltage:_____

Figure 57-2. Many modern battery testers will go through an automatic test sequence and display battery condition as a scope pattern. Follow the tester manufacturer's procedures to make battery tests.

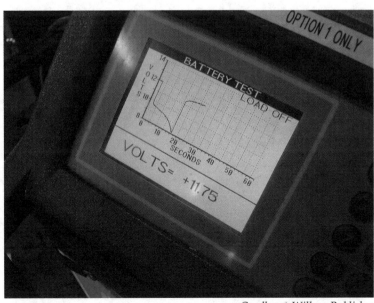

Goodheart-Willcox Publisher

> **Caution**
>
> If the voltage is below 12 volts, charge the battery before making further tests.

☐ 6. Use the electrical system tester to drop the voltage to 9.6 volts and record the amperage draw.

Amperage draw at 9.6 volts:_____

☐ 7. Compare the readings with specifications.

Do the readings indicate a problem? Yes ___ No ___

If Yes, describe the problem: _____

_____

_____

Perform a Conductance Test (Optional)

☐ 1. Obtain a conductance tester.

> **Note**
>
> Not all battery manufacturers publish conductance specifications. Check the tester or battery manufacturer's service information to determine whether a conductance specification is available for the battery that you are testing.

☐ 2. Obtain the conductance specification and enter here.

Normal or maximum reading:_____

Lowest reading or largest percent deviation allowed:_____

Specification source:_____

☐ 3. Connect the tester to the battery terminals.

☐ 4. Using the tester keypad, enter battery information as directed by the tester screen.

☐ 5. Once all information is entered, the tester will go through an automated test sequence.

> **Warning**
>
> Conductance testers send a small AC voltage through the battery. Do not disconnect the tester during the test sequence, as a spark may result.

☐ 6. Read the conductance from the tester screen.

Conductance reading:_____

☐ 7. Disconnect the tester from the battery terminals.

Job 57—Inspect and Test a Battery (continued)

☐ 8. Compare the conductance reading with the specification(s).
Is battery conductance acceptable? Yes ___ No ___
If No, explain:_____
_____

Is there any indication of shorts or open circuits? Yes ___ No ___
If Yes, explain:_____
_____

Job Wrap Up

☐ 1. Return all tools and equipment to storage.

☐ 2. Clean the work area.

☐ 3. Did you encounter any problems during this procedure? Yes ___ No ___
If Yes, describe the problems: _____
_____
_____

What did you do to correct the problems?_____
_____
_____

☐ 4. Have your instructor check your work and sign this job sheet.

Performance Evaluation—Instructor Use Only

Did the student complete the job in the time allotted? Yes ___ No ___
If No, which steps were not completed?_____
How would you rate this student's overall performance on this job?_____
5–Excellent, 4–Good, 3–Satisfactory, 2–Unsatisfactory, 1–Poor
Comments: _____
_____
_____

INSTRUCTOR'S SIGNATURE _____

Notes

Job

Service a Battery

58

After completing this job, you will be able to clean and charge a battery.

Instructions

As you read the job instructions, answer the questions and perform the tasks. Print your answers neatly and use complete sentences. Consult the proper service literature and ask your instructor for help as needed.

> **Warning**
> ⚠ Before performing this job, review all pertinent safety information in the text and discuss safety procedures with your instructor.

Procedures

> **Warning**
> ⚠ Before performing service on a 12-volt battery installed in a hybrid vehicle, disconnect the high-voltage system according to manufacturer's instructions. Then wait at least five minutes to ensure that any high-voltage capacitors have discharged.

☐ 1. Obtain a vehicle with a battery in need of service.

☐ 2. Attach a memory saver to the vehicle cigarette lighter or other auxiliary power outlet.

☐ 3. Protect the vehicle's painted surfaces with a fender cover.

☐ 4. Remove the battery negative cable. This will eliminate any chance of an electrical short while removing the positive cable.

☐ 5. Remove the positive cable.

☐ 6. Remove the battery hold-down hardware.

☐ 7. Remove the battery from the vehicle.

☐ 8. Clean the battery cable ends with a solution of baking soda and water, or a commercial cleaning product.

☐ 9. Clean the battery top and terminals with a solution of baking soda and water, or a commercial cleaning product.

> **Warning**
>
> Do not allow the cleaning solution to enter the battery cells.

☐ 10. Rinse the battery with clean water and dry it thoroughly.

☐ 11. Inspect the battery tray and hold-down hardware, **Figure 58-1**.
Are the battery tray and hardware clean and in good condition? Yes ___ No ___
If No, clean, repaint, or replace the tray and hardware as needed.

☐ 12. Reinstall the battery in the vehicle.

☐ 13. Install the battery hold-down hardware.

☐ 14. Install and tighten the positive battery cable on the battery positive terminal.

☐ 15. Install and tighten the negative battery cable on the battery negative terminal.

☐ 16. Remove the memory saver.

Identify Electronic Parts That Require Reprogramming after Battery Removal

> **Note**
>
> Some electronic modules rely on battery voltage to maintain their programming. If a memory saver was not installed before the battery was removed, or if battery voltage becomes extremely low, the technician must reprogram these electronic modules after the battery problem has been corrected. The most common electronic modules needing reprogramming are the engine and drive train modules, body (sound system, climate control, clock) modules, and security system modules.

Figure 58-1. Check that the battery tray is not corroded or damaged.

Goodheart-Willcox Publisher

Job 58—Service a Battery (continued)

☐ 1. Refer to the service information to determine the following:
- Which electronic modules require reprogramming?
- What is the proper reprogramming procedures for each module?

☐ 2. Perform the necessary reprogramming procedures as outlined in the service information.
- Attach a scan tool as explained in Job 74 and follow scan tool directions.

Describe the needed operations: _____

_____

_____

- Turn the ignition switch to the *On* position and push buttons on the sound system or climate control.

Describe the needed operations: _____

_____

_____

_____

_____

Charge a Battery

☐ 1. Attach the clamps of the battery charger to the battery terminals.

☐ 2. Make sure the battery charger is plugged into an electrical outlet.

☐ 3. Set the battery charger controls to the charge rate desired:

Fast:___ Slow:___ Trickle:___ Other (specify):_____

☐ 4. Set the battery charger timer to the required time.

☐ 5. Allow the battery to charge.

☐ 6. When the required time has elapsed, turn off the charger controls.

☐ 7. Remove the battery charger clamps from the battery terminals.

Job Wrap Up

☐ 1. Return all tools and equipment to storage.

☐ 2. Clean the work area.

☐ 3. Did you encounter any problems during this procedure? Yes ___ No ___

If Yes, describe the problems: _____

_____

_____

What did you do to correct the problems?_____

_____

_____

☐ 4. Have your instructor check your work and sign this job sheet.

Performance Evaluation—Instructor Use Only

Did the student complete the job in the time allotted? Yes ___ No ___

If No, which steps were not completed?_____

How would you rate this student's overall performance on this job?_____

5–Excellent, 4–Good, 3–Satisfactory, 2–Unsatisfactory, 1–Poor

Comments: _____

_____

_____

INSTRUCTOR'S SIGNATURE _____

Job

Jump-Start a Vehicle

59

After completing this job, you will be able to jump-start a vehicle using jumper cables and a booster battery or an auxiliary power source.

Instructions

As you read the job instructions, answer the questions and perform the tasks. Print your answers neatly and use complete sentences. Consult the proper service literature and ask your instructor for help as needed.

> **Warning**
>
> ⚠ Before performing this job, review all pertinent safety information in the text and discuss safety procedures with your instructor.

Procedures

☐ 1. Obtain a vehicle to be used in this job. Your instructor may direct you to perform this job on a shop vehicle.

☐ 2. Gather the tools needed to perform this job.

> **Caution**
>
> ◇ A modern vehicle with a completely dead battery cannot be push started. Attempting to start a vehicle with a weak battery can damage the catalytic converter. Always use jumper cables or install a fully charged battery.

Jump-Start a Vehicle with Jumper Cables

☐ 1. Position the boost vehicle so the jumper cables will reach both batteries.

☐ 2. Attach one jumper cable clamp to the positive terminal of the booster battery.

☐ 3. Attach one jumper cable clamp to the positive terminal of the discharged battery.

> **Warning**
>
> ⚠ Be sure to attach the jumper cables positive to positive and negative to negative.

☐ 4. Attach one jumper cable clamp to the negative terminal of the booster battery.

☐ 5. Attach the final jumper cable clamp to a ground on the engine of the vehicle being jump-started.

> **Warning**
>
> ⚠ Do not attach the jumper cable to the battery negative cable, as a spark could ignite any hydrogen gas that has collected near the top of the battery.

☐ 6. Start the engine of the booster vehicle.

☐ 7. Start the engine of the vehicle with the discharged battery.

☐ 8. Disconnect the negative cable clamp on the vehicle being jump-started. Keep the jumper cable clamp in your hand and away from the engine compartment. Then, disconnect the negative cable clamp on the booster vehicle.

☐ 9. Disconnect both positive cable clamps.

Use an Auxiliary Power Source to Jump-Start a Vehicle

☐ 1. Obtain an auxiliary power source.

☐ 2. Attach the positive auxiliary power source cable clamp to the positive terminal of the discharged battery.

☐ 3. Attach the negative auxiliary power source cable clamp to a ground on the engine.

> **Warning**
>
> ⚠ Do not attach the cable to the battery negative cable, as a spark could ignite any hydrogen gas that has collected near the top of the battery.

☐ 4. Start the vehicle's engine.

☐ 5. Switch off the auxiliary power source.

☐ 6. Disconnect the negative cable clamp.

☐ 7. Disconnect the positive cable clamp.

Job 59—Jump-Start a Vehicle (continued)

Job Wrap Up

☐ 1. Return all tools and equipment to storage.

☐ 2. Clean the work area.

☐ 3. Did you encounter any problems during this procedure? Yes ___ No ___

If Yes, describe the problems: _____

_____

_____

What did you do to correct the problems?_____

_____

_____

☐ 4. Have your instructor check your work and sign this job sheet.

Performance Evaluation—Instructor Use Only

Did the student complete the job in the time allotted? Yes ___ No ___

If No, which steps were not completed?_____

How would you rate this student's overall performance on this job?_____

5–Excellent, 4–Good, 3–Satisfactory, 2–Unsatisfactory, 1–Poor

Comments: _____

_____

_____

INSTRUCTOR'S SIGNATURE _____

Notes

Job

Inspect, Test, and Diagnose a Starting System

60

After completing this job, you will be able to diagnose a starter and related starting system components.

Instructions

As you read the job instructions, answer the questions and perform the tasks. Print your answers neatly and use complete sentences. Consult the proper service literature and ask your instructor for help as needed.

> ### Warning
> ⚠️ Before performing this job, review all pertinent safety information in the text and discuss safety procedures with your instructor.

Procedures

☐ 1. Obtain a vehicle to be used in this job. Your instructor may direct you to perform this job on a shop vehicle.

☐ 2. Gather the tools needed to perform the following job.

☐ 3. Try to start the vehicle.

Did the vehicle start? Yes ___ No ___

Describe any unusual conditions you noticed while attempting to start the vehicle:

_____

_____

Determine Whether the Starting Problem Is Electrical or Mechanical

☐ 1. Attempt to turn the engine with flywheel turner or socket and breaker bar at the front of the crankshaft.

Can the engine be turned? Yes ___ No ___

2. Determine from the actions in step 1 whether the problem is electrical or mechanical.

Electrical ___ Mechanical ___

Explain your answer:_____

_____

_____

> **Note**
>
> If the engine has a mechanical problem, consult your instructor about what steps to take.

Test the Starter's Electrical Properties

1. Obtain the needed starting and charging system tester(s).

2. Obtain the correct electrical specifications for the vehicle you are testing.

3. Attach the starting and charging system tester to the vehicle according to the manufacturer's instructions. **Figure 60-1** shows how an inductive pick up is attached to read amperage draw.

4. Check the battery voltage and general battery condition.

   What was the voltage reading?_____

   Were problems found with the battery condition? Yes ___ No ___

   If Yes, describe them: _____

   _____

5. Disable the ignition or fuel system as necessary to prevent the engine from starting.

6. Have an assistant crank the engine.

Figure 60-1. In this photograph, a multimeter is being used with an inductive pick up to measure amperage. Always clamp the pick up over the negative battery cable.

Inductive pick up

Goodheart-Willcox Publisher

Job 60—Inspect, Test, and Diagnose a Starting System (continued)

☐ 7. Using the tester, check the starter current draw and battery voltage as the starter is operated.

Record the amperage draw:_____ amps.

Record the voltage drop:_____ volts. See **Figure 60-2**.

☐ 8. Compare the readings with specifications.

Does there appear to be a problem? Yes ___ No ___

If Yes, what is the problem?_____

_____

_____

Use Waveforms to Determine Electrical Problems

> **Note**
>
> Starters produce a distinctive waveform, usually called a sawtooth waveform, and are good candidates for waveform analysis.

☐ 1. Obtain a waveform meter and set it to read DC voltage. Make other adjustments as necessary.

☐ 2. Attach the positive lead of the waveform meter to a positive battery cable connection.

☐ 3. Attach the negative lead of the waveform meter to a metal engine component.

☐ 4. Operate the starter and note the waveform.

Figure 60-2. The cranking voltage shown on this system indicates a good battery and starter. Also check starter amperage draw when possible.

Goodheart-Willcox Publisher

☐ 5. Draw the waveform in the space below.

☐ 6. Compare the waveform to a known good waveform.

Does the waveform match the known good waveform? Yes ___ No ___

If No, how does it differ? _____

_____

_____

What could be causing the incorrect waveform? _____

_____

_____

Make Starting Circuit Voltage Drop Tests

☐ 1. Set a multimeter to read voltage.

☐ 2. Place the leads of the multimeter on either side of the connection to be tested, **Figure 60-3**.

Figure 60-3. Place the multimeter leads on either side of the connection to be tested. Modern multimeters will record positive or negative voltage, so polarity is not important.

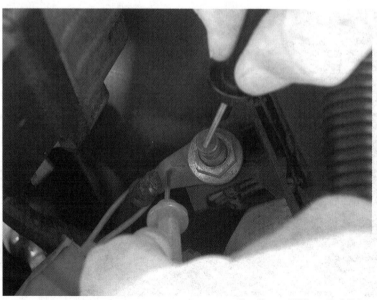

Goodheart-Willcox Publisher

Job 60—Inspect, Test, and Diagnose a Starting System (continued)

☐ 3. Have an assistant crank the engine.

☐ 4. Observe and record the voltage reading on the multimeter. This reading is the voltage drop.

Voltage drop:_____

☐ 5. Compare the voltage drop to specifications.

Is the voltage drop excessive? Yes ___ No ___

If Yes, what should be done? _____

_____

Check the Starting System Wiring

☐ 1. Obtain system wiring diagrams.

☐ 2. Using the wiring diagram as a guide, inspect all starting system–related wires. Place a check mark next to any of the following conditions that you observe:

☐ Insulation is discolored and/or swollen (overheating).

☐ White or green deposits are visible on exposed wires (corrosion).

☐ Connectors are partially melted or their metal is discolored (overheating).

☐ Connectors are loose or disconnected.

If any problems were found, describe the location and the corrective action to be taken: _____

_____

_____

☐ 3. To make resistance checks of a wire or connector, obtain a multimeter and set it to read resistance.

☐ 4. Disconnect the wire or connector to be tested from the vehicle's electrical system.

☐ 5. Place the leads of the multimeter on each end of the wire or connector to be checked and observe the reading.

Reading:_____ ohms.

☐ 6. Compare the reading taken in step 5 to specifications.

Does the wire or connector have excessively high resistance? Yes ___ No ___

If Yes, what should be done next?_____

Test a Solenoid or Relay

☐ 1. Inspect the solenoid or relay for obvious damage.

Did you find any damage? Yes ___ No ___

☐ 2. Obtain a non-powered test light or multimeter. If a multimeter is to be used, set it to read voltage.

☐ 3. Using the test light or multimeter, determine whether voltage is available to the solenoid or relay.

Is voltage available to the solenoid? Yes ___ No ___

If Yes, go to step 7.

If No, go to step 4.

☐ 4. If voltage is not available, probe backward to the spot in the circuit where voltage is available.

Describe the spot where voltage stops: _____

_____

_____

☐ 5. Check the wiring or components at the spot where voltage becomes available. Wiring can be broken internally, so inspect it carefully. Components include connectors, fuses, circuit breakers, and fusible links.

Describe any defects found: _____

_____

_____

☐ 6. Repair the problem to provide power to the relay or solenoid.

☐ 7. If voltage is available to the device, have an assistant operate the circuit. Listen for a clicking noise, or note whether:

• The relay transfers power to the starter. Yes ___ No ___

• The solenoid operates the starter. Yes ___ No ___

If the relay or solenoid now operates, no further checking is needed.

If the relay or solenoid does not operate, obtain a multimeter and set it to read resistance.

☐ 8. Obtain resistance specifications for the relay or solenoid.

Terminals to check:_____ and _____

Resistance range:_____ ohms

Terminals to check:_____ and _____

Resistance range:_____ ohms

Terminals to check:_____ and _____

Resistance range:_____ ohms

☐ 9. Follow the manufacturer's directions to measure the resistance of the relay or solenoid.

Terminals checked:_____ and _____

Resistance reading:_____ ohms

Terminals checked:_____ and _____

Resistance reading:_____ ohms

Terminals checked:_____ and _____

Resistance reading:_____ ohms

Is the resistance reading within specifications? Yes ___ No ___

In your own words, describe what the readings mean: _____

_____

_____

What actions should be taken to correct the problem? _____

_____

_____

Job 60—Inspect, Test, and Diagnose a Starting System (continued)

Test a Suspected Ignition Switch or Neutral Safety Switch

☐ 1. Use a non-powered test light or multimeter set to read voltage to determine whether voltage is available to the switch.

 If voltage is available, go to step 7. If voltage is not available, go to step 2.

☐ 2. If voltage is not available, probe backward to the spot in the circuit where voltage is available.

 Describe the spot where voltage stops: _____

 _____

☐ 3. At the spot where voltage becomes available, check the wiring or components. Wiring can be broken internally, so inspect it carefully. Components include connectors, fuses, circuit breakers, and fusible links.

 Describe any defects found: _____

 _____

☐ 4. Repair the problem to provide power to the ignition or neutral safety switch.

☐ 5. Move the probe or multimeter lead to the output terminal of the switch. Have an assistant operate the circuit while you observe the meter or probe.

 Does voltage pass through the switch during operation? Yes ___ No ___

 If Yes, no further checking is needed.

 If No, obtain a multimeter and set it to read resistance.

> **Note**
>
> An ignition switch is a three- or four-position switch with two or three output terminals. One output terminal should have power when the switch is in the *Start* position. Another output terminal should have power when the switch is in the *On* position. The third output terminal should have power when the switch is in the *Accessories* position.

☐ 6. Obtain resistance specifications for the switch.

 Terminals to check:_____ and _____
 Resistance range:_____ ohms
 Terminals to check:_____ and _____
 Resistance range:_____ ohms
 Terminals to check:_____ and _____
 Resistance range:_____ ohms

☐ 7. Follow the manufacturer's directions to measure the resistance of the switch.

Terminals checked:_____ and _____

Resistance reading:_____ ohms

Terminals checked:_____ and _____

Resistance reading:_____ ohms

Terminals checked:_____ and _____

Resistance reading:_____ ohms

Is the resistance reading within specifications? Yes ___ No ___

In your own words, describe what the readings mean: _____

_____

_____

What actions should be taken to correct the problem? _____

_____

_____

Job Wrap Up

☐ 1. Return all tools and equipment to storage.

☐ 2. Clean the work area.

☐ 3. Did you encounter any problems during this procedure? Yes ___ No ___

If Yes, describe the problems: _____

_____

_____

What did you do to correct the problems?_____

_____

_____

☐ 4. Have your instructor check your work and sign this job sheet.

Performance Evaluation—Instructor Use Only

Did the student complete the job in the time allotted? Yes ___ No ___

If No, which steps were not completed?_____

How would you rate this student's overall performance on this job?_____

5–Excellent, 4–Good, 3–Satisfactory, 2–Unsatisfactory, 1–Poor

Comments: _____

_____

INSTRUCTOR'S SIGNATURE _____

Job

Replace a Starter

61

After completing this job, you will be able to replace a starter.

Instructions

As you read the job instructions, answer the questions and perform the tasks. Print your answers neatly and use complete sentences. Consult the proper service literature and ask your instructor for help as needed.

> **Warning**
>
> ⚠ Before performing this job, review all pertinent safety information in the text and discuss safety procedures with your instructor.

Procedures

☐ 1. Obtain a vehicle to be used in this job. Your instructor may direct you to perform this job on a shop vehicle.

☐ 2. Gather the tools needed to perform the following job.

☐ 3. Remove the battery negative cable.

☐ 4. Raise the vehicle.

> **Warning**
>
> ⚠ The vehicle must be raised and supported in a safe manner. Always use approved lifts or jacks and jack stands.

☐ 5. Remove inspection covers, exhaust components, and skid plates as necessary to gain access to the starter.

☐ 6. Remove the starter wiring, **Figure 61-1**. Depending on the design, you may have to perform this step after completing step 7.

Figure 61-1. If possible, remove the starter wiring before removing the starter. Most modern starters have only two wires.

Goodheart-Willcox Publisher

☐ 7. Remove the starter fasteners, **Figure 61-2**.

 Note

If adjusting shims are used at the starter, note their position and save them for reinstallation.

Figure 61-2. This starter is held to the engine block with two fasteners. Others are attached to the transmission housing.

Goodheart-Willcox Publisher

Job 61—Replace a Starter (continued)

☐ 8. Remove the starter from the vehicle.

☐ 9. Compare the old and replacement starters.

☐ 10. Inspect the flywheel teeth.

Did you find damage or excessive wear on the flywheel teeth? Yes ___ No ___
If Yes, the flywheel must be replaced.

☐ 11. Place the starter in position.

☐ 12. Reinstall the wires if this must be done before step 13.

☐ 13. Install any adjusting shims and then install and tighten the starter fasteners. Reinstall any remaining starter wiring.

☐ 14. Reinstall any inspection covers or skid plates that were removed.

☐ 15. Lower the vehicle and reconnect the battery negative cable.

☐ 16. Check starter operation.

> **Note**
>
> If the starter is noisy, and uses adjustment shims, add or remove shims until the starter operates quietly.

Job Wrap Up

☐ 1. Return all tools and equipment to storage.

☐ 2. Clean the work area.

☐ 3. Did you encounter any problems during this procedure? Yes ___ No ___
If Yes, describe the problems: _____
_____

What did you do to correct the problems?_____
_____

☐ 4. Have your instructor check your work and sign this job sheet.

Performance Evaluation—Instructor Use Only

Did the student complete the job in the time allotted? Yes ___ No ___
If No, which steps were not completed?_____
How would you rate this student's overall performance on this job?_____
5–Excellent, 4–Good, 3–Satisfactory, 2–Unsatisfactory, 1–Poor
Comments: _____
_____

INSTRUCTOR'S SIGNATURE _____

Notes

Job 62

Inspect, Test, and Diagnose a Charging System

After completing this job, you will be able to inspect, test, and diagnose a vehicle's charging system.

Instructions

As you read the job instructions, answer the questions and perform the tasks. Print your answers neatly and use complete sentences. Consult the proper service literature and ask your instructor for help as needed.

> **Warning**
>
> Before performing this job, review all pertinent safety information in the text and discuss safety procedures with your instructor.

Procedures

☐ 1. Obtain a vehicle to be used in this job. Your instructor may direct you to perform this job on a shop vehicle.

☐ 2. Gather the tools needed to perform the following job.

Check the Operation of the Charging System

☐ 1. Obtain the needed starting and charging system tester.

☐ 2. Obtain the correct electrical specifications for the vehicle that you are testing.

☐ 3. Inspect the alternator drive belt.

Is the belt properly tightened? Yes ___ No ___

Is the belt in good condition? Yes ___ No ___

If you answered No to either of these questions, explain your answer: _____

_____

If the belt is not properly tightened or is damaged, see the belt maintenance information in Job 14.

> **Note**
>
> The belt driving the alternator must be in good condition before the charging system can be checked.

☐ 4. Attach the starting and charging system tester to the vehicle according to the manufacturer's instructions.

☐ 5. Check the battery voltage and general battery condition.

What was the voltage reading?_____

Were problems found with the battery condition or voltage? Yes ___ No ___

If Yes, describe them: _____

_____

> **Caution**
>
> If the battery is discharged or defective, the charging system cannot be adequately tested.

☐ 6. Start the vehicle and check charging system operation. **Figure 62-1** shows idle voltage under load and no load conditions.

What is the charging system voltage at idle?_____ volts

What is the charging system voltage at 2500 rpm?_____ volts

What was the maximum charging system amperage?_____ amps

☐ 7. Compare the charging system readings with system specifications.

Are all of the readings within specifications? Yes ___ No ___

If No, list the out-of-specification readings and describe the possible causes: _____

_____

Figure 62-1. Comparing the charging voltage under load and no load conditions gives a good indication of charging system operation.

Goodheart-Willcox Publisher

Job 62—Inspect, Test, and Diagnose a Charging System (continued)

☐ 8. Check the alternator stator and diodes (if this test can be made). The tester in **Figure 62-2** indicates whether the diodes are operating properly. Other testers require that you interpret a waveform.

Are the stator and diodes OK? Yes ___ No ___

What possible defects have you identified? _____

_____

☐ 9. If your readings are out of the specified range, make further checks. On some vehicles, it is possible to bypass the voltage regulator. On other vehicles, the charging system can be diagnosed with a scan tool.

Were further checks possible? Yes ___ No ___

If Yes, what did they reveal? _____

_____

_____

_____

Perform Voltage Drop Tests

☐ 1. Obtain a multimeter and set it to read voltage.

☐ 2. Place the leads of the multimeter on either side of the connection to be tested.

☐ 3. Start the engine.

☐ 4. Observe and record the voltage reading on the multimeter. This is the voltage drop.

Voltage drop:_____ volts

Figure 62-2. Testing the diode condition ensures that the charging system is operating properly.

Goodheart-Willcox Publisher

5. Compare the voltage drop to specifications.
   Is the voltage drop excessive? Yes ___ No ___
   If Yes, what action should be taken? _____

   _____

Use Waveforms to Determine Electrical Problems

> **Note**
>
> Alternator stators produce a distinctive waveform and alternators are good candidates for waveform analysis.

1. Obtain a waveform meter and set it to read dc voltage. Make other adjustments as necessary.
2. Attach the positive lead of the waveform meter to the stator terminal of the alternator to be tested.
3. Attach the negative lead of the waveform meter to a metal part on the engine.
4. Start the engine and note the alternator waveform.
5. Draw the waveform in the space below.

6. Compare the waveform to a known good waveform.
   Does the waveform match the known good waveform? Yes ___ No ___
   If No, how does it differ? _____

   _____

   _____

   What could be causing the incorrect waveform? _____

   _____

   _____

   _____

Job 62—Inspect, Test, and Diagnose a Charging System (continued)

Job Wrap Up

☐ 1. Return all tools and equipment to storage.

☐ 2. Clean the work area.

☐ 3. Did you encounter any problems during this procedure? Yes ___ No ___

If Yes, describe the problems: _____

_____

What did you do to correct the problems?_____

_____

☐ 4. Have your instructor check your work and sign this job sheet.

Performance Evaluation—Instructor Use Only

Did the student complete the job in the time allotted? Yes ___ No ___

If No, which steps were not completed?_____

How would you rate this student's overall performance on this job?____

5–Excellent, 4–Good, 3–Satisfactory, 2–Unsatisfactory, 1–Poor

Comments: _____

_____

INSTRUCTOR'S SIGNATURE _____

Notes

Job

Replace an Alternator

63

After completing this job, you will be able to replace a vehicle's alternator.

Instructions

As you read the job instructions, answer the questions and perform the tasks. Print your answers neatly and use complete sentences. Consult the proper service literature and ask your instructor for help as needed.

> **Warning**
>
> ⚠ Before performing this job, review all pertinent safety information in the text and discuss safety procedures with your instructor.

Procedures

- [ ] 1. Obtain a vehicle to be used in this job. Your instructor may direct you to perform this job on a shop vehicle.
- [ ] 2. Gather the tools needed to perform the following job.
- [ ] 3. Remove the battery negative cable.
- [ ] 4. Remove the alternator drive belt. Refer to the belt service information in Job 14.
- [ ] 5. Remove the alternator wiring connectors.
- [ ] 6. Remove the alternator fasteners.
- [ ] 7. Remove the alternator from the vehicle.
- [ ] 8. Compare the old and replacement alternators.
- [ ] 9. Place the alternator in position on the engine, **Figure 63-1**.
- [ ] 10. Install the alternator fasteners and any adjusting shims.
- [ ] 11. Reinstall the alternator wire connectors.
- [ ] 12. Reinstall the alternator drive belt.
- [ ] 13. Adjust the drive belt if necessary and tighten the alternator fasteners.
- [ ] 14. Reconnect the battery negative cable.
- [ ] 15. Start the engine and check alternator operation.

Figure 63-1. Carefully place the alternator in position.

Goodheart-Willcox Publisher

Job Wrap Up

☐ 1. Return all tools and equipment to storage.

☐ 2. Clean the work area.

☐ 3. Did you encounter any problems during this procedure? Yes ___ No ___
If Yes, describe the problems: _____
_____
_____

What did you do to correct the problems?_____
_____
_____

☐ 4. Have your instructor check your work and sign this job sheet.

Performance Evaluation—Instructor Use Only

Did the student complete the job in the time allotted? Yes ___ No ___
If No, which steps were not completed?_____
How would you rate this student's overall performance on this job?_____
5–Excellent, 4–Good, 3–Satisfactory, 2–Unsatisfactory, 1–Poor
Comments: _____
_____
_____

INSTRUCTOR'S SIGNATURE _____

Job

64

Diagnose Lighting System Problems

After completing this job, you will be able to diagnose problems in a vehicle's lighting systems.

Instructions

As you read the job instructions, answer the questions and perform the tasks. Print your answers neatly and use complete sentences. Consult the proper service literature and ask your instructor for help as needed.

> **Warning**
>
> ⚠ Before performing this job, review all pertinent safety information in the text and discuss safety procedures with your instructor.

Procedures

- ☐ 1. Obtain a vehicle to be used in this job. Your instructor may direct you to perform this job on a shop vehicle.
- ☐ 2. Gather the tools needed to perform the following job.
- ☐ 3. Obtain the needed system wiring diagrams.

General Light Service

- ☐ 1. Remove the non-functioning bulb and socket from the housing.
- ☐ 2. Inspect the bulb. Most burned out bulbs will be obviously bad. A defective filament will vibrate when the bulb is lightly shaken.

    Is the bulb burned out? Yes ___ No ___

    If Yes, replace the bulb and recheck its operation.

☐ 3. Visually check lamp sockets for the following: Place a check mark in all that apply.

    ☐ Cracked or overheated plastic socket body.

    ☐ Dented, crushed, or otherwise deformed metal socket body.

    ☐ Corrosion in metal socket body.

    ☐ Bent or broken tabs, slots, or other locking devices.

    ☐ Corroded electrical connectors.

    ☐ Disconnected electrical connectors.

☐ 4. If the bulb and socket appear to be good, use a non-powered test light to check the power and ground circuits at the electrical connector. The control switch should be in the on position. **Figure 64-1** shows a typical procedure.

Are power and ground available at the connector? Yes ___ No ___

If No, go to step 4.

If Yes, reconnect the socket and test it for power and ground.

Are power and a good ground available at the socket? Yes ___ No ___

If No, replace the socket and recheck its operation.

If Yes, replace the bulb and recheck operation.

Note

Some older vehicles had a single wire to the bulb socket. The sockets were directly grounded to the vehicle.

Figure 64-1. The electrical connector should be checked to ensure that power is available and that the circuit is grounded. Modern vehicles with many plastic and fiberglass parts usually have a separate ground wire.

Goodheart-Willcox Publisher

Job 64—Diagnose Lighting System Problems (continued)

☐ 5. Trace the lighting circuit in the proper wiring diagram and answer the following questions:

In the light's circuit, what light control switches does the current pass through?____

_____

In the light's circuit, what relays, circuit breakers, and resistors does power pass through? _____

_____

What frame or body parts are part of the light's ground circuit? These are the body parts that current passes through on its way back to the battery's negative terminal.

_____

_____

Is the circuit a parallel, series, or series-parallel type?_____

☐ 6. After referring to the wiring diagram, redraw the circuit, eliminating any wiring that is not directly related to the circuit.

☐ 7. Using the wiring diagram, perform checks to identify the wiring or electrical device that caused the light to fail.

Describe the problem and the actions taken to correct it:_____

_____

_____

> **Note**
> On older vehicles, a wire often becomes disconnected or a connector plug develops high resistance. This is especially common with taillights and marker lights where the connector is exposed to water and dirt.

Diagnose a Brake Light Problem

☐ 1. Check for the proper operation of the brake light system.

Does the brake light system function properly? Yes ___ No ___

If No, describe the problem: _____

_____

_____

> **Note**
> Diagnose the problem using the procedures in one of the following sections. Brake light problems fall into four categories:
>
> • Some brake lights do not light when the brake pedal is depressed.
> • No brake lights come on when the brake pedal is depressed.
> • The brake lights are on at all times.
> • The front parking lights flash when the brakes are applied.
>
> The diagnosis and service of these problems is discussed in the sections that follow.

Brake Lights Do Not Light

☐ 1. Ensure that the suspected defective light is supposed to come on when the pedal is pressed. Many modern rear light systems use double filament bulbs for the turn signals and brake lights and separate single filament bulbs for the taillights.

☐ 2. Remove the bulb and inspect it as was explained earlier in *General Light Service* section of this job.

Is the bulb burned out? Yes ___ No ___

If Yes, replace the bulb and recheck operation.

> **Note**
> The double filament brake light bulbs used on older vehicles may have a burned-out brake light filament but a good taillight filament, or vice versa. If either filament is broken, replace the bulb.

☐ 3. If the bulb appears to be good, check for power at the center terminal of the socket using a non-powered test light.

If power is reaching a good bulb, and it still does not light, go to step 4.

If power is not reaching the bulb, check the wiring between the switch and light.

☐ 4. Inspect the socket for the following conditions. Check all that apply.

☐ Socket is properly grounded (check with ohmmeter).

☐ Bulb contacts are not worn, melted, or corroded.

☐ There is no grease or rust in the bulb socket.

☐ 5. If the inspection in step 4 turned up any problems, repair or replace the socket as necessary, then recheck bulb operation.

> **Note**
> On some older vehicles, a faulty turn signal switch may cause the lights to be off on one side of the vehicle.

All Brake Lights Are Off

> **Note**
> When none of the brake lights work, it is unlikely that all of the bulbs have burned out at once. Almost always the defect is in a main electrical device, either the brake light switch or the fuse.

☐ 1. Check the fuse controlling the brake lights. If other electrical devices served by this fuse are also inoperative, you can conclude that the fuse is probably blown even before looking at it.

Is the fuse blown? Yes ___ No ___

If Yes, replace the fuse and recheck brake light operation.

Job 64—Diagnose Lighting System Problems (continued)

> **Caution**
>
> If the fuse is blown, you must determine what caused the electrical overload.
>
> Do not simply replace the fuse and let the vehicle go.

☐ 2. If the fuse is OK, disconnect the brake light switch. **Figure 64-2** shows a modern brake light switch. Be sure to disconnect the proper connector.

> **Caution**
>
> Do not confuse the brake light switch with the cruise control release switch.

☐ 3. Check the operation of the brake light switch. Use a multimeter or a powered test light.

Does the switch have infinite resistance (test light off) when the pedal is in the unapplied position? Yes ___ No ___

Does the switch have low resistance (test light on) when the brake pedal is lightly pressed? Yes ___ No ___

If the answer is No to either of these questions, adjust or replace the switch as necessary.

If the answer to both of these questions is Yes, look for disconnected, broken, or shorted wiring.

Figure 64-2. The brake light switch on modern vehicles may have inputs to the cruise control and ABS systems. Be sure that you locate the brake light connector before beginning any electrical tests.

Goodheart-Willcox Publisher

Brake Lights On at All Times

☐ 1. Unplug the brake light switch.

Do the lights go off? Yes ___ No ___

If Yes, adjust or replace the brake light switch.

If No, check for shorted wiring.

Front Parking Lights Flash When Brakes Are Applied

☐ 1. Observe the brake light bulbs as an assistant presses on the brake pedal.

Do any bulbs illuminate weakly or not at all? Yes ___ No ___

If Yes, go to step 2.

If No, go to step 4.

☐ 2. Remove and check the bulb.

Is the bulb a dual filament type? Yes ___ No ___

If Yes, go to step 3.

If No, go to step 4.

☐ 3. Closely observe the bulb filaments.

Has one of the filaments broken and fused to the other? Yes ___ No ___

If Yes, this is the source of the problem. Replace the bulb and recheck operation.

If No, go to step 4.

☐ 4. Check for a short between the brake and taillight wiring.

Note

If the vehicle is an older model with dual filament bulbs, disconnect the turn signal harness.

☐ 5. Correct any problems and recheck operation.

Diagnose Problems in Hazard and Turn Signals

☐ 1. Determine which of the following problems is occurring:

☐ Hazard and/or turn signal lights do not illuminate. Go to step 2.

☐ Hazard and/or turn signal lights illuminate but do not flash. Go to step 5.

☐ Hazard and/or turn signal lights flash slowly or only one side flashes. Go to step 8.

☐ 2. If the hazard/turn signal lights do not illuminate, check the fuse.

Is the fuse blown? Yes ___ No ___

If Yes, determine the cause of the overload and correct it. Then, replace the fuse and recheck operation.

If No, reinstall the fuse and go to step 3.

☐ 3. Using wiring diagrams as needed, trace the wiring and determine whether any wires are disconnected or have high resistance.

Were any wiring problems found? Yes ___ No ___

If Yes, correct the problems and recheck operation. Describe the problems found and what you did to correct them. _____

_____

_____

If No, go to step 4.

Job 64—Diagnose Lighting System Problems (continued)

☐ 4. Check for defective electrical devices such as the flasher unit or control switch.

Were any electrical device problems found? Yes ___ No ___

If Yes, correct as needed and recheck operation.

List the faulty components and describe how the problem was corrected: _____

_____

If No, repeat steps 2 through 4 to locate the problem.

☐ 5. Check the turn signal flasher by substituting a unit known to be good.

Does this solve the problem? Yes ___ No ___

If Yes, replace the flasher and recheck operation.

If No, go to step 6.

☐ 6. Using wiring diagrams as needed, trace the wiring and determine whether any wires are disconnected or have high resistance.

Were any wiring problems found? Yes ___ No ___

If Yes, correct as needed and recheck operation. Describe the problems found and what you did to correct them: _____

_____

_____

No, go to step 7.

☐ 7. Check bulb sockets for corrosion and lack of ground. See **Figure 64-3**.

Were any problems found? Yes ___ No ___

If Yes, correct as needed and recheck operation. Describe the problems found and what you did to correct them: _____

_____

_____

_____

Figure 64-3. If the turn signals do not operate on one side, check the bulb sockets for looseness and corrosion. The burned plastic on this socket may indicate a connection that has overheated.

Goodheart-Willcox Publisher

☐ If No, recheck the flashers and wiring until the problem is located.

☐ 8. Using wiring diagrams as needed, determine the following:

- Do any wires have high resistance? Yes ___ No ___
- Are any bulb sockets corroded? Yes ___ No ___
- Are any bulb sockets not properly grounded? Yes ___ No ___

If the answer to any of the above is Yes, correct the problems and recheck turn signal operation. Describe the problems found and what you did to correct them:

_____

_____

_____

If the answer to any of the questions is No, go to step 9.

☐ 9. Ensure that the proper flasher is being used.

Is the flasher correct? Yes ___ No ___

If No, install the proper flasher and recheck operation.

If Yes, recheck wiring and wiring sockets until the problem is located.

Job Wrap Up

☐ 1. Return all tools and equipment to storage.

☐ 2. Clean the work area.

☐ 3. Did you encounter any problems during this procedure? Yes ___ No ___

If Yes, describe the problems: _____

_____

_____

What did you do to correct the problems?_____

_____

_____

☐ 4. Have your instructor check your work and sign this job sheet.

Performance Evaluation—Instructor Use Only

Did the student complete the job in the time allotted? Yes ___ No ___

If No, which steps were not completed?_____

How would you rate this student's overall performance on this job?____

5–Excellent, 4–Good, 3–Satisfactory, 2–Unsatisfactory, 1–Poor

Comments: _____

_____

_____

INSTRUCTOR'S SIGNATURE _____

Job

Replace and Aim Headlights

65

After completing this job, you will be able to replace and aim a vehicle's headlights.

Instructions

As you read the job instructions, answer the questions and perform the tasks. Print your answers neatly and use complete sentences. Consult the proper service literature and ask your instructor for help as needed.

> **Warning**
>
> ⚠ Before performing this job, review all pertinent safety information in the text and discuss safety procedures with your instructor.

Procedures

☐ 1. Obtain a vehicle to be used in this job. Your instructor may direct you to perform this job on a shop vehicle.

☐ 2. Gather the tools needed to perform the following job.

Replace a Headlight

Sealed Beam Headlights

☐ 1. If necessary, open the vehicle hood to gain access to headlight attachments.

☐ 2. Remove any trim that blocks access to the headlight fasteners.

☐ 3. Remove the fasteners holding the headlight to the headlight housing.

> **Caution**
>
> ◇ Do not move the headlight adjusting screws, this will affect headlight aim.

☐ 4. Carefully remove the headlight from the headlight housing.

☐ 5. Remove the electrical connector.

☐ 6. Compare the old and new headlight to ensure that they are the same size and have the same number of electrical contacts.

☐ 7. Install the electrical connector on the new headlight.

☐ 8. Place the headlight in position in the headlight housing.

☐ 9. Install and tighten the headlight fasteners.

☐ 10. Check headlight operation. If the light does not operate, recheck the electrical connection.

☐ 11. Replace any trim that was removed.

☐ 12. Close the hood if necessary.

Replaceable Bulb Headlights

> **Warning**
>
> ⚠ Many modern vehicles have high-intensity discharge (HID or Xenon) headlights. The igniters used on high-intensity discharge headlights produce potentially hazardous voltages. The bulbs can reach temperatures of over 1300°F (2000°C) when operating. Do not touch a high-intensity discharge bulb when it is illuminated. Before working on any modern headlight system, first determine whether it is a high-intensity discharge type.

☐ 1. Open the vehicle hood to gain access to the bulb.

☐ 2. Remove any parts that block access to the bulb socket.

> **Warning**
>
> ⚠ If the headlight system is a high-intensity discharge type, disconnect the battery cable or igniter low-voltage harness and wait several minutes before going to step 3. This will ensure that any high voltage has been discharged and that the bulb has had time to cool.

☐ 3. Remove the bulb:

- Remove the lock ring holding the bulb and socket to the headlight housing, **Figure 65-1**, then pull the bulb from the housing.
 or
- Twist the bulb and socket assembly approximately 1/4 turn counterclockwise, **Figure 65-2**, then pull the bulb from the housing.

☐ 4. Remove the bulb by pulling it from the socket, **Figure 65-3**.

☐ 5. Push the new bulb into place, using a clean shop towel on the glass portion.

> **Caution**
>
> ◇ Do not touch the glass of the new bulb. Body oils on the bulb may cause it to shatter when illuminated.

☐ 6. Reinstall the bulb and socket into the housing. Tighten the lock ring if necessary.

☐ 7. Check headlight operation. If the light does not operate, recheck the electrical connection.

Job 65—Replace and Aim Headlights (continued)

Figure 65-1. Unscrew the lock ring to release the bulb and socket assembly.

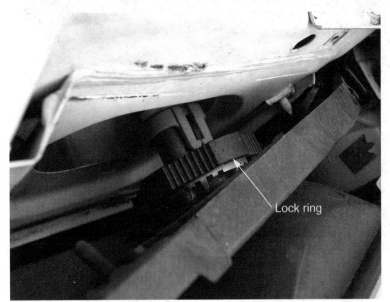

Lock ring

Goodheart-Willcox Publisher

☐ 8. Replace any other parts that were removed.

☐ 9. Close the hood if necessary.

Aim the Headlights

☐ 1. Place the vehicle on a level floor.

☐ 2. Test and correct headlight operation on high and low beams.

Figure 65-2. Rotate the socket about 1/4 turn to release it from the housing.

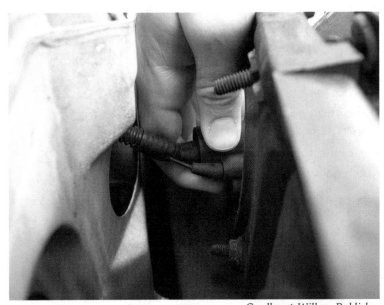

Goodheart-Willcox Publisher

Figure 65-3. Once the bulb is exposed, it can be pulled from the socket. Do not touch the new bulb with your bare hands.

Goodheart-Willcox Publisher

☐ 3. Make sure all tires are the same size and type and properly inflated. Correct as needed.

☐ 4. Remove any excessive loads from the vehicle trunk or bed.

☐ 5. Locate the headlight adjusters. It may be necessary to open the hood to gain access to the adjusters.

☐ 6. Install the aimers on or in front of the vehicle headlights as needed.

> **Note**
>
> Some vehicles have built-in headlight aiming bubbles, such as the one in **Figure 65-4**. Follow the manufacturer's instructions to adjust the lights.

☐ 7. Compensate (adjust) the headlight aimers as needed.

☐ 8. Turn on the vehicle headlights. Depending on the manufacturer's instructions, set the headlights to either high or low beam.

☐ 9. Determine whether the headlights require adjustment.

Do the headlights need adjustment? Yes ___ No ___
If No, go to step 11.

☐ 10. Adjust the headlights as needed and recheck.

Briefly describe what was done to adjust the headlights: _____

_____

☐ 11. Turn off the headlights and close the hood.

☐ 12. Remove the headlight aimers, if necessary.

Job 65—Replace and Aim Headlights (continued)

Figure 65-4. On some vehicles, bubble-type headlight aiming devices are built into the headlight assembly.

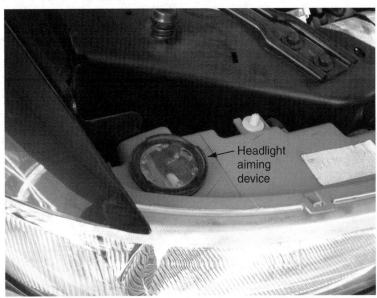

Goodheart-Willcox Publisher

Job Wrap Up

☐ 1. Return all tools and equipment to storage.

☐ 2. Clean the work area.

☐ 3. Did you encounter any problems during this procedure? Yes ___ No ___
If Yes, describe the problems: _____

_____

What did you do to correct the problems?_____
_____w
_____

☐ 4. Have your instructor check your work and sign this job sheet.

Notes

Job

Check the Operation of Anti-Theft and Keyless Entry Systems

66

After completing this job, you will be able to diagnose anti-theft and keyless entry systems. You will also be able to remove and reinstall a door panel.

Instructions

As you read the job instructions, answer the questions and perform the tasks. Print your answers neatly and use complete sentences. Consult the proper service literature and ask your instructor for help as needed.

> **Warning**
>
> ⚠ Before performing this job, review all pertinent safety information in the text and discuss safety procedures with your instructor.

Procedures

1. Obtain a vehicle to be used in this job. Your instructor may direct you to perform this job on a shop vehicle.
2. Gather the tools needed to perform this job.
3. Obtain wiring diagrams or other service literature as needed.

Diagnose an Anti-Theft System That Uses a Key Resistor

> **Note**
>
> Security system problems may or may not illuminate the security light. Security system problems usually will be noticed as failure of the vehicle to start. Later systems can be diagnosed by attaching a scan tool to the vehicle diagnostic connector and accessing trouble codes.

1. Disconnect the security system wires at the base of the steering column.
2. Insert the key in the ignition switch.
3. Obtain a multimeter and set it to the resistance (ohms) position.

☐ 4. Turn the ignition switch to the *On* position and determine which security system wires complete the circuit through the ignition switch and key.

☐ 5. Use the multimeter to check continuity and resistance values through the ignition switch and key.

   Resistance reading:_____

   Resistance value specified in the service literature:_____

☐ 6. Repeat step 5 while wiggling the key and turning it between the on and start positions.

   Does the resistance value remain constant? Yes ___ No ___

   If the multimeter shows no continuity (infinite resistance) or intermittent continuity, the switch contacts or the key resistor are probably bad. No continuity can be caused by a bad key resistor or contacts. Intermittent continuity is most likely caused by loose or corroded contacts. Make repairs as needed, reconnect the wiring, and recheck system operation.

Diagnose a Remote Keyless Entry System

☐ 1. Check that the power door lock system operates properly from the door controls.

   Are the power door locks operating properly? Yes ___ No ___

   If Yes, go to step 2.

   If No, correct the door lock system. Then, recheck keyless entry system operation.

☐ 2. Check for radio interference from nearby electrical devices or signal blockage from other vehicles, trees, shrubbery, or buildings.

☐ 3. If the power door locks are working properly and there is no radio interference, try to operate the system using two different transmitters.

   If the system operates from one transmitter only, go to step 4.

   If the system will not operate from either transmitter, go to step 6.

☐ 4. Replace the battery of the suspect transmitter, **Figure 66-1**, and recheck operation.

   Does the transmitter now operate the door locks? Yes ___ No ___

   If Yes, go to the *Job Wrap Up* section.

   If No, go to step 5.

☐ 5. Replace the transmitter and recheck.

   Does the transmitter now operate the door locks? Yes ___ No ___

   If Yes, go to the *Job Wrap Up* section.

   If No, go to step 6.

☐ 6. Check the control module fuse.

   Is the fuse OK? Yes ___ No ___

   If Yes, go to step 7.

   If No, replace the fuse and recheck keyless entry system operation.

> **Caution**
>
> ⚠ If the fuse is blown, you must determine what caused the electrical overload. Do not simply replace the fuse and let the vehicle go.

Job 66—Check the Operation of Anti-Theft and Keyless Entry Systems (continued)

Figure 66-1. Most transmitter batteries can be replaced by prying the case apart to expose the battery. Be careful not to damage the electronic circuitry while changing the battery.

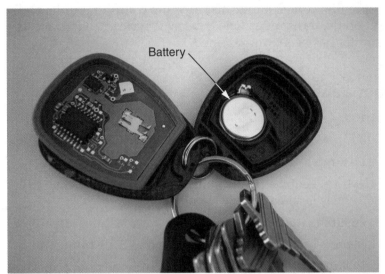

Goodheart-Willcox Publisher

☐   7.   Check the control module wiring for defects and loose connectors, **Figure 66-2**.
Were problems found in the wiring? Yes ___ No ___
If No, go to step 8.
If Yes, repair the wires as needed and recheck keyless entry system operation.

Figure 66-2. A typical control module located under a side trim panel. Check the service information to determine the location of the control module on the vehicle that you are working on.

Goodheart-Willcox Publisher

☐ 8. Replace the control module and recheck keyless entry system operation. When replacing the control module, make sure that the FCC model number on the original and replacement are the same.

> ### Note
> It may be necessary to program the new transmitter. Ground the programming connector located near the control module, and push any button on the transmitter. The locks will cycle once to indicate that the transmitter has been programmed.

Remove a Door Panel

☐ 1. Remove the battery negative cable.

☐ 2. Remove the door panel armrest. If the armrest is part of the panel, skip this step.

☐ 3. Remove the pull strap if used.

☐ 4. Remove the electrical switches controlling windows, door locks, and power mirrors, if the vehicle is so equipped.

☐ 5. Remove any remaining hardware, such as door and window handles.

☐ 6. Remove the fasteners holding the door panel to the door frame.

☐ 7. Carefully pull the door panel from the door frame. Some door panels must be lifted to disengage them from the window sill or internal slot. See **Figure 66-3**.

☐ 8. Remove the inner vapor barrier.

Reinstall a Door Panel

☐ 1. Reinstall the vapor barrier.

☐ 2. Place the door panel in position and reinstall the fasteners.

☐ 3. Reinstall the door hardware and electrical switches.

Figure 66-3. After removing all connectors and fasteners, lift the door panel up to remove it.

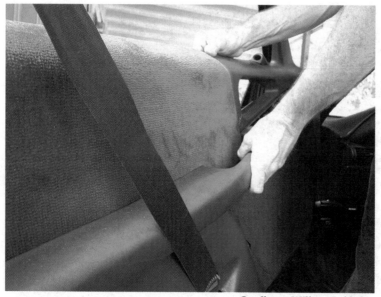

Goodheart-Willcox Publisher

Job 66—Check the Operation of Anti-Theft and Keyless Entry Systems (continued)

☐ 4. Reinstall the pull strap and armrest, if necessary.

☐ 5. Reconnect the battery negative cable.

Job Wrap Up

☐ 1. Return all tools and equipment to storage.

☐ 2. Clean the work area.

☐ 3. Did you encounter any problems during this procedure? Yes ___ No ___

If Yes, describe the problems: _____

_____

_____

What did you do to correct the problems?_____

_____

_____

☐ 4. Have your instructor check your work and sign this job sheet.

Performance Evaluation—Instructor Use Only

Did the student complete the job in the time allotted? Yes ___ No ___

If No, which steps were not completed?_____

How would you rate this student's overall performance on this job?_____

5–Excellent, 4–Good, 3–Satisfactory, 2–Unsatisfactory, 1–Poor

Comments: _____

_____

_____

INSTRUCTOR'S SIGNATURE _____

Notes

Job 67

Diagnose Instrument Panel Warning Light Problems

After completing this job, you will be able to diagnose an instrument panel warning light problem.

Instructions

As you read the job instructions, answer the questions and perform the tasks. Print your answers neatly and use complete sentences. Consult the proper service literature and ask your instructor for help as needed.

> **Warning**
>
> ⚠ Before performing this job, review all pertinent safety information in the text and discuss safety procedures with your instructor.

Procedures

☐ 1. Obtain a vehicle to be used in this job. Your instructor may direct you to perform this job on a shop vehicle.

☐ 2. Gather the tools needed to perform this job.

Diagnose Instrument Panel Warning Light Problems

> **Note**
>
> There are two kinds of warning light problems:
>
> - The warning light does not light at any time.
> - The warning light is on at all times.
>
> Refer to the appropriate section of this job based on the type of problem you are trying to diagnose.

Warning Light Does Not Light

☐ 1. Check the fuse.

Is the fuse blown? Yes ___ No ___

2. If the fuse is blown, determine the cause of the electrical overload, correct it, and recheck warning light operation.

3. If the fuse is good, remove the connector to the electrical switch or sensor that operates the light.

4. Using a fused jumper wire, ground the switch or sensor connector, **Figure 67-1**.

   Does the light come on? Yes ___ No ___

   If Yes, the switch or sensor is defective. Adjust or replace as necessary and recheck.

   If No, go to step 5.

Note

 Most warning light switches and sensors operate by completing a ground through the light. Some switches, such as parking brake switches, can become misadjusted. The electrical connector may be disconnected or the switch or sensor may not be grounded. Pursue all possibilities before deciding that the switch or sensor is defective.

---

5. Check the warning light bulb. To reach the bulb, it may be necessary to partially disassemble the dashboard. The bulb may be burned out, or may have fallen out of its socket.

   Is the bulb OK? Yes ___ No ___

   If Yes, go to step 6.

   If No, replace the bulb and recheck warning light operation.

Note

 In some cases, someone has removed the bulb because it was on at all times. Install a new bulb and find out why it is on all the time using the procedure in the *Warning Light Is Always On* section of this job.

Figure 67-1. Grounding the sensor connector completes the circuit through the instrument panel warning light to ground. If the light circuit is OK, the light will come on.

Goodheart-Willcox Publisher

Job 67—Diagnose Instrument Panel Warning Light Problems (continued)

☐ 6. Obtain the proper wiring diagram and trace the following:
- Power from the vehicle's positive battery terminal to the warning light fuse.
- Power from the warning light fuse to the warning light bulb.
- Power from the warning light bulb to the switch or sensor.
- Power from the switch or sensor to ground.

☐ 7. Using the wiring diagram, draw the warning light circuit, eliminating any wiring that is not directly related to the circuit.

☐ 8. Refer to your wiring diagram.

Could a wiring problem cause the light to fail to illuminate? Yes ___ No ___

If Yes, check and repair the wiring as necessary and recheck operation.

If No, recheck the lights, fuses, and sensors as necessary.

Warning Light Is Always On

> **Note**
>
> This procedure assumes that the vehicle has no mechanical problems that would illuminate the light.

☐ 1. Determine which vehicle systems operate the light. See **Figure 67-2**.

☐ 2. Unplug the connector at the switch or sensor that operates the light, **Figure 67-3**.

Does the light go out? Yes ___ No ___

If Yes, go to step 3.

If No, go to step 4.

☐ 3. Replace or adjust the switch/sensor as necessary and recheck the warning light operation.

Did replacing the switch/sensor fix the problem? Yes ___ No ___

If Yes, skip to step 5.

Figure 67-2. This light indicates that the windshield washer fluid level is low. If it is on and filling the washer fluid reservoir does not cause the warning light to go out, something is wrong with the light circuit.

Goodheart-Willcox Publisher

Figure 67-3. Unplug the sensor. If the light goes out, the sensor is defective. If the light stays on, the sensor is OK.

Goodheart-Willcox Publisher

4. If the light stays on, reattach the connector and, using the proper wiring diagram, look for a wire that has grounded against the vehicle body.

Did you locate a problem? Yes ___ No ___

If Yes, repair the wiring and recheck warning light operation.

If No, repeat this step until the problem is located.

Reset a Maintenance Indicator Light

> **Note**
>
> Indicator light resetting procedures vary between manufacturers, but procedures are almost always given in the owner's manual. For the purposes of this job, a general procedure is outlined below.

1. Turn the ignition switch to the *On* position.
2. Operate and hold a dashboard control until the light goes off, or begins blinking.
3. Turn the ignition switch to the *Off* position while continuing to hold the dashboard control.
4. Turn the ignition switch back to the *On* position and determine whether the light goes off within a few seconds.

Did the light go off? Yes ___ No ___

If No, perform the resetting procedure again.

How did the actual procedure differ from the general procedure given here? _____

_____

_____

Job 67—Diagnose Instrument Panel Warning Light Problems (continued)

Job Wrap Up

☐ 1. Return all tools and equipment to storage.

☐ 2. Clean the work area.

☐ 3. Did you encounter any problems during this procedure? Yes ___ No ___

If Yes, describe the problems: _____

_____

What did you do to correct the problems?_____

_____

☐ 4. Have your instructor check your work and sign this job sheet.

Performance Evaluation—Instructor Use Only

Did the student complete the job in the time allotted? Yes ___ No ___

If No, which steps were not completed?_____

How would you rate this student's overall performance on this job?____

5–Excellent, 4–Good, 3–Satisfactory, 2–Unsatisfactory, 1–Poor

Comments: _____

_____

INSTRUCTOR'S SIGNATURE _____

Notes

Job

68

Check and Correct the Operation Windshield Washers and Wipers

After completing this job, you will be able to diagnose and service windshield washers and wipers.

Instructions

As you read the job instructions, answer the questions and perform the tasks. Print your answers neatly and use complete sentences. Consult the proper service literature and ask your instructor for help as needed.

> **Warning**
>
> Before performing this job, review all pertinent safety information in the text and discuss safety procedures with your instructor.

Procedures

☐ 1. Obtain a vehicle to be used in this job. Your instructor may direct you to perform this job on a shop vehicle.

☐ 2. Gather the tools needed to perform this job.

☐ 3. Obtain the needed system wiring diagrams.

Diagnose Windshield Wiper Motor Problems

> **Note**
>
> For specific windshield wiper problems such as failure to park, incorrect operation at certain speeds only, or failure to stop, consult the manufacturer's service literature.

☐ 1. Ensure that the wiper motor fuse or circuit breaker is not blown or tripped.

Is the fuse OK? Yes ___ No ___

2. Disconnect the windshield wiper motor connector. The wiper motor may be located on the engine firewall (bulkhead) or under a cover between the firewall and windshield, **Figure 68-1**. Remove the plastic cover as needed to gain access to the motor.

3. Turn the ignition switch to the *On* position.

4. Place the windshield wiper control switch in the *On* position.

5. Connect a non-powered test light to the power wire at the wiper motor's electrical connector.

   Does the test light illuminate? Yes ___ No ___

   If No, trace the wiring between the fuse and motor to isolate the problem.

   If Yes, go to step 6.

6. Check the ground at the motor.

   Is the motor properly grounded? Yes ___ No ___

   If No, repair the ground and retest.

   If Yes, go to step 7.

7. Connect one lead of a fused jumper wire to the input terminal of the motor.

8. Connect the other lead of the jumper wire to the battery positive terminal.

   Does the motor operate? Yes ___ No ___

   If Yes, repeat step 5 to isolate the problem.

   If No, go to step 10.

   If the motor operates but the wipers do not move, check for disconnected linkage or a broken motor shaft.

9. Check the wiper linkage for binding and lack of lubrication.

   Is the linkage clean and lubricated? Yes ___ No ___

   If No, clean and lubricate it until it works freely, then recheck.

   If Yes, go to step 10.

10. Replace the motor and recheck its operation.

Figure 68-1. The wiper motor on many newer vehicles is located under a plastic cover between the firewall and windshield.

Goodheart-Willcox Publisher

Job 68—Check and Correct the Operation Windshield Washers and Wipers (continued)

Replace a Wiper or Blade Insert

☐ 1. Turn the ignition switch to the *On* position.

☐ 2. Turn the windshield wiper switch to the *On* position.

☐ 3. Turn the ignition switch to the *Off* position when wiper arms reach a place on the windshield where they can be easily reached.

☐ 4. Lift the wiper from the glass and detach the retainer. The retainer type depends on whether the wiper rubber insert or the entire wiper assembly is being replaced.

Describe the type of retainer: _____

☐ 5. Remove the blade insert or wiper assembly as needed.

☐ 6. Install the replacement part.

☐ 7. Install the retainer and ensure that it is securely latched.

☐ 8. Pour a slight amount of water on the windshield.

☐ 9. Turn the ignition switch to the *On* position and note wiper operation.

☐ 10. Turn the wiper and ignition switches to the *Off* position.

Diagnose Windshield Washer Operation

☐ 1. Operate the washer control switch and determine whether the pump runs.

Does the pump run? Yes ___ No ___

If No, go to step 2.

If the pump motor runs, but does not pump fluid, check the following:

- Is there enough fluid in the reservoir? Yes ___ No ___

- Are the hoses connected? Yes ___ No ___

- Are the hoses or jet nozzles clear (not plugged)? Yes ___ No ___

If the answer to any of the above questions is No, correct as necessary and retest pump operation.

If the answer to all of the above questions is Yes, go to step 6.

☐ 2. If the pump circuit is controlled through a fuse, check the fuse condition.

Is the fuse OK? Yes ___ No ___

If No, replace it and recheck washer operation.

If Yes, go to step 3.

☐ 3. If the fuse is good, attach a non-powered test light to the washer input terminal of the wiring harness. **Figure 68-2** shows the connector of a typical reservoir-mounted washer pump.

> ### Note
>
> SUVs, station wagons, and vans may have an extra washer pump for the rear window. Determine which pump requires testing before proceeding.

Figure 68-2. Modern washer pumps are installed on the reservoir tank.

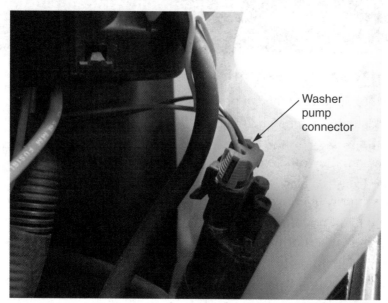

Washer
pump
connector

Goodheart-Willcox Publisher

☐ 4. Operate the washer switch and note whether the test light illuminates.
Does the test light illuminate? Yes ___ No ___
If Yes, go to step 5.
If No, check the wiring between the fuse and the pump motor.

☐ 5. Check that the pump motor is properly grounded.
Is the motor properly grounded? Yes ___ No ___
If No, repair the ground and retest.
If Yes, go to step 6.

☐ 6. Replace the pump motor and retest.

Job Wrap Up

☐ 1. Return all tools and equipment to storage.

☐ 2. Clean the work area.

☐ 3. Did you encounter any problems during this procedure? Yes ___ No ___
If Yes, describe the problems: _____

_____

What did you do to correct the problems?_____

_____

☐ 4. Have your instructor check your work and sign this job sheet.

Job 68—Check and Correct the Operation Windshield Washers and Wipers (continued)

Performance Evaluation—Instructor Use Only

Did the student complete the job in the time allotted? Yes ___ No ___

If No, which steps were not completed?_____

How would you rate this student's overall performance on this job?_____

5–Excellent, 4–Good, 3–Satisfactory, 2–Unsatisfactory, 1–Poor

Comments: _____
_____
_____

INSTRUCTOR'S SIGNATURE _____

Notes

Job

Inspect an Air Conditioning System

69

After completing this job, you will be able to inspect various components of a vehicle's heating and air conditioning system.

Instructions

As you read the job instructions, answer the questions and perform the tasks. Print your answers neatly and use complete sentences. Consult the proper service literature and ask your instructor for help as needed.

> **Warning**
> ⚠ Before performing this job, review all pertinent safety information in the text and discuss safety procedures with your instructor.

Procedures

☐ 1. Obtain a vehicle to be used in this job. Your instructor may direct you to perform this job on a shop vehicle.

☐ 2. Gather the tools needed to perform the following job.

Visually Inspect Under-Hood Air Conditioning Components

☐ 1. Open the vehicle hood.

☐ 2. Visually check the air conditioning system for obvious refrigerant leaks. Leaks are indicated by oil on air conditioning components.

Did you find any refrigerant leaks? Yes ___ No ___

If Yes, describe the leak locations: _____

_____

☐ 3. Examine the air conditioning compressor's drive belt.

Is the compressor drive belt tension acceptable? Yes ___ No ___

If No, check the condition of any tensioners and mounting hardware and then adjust the belt tension. Refer to Job 14 as needed.

Is the compressor drive belt condition acceptable? Yes ___ No ___

If No, describe the damage: _____

_____

☐ 4. Examine the refrigeration hoses and fittings.

Is frayed rubber evident on any hoses? Yes ___ No ___

Are cuts evident on any hoses? Yes ___ No ___

Did you find evidence of leaks on any hoses or fittings? Yes ___ No ___

Are any of the refrigerant hose fittings damaged? Yes ___ No ___

If you answered Yes to any of these questions, describe the defects: _____

_____

_____

☐ 5. Check other accessible air conditioning system components for defects.

Does the compressor clutch appear to be in good condition? Yes ___ No ___

If No, describe the defects: _____

_____

Do you see any dirt or other debris on the condenser? Yes ___ No ___

If Yes, carefully clean the condenser.

Do you see any visible damage to the condenser or accumulator/receiver-drier?
Yes ___ No ___

If Yes, describe the damage: _____

_____

Is the evaporator drain obstructed? Yes ___ No ___

If Yes, consult your instructor.

> ### Note
> If condensation is dripping from under the vehicle, it can be assumed that the drain is open. However, if sloshing noises are heard or the front carpet of the vehicle is wet, the drain hose must be visually inspected.

Is refrigerant oil visible? Yes ___ No ___

If Yes, consult your instructor.

☐ 6. Operate the air conditioning and heater.

Does the air smell musty or moldy? Yes ___ No ___

If Yes, there is likely microbial growth in the evaporator case. The evaporator case must be cleaned and disinfected. Consult your instructor.

Does the air smell like coolant? Yes ___ No ___

If Yes, the heater core may be leaking. Consult you instructor.

Does the air smell oily? Yes ___ No ___

If Yes, there may be a massive refrigerant leak in the evaporator. Consult you instructor.

Job 69—Inspect an Air Conditioning System (continued)

Were any other unusual odors detected? Yes ___ No ___

Describe the odor and inform your instructor:_____

_____

_____

Inspect Ducts, Hoses, and Outlet Vents

☐ 1. Remove instrument panel components or cover panels as necessary to access the air handling system ductwork and hoses.

☐ 2. Make a visual inspection of the ducts and hoses. Check carefully for misaligned or disconnected ducts, torn hoses, and loose connections.

Were any problems noted? Yes ___ No ___

If Yes, describe the problems: _____

_____

☐ 3. Inspect the air handling system outlet vents for the following problems:

- Stuck or broken shutoff flaps.
- Stuck outlets.
- Stuck or broken outlet vent fins.
- Other outlet vent damage.

Were any problems noted? Yes ___ No ___

If Yes, describe the problems: _____

_____

☐ 4. Consult with your instructor about what repair steps to take.

Repairs to be made: _____

_____

☐ 5. Make repairs as necessary.

☐ 6. Recheck airflow and overall HVAC system operation.

Inspect/Replace Cabin Filter

> **Note**
>
> The cabin filter should be changed every 12,000–15,000 miles (19,000–24,000 km) or whenever the system airflow becomes sluggish.

☐ 1. Determine the cabin filter location. **Figure 69-1** shows the most common cabin filter locations. The location may be shown in the owners' manual or a parts catalog.

Where is the cabin filter located?_____

> **Note**
>
> The following two sections are arranged by the filter location. Follow the procedure in the section that is appropriate for the filter you are replacing. Disregard the other procedure.

Figure 69-1. Common cabin air filter locations are shown here. A—Inside the glove box. B—Under the hood. C—Under the dash.

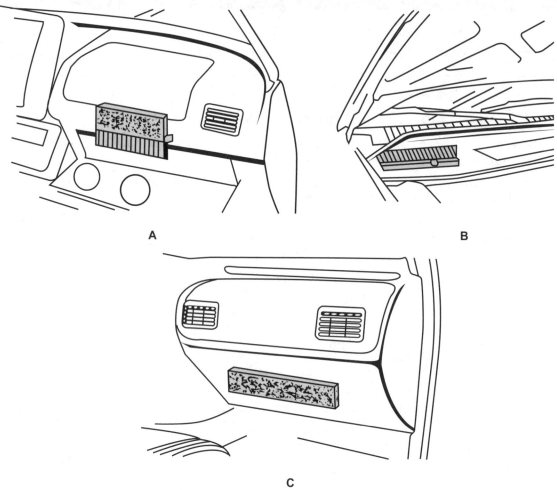

A

B

C

Goodheart-Willcox Publisher

Cabin Filter Located in the Passenger Compartment

1. If the cabin filter is located in the passenger compartment under the glove compartment, remove the kick panel covering the filter housing then loosen the housing. If the cabin filter is located behind the glove compartment, open the glove compartment and the filter access doors.

2. Remove the cabin filter.

> **Note**
>
> Some vehicles have two filters installed in the housing. Both filters should be changed. Remove the top filter by pulling it forward, then pull the second filter upward into the space previously occupied by the first filter and remove it.

3. Observe the cabin filter condition and describe it in the space provided.

_____

_____

_____

Job 69—Inspect an Air Conditioning System (continued)

> **Caution**
>
> This type of filter usually cannot be successfully cleaned. If the filter is dirty, it should be replaced.

☐ 4. Install the new filter(s) or reinstall the inspected filter(s).

> **Note**
>
> If the housing has two filters, slide the first new filter into the place occupied by the top filter, and then push it downward into place. Next, install the other new filter in the top position.

☐ 5. Reinstall the kick panel or close the access door and glove compartment door.

Cabin Filter Located in Cowl

☐ 1. If necessary, place the windshield wipers in the straight up position.

☐ 2. Open the hood and remove the right side cowl cover to expose the cabin air filter.

☐ 3. Pull on the removal tab to remove the filter from the recess.

☐ 4. Install the new filter and make sure that it is fully seated in the recess.

☐ 5. Reinstall the cowl cover.

☐ 6. Close the hood.

☐ 7. Park the windshield wipers.

☐ 8. Recheck airflow and overall system operation.

Job Wrap Up

☐ 1. Return all tools and equipment to storage.

☐ 2. Clean the work area.

☐ 3. Did you encounter any problems during this procedure? Yes ___ No ___

   If Yes, describe the problems: _____

   _____

   _____

   What did you do to correct the problems?_____

   _____

   _____

☐ 4. Have your instructor check your work and sign this job sheet.

Performance Evaluation—Instructor Use Only

Did the student complete the job in the time allotted? Yes ___ No ___
If No, which steps were not completed?_____
How would you rate this student's overall performance on this job?_____
5–Excellent, 4–Good, 3–Satisfactory, 2–Unsatisfactory, 1–Poor
Comments: _____
_____
_____
INSTRUCTOR'S SIGNATURE _____

Job
Perform a Vacuum Test and a Power Balance Test

70

After completing this job, you will be able to perform a vacuum test and a power balance test as part of the diagnostic process.

Instructions

As you read the job instructions, answer the questions and perform the tasks. Print your answers neatly and use complete sentences. Consult the proper service literature and ask your instructor for help as needed.

> **Warning**
>
> Before performing this job, review all pertinent safety information in the text and discuss safety procedures with your instructor.

Procedures

☐ 1. Obtain a vehicle to be used in this job. Your instructor may direct you to perform this job on a shop vehicle or engine.

☐ 2. Gather the tools needed to perform the following job.

Engine Vacuum Test

☐ 1. Attach a vacuum gauge to the engine. The easiest way to do this is to remove an engine vacuum line and attach the vacuum gauge hose. If a vacuum line cannot be removed or if removing any hose would affect engine operation, the gauge should be connected to the vacuum circuit without interrupting it. This can be accomplished by removing one of the engine's vacuum lines, inserting a length of vacuum hose with a T fitting, and then attaching the vacuum gauge hose to the open nipple on the fitting. It can also be accomplished by removing a fitting from the intake manifold and temporarily installing a hose fitting that allows the gauge to be connected between the vacuum line and the manifold.

☐ 2. Start the engine and allow it to idle.

Figure 70-1. Compare the vacuum gauge readings for the engine you are testing with the readings shown here.

Vacuum Gauge Readings

Note: White needle indicates steady vacuum. Red needle indicates fluctuating vacuum.

Needle steady and within specifications.

Cause: Normal vacuum at idle.

Needle very low and steady.

Cause: Vacuum or intake manifold leak.

Needle normal at idle, but fluctuates as engine speed is increased.

Cause: Weak valve spring.

Needle jumps to almost zero when throttle is opened and comes back to just over normal vacuum when closed.

Cause: Normal acceleration and deceleration reading.

Needle slowly drops from normal as engine speed is increased.

Cause: Restricted exhaust (compare at idle and 2500 rpm).

Needle steady, but low at idle.

Cause: Improper valve or ignition timing.

Needle has small pulsation at idle.

Cause: Insufficient spark plug gap.

Needle occasionally makes a sharp fast drop.

Cause: Sticking valve.

Needle regularly drops 4 to 8 inches.

Cause: Blown head gasket or excessive block-to-head clearance.

Needle slowly drifts back and forth.

Cause: Improper air-fuel mixture.

Needle drops regularly; may become steady as engine speed is increased.

Cause: Burned valve, worn valve guide, insufficient tappet clearance.

Needle drops to zero when engine is accelerated and snaps back to higher than normal on deceleration.

Cause: Worn piston rings or diluted oil.

Goodheart-Willcox Publisher

Job 70—Perform a Vacuum Test and a Power Balance Test (continued)

☐ 3. Refer to the chart in **Figure 70-1** to diagnose engine problems. If necessary, increase engine speed to make further checks.

What conclusions can you make from reading the vacuum gauge?_____

_____

_____

_____

_____

_____

☐ 4. Turn off the engine.

☐ 5. Remove the vacuum gauge and reattach vacuum hoses or fittings as necessary. If you used a T fitting to attach the vacuum gauge hose, remove the T fitting and reconnect the vacuum line.

Power Balance Test

☐ 1. Attach a power balance testing device. This can be a scan tool or engine analyzer with the capability of shutting down the ignition or fuel injector on individual cylinders.

☐ 2. Start the engine and set the engine speed to fast idle before beginning the test.

☐ 3. Kill (disable) each cylinder in turn and record the engine speed as each cylinder is disabled.

Cylinder # 1:_____rpm.   Cylinder # 2:_____rpm.
Cylinder # 3:_____rpm.   Cylinder # 4:_____rpm.
Cylinder # 5:_____rpm.   Cylinder # 6:_____rpm.
Cylinder # 7:_____rpm.   Cylinder # 8:_____rpm.
Cylinder # 9:_____rpm.   Cylinder # 10:_____rpm.
Cylinder # 11:_____rpm.   Cylinder # 12:_____rpm.

☐ 4. Return the engine to its normal idle speed and turn it off.

☐ 5. Compare the rpm drops for all cylinders.

Did the rpm fail to drop when any cylinder was disabled? Yes ___ No ___

If Yes, what was the number of the cylinder(s) that did not drop?_____

What do you think could cause the readings that you observed?_____

_____

_____

_____

_____

☐ 6. Remove the test equipment leads from the engine.

Job Wrap Up

☐   1.   Return all tools and equipment to storage.

☐   2.   Clean the work area.

☐   3.   Did you encounter any problems during this procedure? Yes ___ No ___

       If Yes, describe the problems: _____

       _____

       What did you do to correct the problems?_____

       _____

       _____

☐   4.   Have your instructor check your work and sign this job sheet.

Performance Evaluation—Instructor Use Only

Did the student complete the job in the time allotted? Yes ___ No ___

If No, which steps were not completed?_____

How would you rate this student's overall performance on this job?_____

5–Excellent, 4–Good, 3–Satisfactory, 2–Unsatisfactory, 1–Poor

Comments: _____

_____

INSTRUCTOR'S SIGNATURE _____

Job
Perform a Cranking Compression Test, Running Compression Test, and a Cylinder Leakage Test

After completing this job, you will be able to perform compression tests and a cylinder leakage test as part of the diagnostic process.

Instructions

As you read the job instructions, answer the questions and perform the tasks. Print your answers neatly and use complete sentences. Consult the proper service literature and ask your instructor for help as needed.

> **Warning**
>
> ⚠ Before performing this job, review all pertinent safety information in the text and discuss safety procedures with your instructor.

Procedures

☐ 1. Obtain a vehicle to be used in this job. Your instructor may direct you to perform this job on a shop vehicle or engine.

☐ 2. Gather the tools needed to perform the following job.

Cranking Compression Test

☐ 1. Remove all spark plugs.

☐ 2. Disable the ignition and fuel systems by any of the following methods:
- Ignition system: ground the coil wire or remove the ignition fuse.
- Fuel system: remove the fuel pump relay or relay control fuse.

> **Note**
>
> It is not necessary to disable the fuel system on engines with carburetors.

☐ 3. Block the throttle valve in the open position.

☐ 4. Install the compression tester in first spark plug opening.

☐ 5. Crank the engine through four compression strokes.

Record the reading: _____

☐ 6. Repeat steps 4 and 5 for all other engine cylinders.

Cylinder # 1:_____   Cylinder # 2:_____

Cylinder # 3:_____   Cylinder # 4:_____

Cylinder # 5:_____   Cylinder # 6:_____

Cylinder # 7:_____   Cylinder # 8:_____

Cylinder # 9:_____   Cylinder # 10:_____

Cylinder # 11:_____   Cylinder # 12:_____

☐ 7. Compare the compression readings for all cylinders.

Is the compression excessively low or high on any cylinder(s)? Yes ___ No ___

If Yes, which cylinders have abnormal readings? _____

What do you think could cause the readings that you observed? Refer to **Figure 71-1** for information about diagnosing compression problems._____

_____

_____

_____

_____

_____

Figure 71-1. The causes of these compression readings apply to any engine. Consult the manufacturer's service literature for any special problem.

Compression Gauge Readings		
Compression Test Results	**Cause**	**Wet Test Results**
All cylinders at normal pressure (no more than 10–15% difference between cylinders)	Engine is in good shape, no problems.	No wet test needed.
All cylinders low (more than 20%)	Burned valve or valve seat, blown head gasket, worn rings or cylinder, valves misadjusted, jumped timing chain or belt, physical damage to engine.	If compression increases, cylinder or rings are worn. No increase, problem caused by valve train. Near zero compression caused by engine damage.
One or more cylinders low (more than 20% difference)	Burned valve, valve seat, damage or wear on affected cylinder(s).	If compression increases, cylinder or rings are worn. No increase, problem caused by valve train. Near zero compression caused by engine damage.
Two adjacent cylinders low (more than 20% difference)	Blown head gasket, cracked block or head.	Little or no increase in pressure.
Compression high (more than 20% difference)	Carbon build-up in cylinder.	Do not wet test for high compression.

Goodheart-Willcox Publisher

Job 71—Perform a Cranking Compression Test, Running Compression Test, and a Cylinder Leakage Test (continued)

☐ 8. If any cylinder had a low compression reading, pour approximately one teaspoon (1 ml) of engine oil in the cylinder and retest the compression.

Did the compression improve? Yes ___ No ___

What is a possible cause? _____

_____

_____

_____

☐ 9. Return the throttle valve to the closed position and replace the fuel pump relay or relay control fuse if it was removed.

☐ 10. Reinstall the spark plugs and reconnect the ignition system.

Running Compression Test

☐ 1. Remove the spark plug of the cylinder to be tested. If the spark plugs were removed for the cranking compression test, reinstall all of them except the plug of the cylinder to be tested.

☐ 2. Install the compression tester in the spark plug hole.

☐ 3. Start the engine.

☐ 4. Compare the compression reading at idle with the static compression reading.

Is the compression approximately 50% of the static compression reading?
Yes ___ No ___

☐ 5. Quickly snap the throttle open and closed.

Does compression rise to about 80% of the static compression reading?
Yes ___ No ___

☐ 6. Repeat steps 4 and 5 for all other engine cylinders.

> **Note**
> Reinstall each plug before moving to the next cylinder. Leaving out any plug other than the plug to be tested will affect readings.

Cylinder # 1:_____   Cylinder # 2:_____

Cylinder # 3:_____   Cylinder # 4:_____

Cylinder # 5:_____   Cylinder # 6:_____

Cylinder # 7:_____   Cylinder # 8:_____

Cylinder # 9:_____   Cylinder # 10:_____

Cylinder # 11:_____   Cylinder # 12:_____

☐ 7. Compare the compression readings for all cylinders.

Is the running compression excessively low or high on any cylinder(s)?
Yes ___ No ___

If Yes, which cylinders have abnormal readings? _____

What do you think could cause the readings that you observed? Possible causes include worn camshaft lobes, excessive carbon deposits on the valves, and worn rings:

_____

_____

_____

_____

_____

☐ 8. Ensure that all plugs have been properly reinstalled and torqued.

☐ 9. Remove all test equipment.

Cylinder Leakage Test

> **Note**
>
> A cylinder leakage test is usually performed when a compression test indicates low compression on a cylinder. Your instructor may direct you to perform this test on a randomly selected cylinder in good condition.

☐ 1. Disable the ignition system to prevent accidental starting.

☐ 2. Attach a shop air hose to the leak tester.

☐ 3. Adjust the tester pressure to the recommended setting. This is usually about 5-10 psi (35.5–68.9 kpa).

Recommended pressure setting: _____ psi or kpa (circle one).

☐ 4. Remove the spark plug from the suspect cylinder.

☐ 5. Bring the suspect cylinder to the top of its compression stroke by feeling for compression as the piston comes up. Some technicians use a whistle to indicate when the compression stroke is occurring.

☐ 6. Install the leak tester hose in the spark plug opening.

☐ 7. Open the valve allowing regulated pressure into the cylinder.

☐ 8. Observe the pressure. It should be at or near the regulated pressure.

Pressure reading: _____ psi or kpa (circle one).

Does this pressure match the regulated pressure? Yes ___ No ___

If No, what is a possible cause? _____

_____

_____

_____

_____

☐ 9. If the pressure is low, refer to the chart in **Figure 71-2**.

After consulting the chart, list the possible engine problem: _____

_____

_____

_____

_____

Job 71—Perform a Cranking Compression Test, Running Compression Test, and a Cylinder Leakage Test (continued)

Figure 71-2. The engine cylinder is supposed to be almost airtight on the top of its compression stroke. Air escaping anywhere is caused by a defect.

Cylinder Leakage Test Results	
Condition	**Possible Causes**
No air escapes from any of the cylinders.	Normal condition, no leakage.
Air escapes from carburetor or throttle body.	Intake valve not seated or damaged.
	Valve train mistimed, possible jumped timing chain or belt.
	Broken or damaged valve train part.
Air escapes from tailpipe.	Exhaust valve not seated or damaged.
	Valve train mistimed.
	Broken or damaged valve train part.
Air escapes from dipstick tube or oil fill opening.	Worn piston rings. Worn cylinder walls.
	Damaged piston.
	Blown head gasket.
Air escapes from adjacent cylinder.	Blown head gasket.
	Cracked head or block.
Air bubbles in radiator coolant.	Blown head gasket.
	Cracked head or block.
Air heard around outside of cylinder.	Cracked or warped head or block.
	Blown head gasket.

Goodheart-Willcox Publisher

☐ 10. Remove the tester hose and reinstall the spark plug.

☐ 11. Repeat steps 4 through 10 on all suspect cylinders.

☐ 12. Analyze the readings of all tested cylinders.
What conclusions can you make? _____
_____
_____
_____

☐ 13. Remove the shop air hose from the tester.

Job Wrap Up

☐ 1. Return all tools and equipment to storage.

☐ 2. Clean the work area.

☐ 3. Did you encounter any problems during this procedure? Yes ___ No ___

If Yes, describe the problems: _____

_____

_____

What did you do to correct the problems?_____

_____

_____

☐ 4. Have your instructor check your work and sign this job sheet.

Performance Evaluation—Instructor Use Only

Did the student complete the job in the time allotted? Yes ___ No ___

If No, which steps were not completed?_____

How would you rate this student's overall performance on this job?____

5–Excellent, 4–Good, 3–Satisfactory, 2–Unsatisfactory, 1–Poor

Comments: _____

_____

INSTRUCTOR'S SIGNATURE _____

Job

Inspect and Test an Ignition System's Secondary Circuit Components and Wiring

After completing this job, you will be able to inspect and test a vehicle's secondary ignition circuit.

Instructions

As you read the job instructions, answer the questions and perform the tasks. Print your answers neatly and use complete sentences. Consult the proper service literature and ask your instructor for help as needed.

> **Warning**
>
> ⚠ Before performing this job, review all pertinent safety information in the text and discuss safety procedures with your instructor.

Procedures

- [ ] 1. Obtain a vehicle to be used in this job. Your instructor may direct you to perform this job on a shop vehicle.
- [ ] 2. Gather the tools needed to perform this job.
- [ ] 3. Determine the type of ignition system to be tested. See **Figure 72-1** for some typical ignition systems. Place a check mark next to the applicable ignition type:
  - [ ] Distributorless (waste spark).
  - [ ] Distributorless with two plugs per cylinder.
  - [ ] Coil-near-plug (uses coil wires).
  - [ ] Coil-on-plug (direct, no plug wires).
  - [ ] Distributor with internal pick up.
  - [ ] Distributor without internal pick up.
- [ ] 4. Locate service information for the ignition system to be tested.

Figure 72-1. Four common types of ignition systems are shown here. A—Distributorless ignition. B—Coil-on-plug ignition. C—Dual ignition (in this design, a combination of coil-over-plug and coil-near-plug systems). D—Distributor-type ignition.

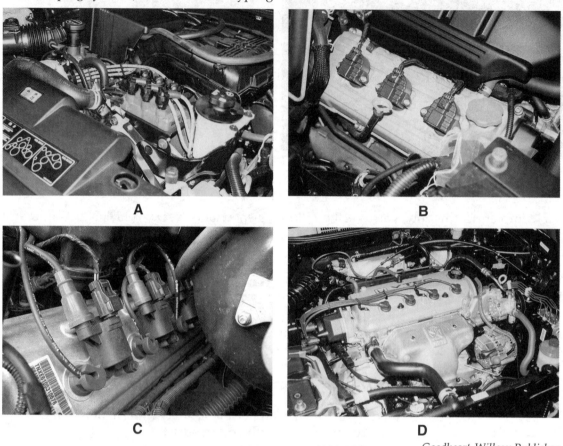

Goodheart-Willcox Publisher

Test for a Spark from the Secondary System

☐ 1. Detach coil or plug wire or remove one coil from its plug.

☐ 2. Attach a spark tester to the wire or coil and ground as applicable.

☐ 3. Have an assistant crank the engine as you observe the spark. Describe the spark produced:

    ☐ No spark is produced.

    ☐ The spark is weak. Describe: _____

    ☐ The spark is acceptable. Describe: _____

> **Caution**
>
> Do not allow the engine to run for more than a few seconds with the spark plug disconnected. Unburned fuel from the dead cylinder can damage the catalytic converter.

☐ 4. If there is no spark or the spark is weak, make further checks to isolate the problem to the primary or secondary ignition system components, as outlined in the following sections of the job.

Job 72—Inspect and Test an Ignition System's Secondary Circuit Components and Wiring (continued)

Read and Interpret Ignition System Waveforms

☐ 1. Obtain one of the following testers, capable of reading ignition system waveforms.

    ☐ Engine analyzer.

    ☐ Oscilloscope.

    ☐ Waveform meter.

☐ 2. Attach the tester leads to the ignition system connections.

Attachment method(s): _____

_____

☐ 3. Set the tester controls to match the ignition system type.

☐ 4. Start the engine and observe the oscilloscope patterns.

☐ 5. Draw the secondary oscilloscope pattern.

☐ 6. Draw the primary oscilloscope pattern.

Do the primary and secondary patterns indicate that the ignition system is operating correctly? Yes ___ No ___

If No, what could be the problem? _____

_____

☐ 7. Stop the engine and remove the tester leads.

Check the Spark Plugs

☐ 1. Remove the spark plugs from the cylinder head.

☐ 2. Visually inspect the spark plugs for excessive wear, fouling, or other signs of damage. List the defects found by cylinder number.

Plug from Cylinder #	Description of Defect
1	
2	
3	
4	
5	
6	
7	
8	
9	
10	
11	
12	

☐ 3. Determine the cause of the plug's condition, replace defective plugs, and retest the ignition system.

Check the Spark Plug Wires

☐ 1. Visually inspect the wires for the defects. Place a check mark next to any that apply.

    ☐ Chafing or other damage.

    ☐ Cracked or split wire insulation.

    ☐ Evidence of flashover or shorting.

    ☐ Damaged boots.

Describe any defects: _____

Job 72—Inspect and Test an Ignition System's Secondary Circuit Components and Wiring (continued)

☐ 2. Use an ohmmeter to check wire resistance. List any defects found by cylinder number.

Wire from Cylinder #	Description of Defect
1	
2	
3	
4	
5	
6	
7	
8	
9	
10	
11	
12	

☐ 3. After consulting with your instructor, replace defective plug wires and recheck the ignition system.

Check the Distributor Cap and Rotor

☐ 1. Remove the cap from the distributor body.

☐ 2. Visually inspect the cap and rotor for carbon tracks and flashover.

☐ 3. Check the cap and rotor for cracks or other evidence of mechanical damage.

☐ 4. After consulting with your instructor, replace defective components as necessary and recheck the ignition system.

Job Wrap Up

☐ 1. Return all tools and equipment to storage.

☐ 2. Clean the work area.

☐ 3. Did you encounter any problems during this procedure? Yes ___ No ___

If Yes, describe the problems: _____

_____

_____

What did you do to correct the problems?_____

_____

_____

☐ 4. Have your instructor check your work and sign this job sheet.

Performance Evaluation—Instructor Use Only

Did the student complete the job in the time allotted? Yes ___ No ___

If No, which steps were not completed?_____

How would you rate this student's overall performance on this job?____

5–Excellent, 4–Good, 3–Satisfactory, 2–Unsatisfactory, 1–Poor

Comments: _____

_____

INSTRUCTOR'S SIGNATURE _____

Job

Use a Scan Tool to Retrieve Trouble Codes and Run Monitors

73

After completing this job, you will be able to use a scan tool to access a vehicle engine or power train computer for diagnosis purposes.

Instructions

As you read the job instructions, answer the questions and perform the tasks. Print your answers neatly and use complete sentences. Consult the proper service literature and ask your instructor for help as needed.

> **Warning**
>
> Before performing this job, review all pertinent safety information in the text and discuss safety procedures with your instructor.

Procedures

☐ 1. Obtain a vehicle to be used in this job. Your instructor may direct you to perform this job on a shop vehicle.

☐ 2. Gather the tools needed to perform this job.

☐ 3. Obtain a scan tool and related service literature for the vehicle selected in step 1.

Type of scan tool:_____

> **Note**
>
> There are many kinds of scan tools. The following procedure is a general guide to scan tool use. Always obtain the service instructions for the scan tool that you are using. If the scan tool literature calls for a different procedure or series of steps from those in this procedure, always perform procedures according to the scan tool literature.

Accessing the Vehicle Computer

☐ 1. Attach the proper test connector cable and power lead to the scan tool.

☐ 2. Ensure that the ignition switch is in the *Off* position.

☐ 3. Locate the correct diagnostic connector.

Diagnostic connector location: _____

☐ 4. Attach the scan tool test connector cable to the diagnostic connector, using the proper adapter if necessary.

☐ 5. Attach the scan tool power lead to the cigarette lighter or battery terminals if necessary.

> **Note**
>
> OBD II scan tools are powered from terminal 16 of the diagnostic connector.

☐ 6. Observe the scan tool screen to ensure that it is working properly.

☐ 7. Enter vehicle information as needed to program the scan tool. Many scan tools can be programmed with the proper vehicle information by entering the vehicle identification number (VIN).

☐ 8. Turn the ignition key to the *On* position.

☐ 9. Retrieve trouble codes and list them in the space provided.

Trouble codes:_____

_____

> **Note**
>
> Vehicle computer systems in good condition will produce a single code to indicate that the engine is not running. If more than one code is produced, check with your instructor before continuing. The computer system and vehicle may have defects that are beyond the scope of this job.

☐ 10. Use the scan tool literature or factory service manual to determine the meaning of the codes.

Code Number	Defect

☐ 11. Start the engine.

Job 73—Use a Scan Tool to Retrieve Trouble Codes and Run Monitors (continued)

☐ 12. Have another student drive the vehicle while you record the following information. If a particular reading is not available, write "NA" in the space.

- Idle RPM: _____

  Is the idle speed within specifications? Yes ___ No ___

- Intake air temperature:_____

  Is the air intake temperature within specifications? Yes ___ No ___

- MAF sensor reading:_____

  Is the MAF sensor reading within specifications? Yes ___ No ___

- MAP sensor reading:_____

  Is the MAP sensor reading within specifications? Yes ___ No ___

- Fuel trim counts at idle:_____ At cruising speed:_____

  Are the fuel trim counts within specifications? Yes ___ No ___

- Does the torque converter lockup clutch apply at cruising speed? Yes ___ No ___

- Speeds at which the shift solenoids are energized:

  First: _____

  Second:_____

  Third: _____

  Fourth: _____

- Coolant temperature at the end of the test:_____°F or °C (circle one)

- Other readings, as required by your instructor:

Type of Reading	Value (Include Units of Measure)	Within Specifications?
		Yes ___ No ___
		Yes ___ No ___
		Yes ___ No ___
		Yes ___ No ___

☐ 13. If a driveability problem is encountered based on the preceding steps, use the scan tool freeze frame feature to capture readings that occur at the time the malfunction occurs.

- Set the scan tool to freeze frame.

- Drive the vehicle until the malfunction occurs.

- Observe the freeze frame data.

Does any freeze frame reading indicate a possible cause of the malfunction? Yes ___ No ___

If Yes, describe: _____

_____

_____

☐ 14. When the testing is complete, turn the ignition switch to the *Off* position.

☐ 15. If your instructor directs, make further checks to isolate the problem(s) revealed by the trouble codes or other readings.

☐ 16. If your instructor directs, repair the problem(s) as necessary. Refer to other jobs as directed.

> **Note**
>
> If the vehicle has an OBD II system, do not erase codes after repairs are completed. Erasing codes will also remove any monitors that have been run, which may cause the vehicle to fail its next emissions test.

☐ 17. After all repairs are complete, operate the vehicle to run the monitors again. If any monitors fail, a trouble code will set, indicating the need for further service. When attempting to set the monitors, keep several points in mind.

- Some monitors are designed to run under certain ambient temperature conditions. In some parts of the United States, these temperatures may not be reached for many months, or ever.

- Monitors may not reset a trouble code until they have run several times. Therefore, it is not possible to determine the status of repairs without keeping the vehicle for an excessive amount of time.

- The vehicle may have to be returned to the owner before all monitors have reset.

- Most state emission inspections require that a certain percentage, usually about 80%, of the monitors to have been run to pass inspection.

Job Wrap Up

☐ 1. Return all tools and equipment to storage.

☐ 2. Clean the work area.

☐ 3. Did you encounter any problems during this procedure? Yes ___ No ___
If Yes, describe the problems: _____

_____

What did you do to correct the problems? _____

_____

☐ 4. Have your instructor check your work and sign this job sheet.

Performance Evaluation—Instructor Use Only

Did the student complete the job in the time allotted? Yes ___ No ___
If No, which steps were not completed? _____
How would you rate this student's overall performance on this job? _____
5–Excellent, 4–Good, 3–Satisfactory, 2–Unsatisfactory, 1–Poor
Comments: _____

_____

_____

INSTRUCTOR'S SIGNATURE _____

Job

Reprogram a Vehicle Computer

74

After completing this job, you will be able to reprogram a vehicle computer using the upload-download or pass-through method.

Instructions

As you read the job instructions, answer the questions and perform the tasks. Print your answers neatly and use complete sentences. Consult the proper service literature and ask your instructor for help as needed.

> ### Warning
> Before performing this job, review all pertinent safety information in the text and discuss safety procedures with your instructor.

Procedures

☐ 1. Obtain a vehicle to be used in this job. Your instructor may direct you to perform this job on a shop vehicle.

☐ 2. Gather the tools needed to perform this job.

Reprogram the Computer

☐ 1. Determine the method to be used to reprogram the vehicle computer.

What reprogramming method will be used? Upload-download ___ Pass-through ___ Each of the methods for reprogramming the computer is covered in one of the following two sections of the job. Follow the procedure in the appropriate section and disregard the other procedure.

Upload-Download Method

> **Note**
>
> This method is sometimes referred to as indirect programming.

☐ 1. If not done previously, ensure that the ignition switch is in the *Off* position and connect the scan tool to the vehicle diagnostic connector.

☐ 2. Observe the scan tool screen and ensure that the tool is operating properly.

☐ 3. If necessary, use the scan tool keypad to enter vehicle information.

☐ 4. Turn the ignition switch to the *On* position if necessary.

☐ 5. Download the existing ECM programming into the scan tool.

Briefly describe the steps taken to download the programming. Be sure to include menus selected and scan tool keys operated. _____

_____

_____

☐ 6. When downloading is complete, turn the ignition switch to the *Off* position and disconnect the scan tool from the vehicle diagnostic connector. **Figure 74-1** shows a scan tool with downloaded ECM programming.

☐ 7. Take the scan tool to the Internet connection, modem, or programming computer. See **Figure 74-2**.

☐ 8. Access the programming database.

Database name: _____

Figure 74-1. Note that this scan tool prompts the technician to take the next step, removing the scan tool from the vehicle and attaching it to the programming computer.

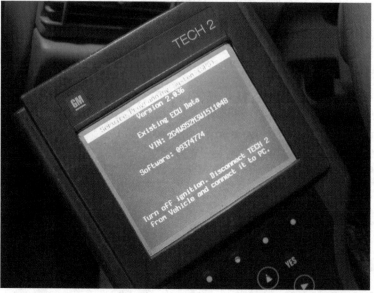

Goodheart-Willcox Publisher

Job 74—Reprogram a Vehicle Computer (continued)

Figure 74-2. Once the scan tool is attached to the programming computer, use the computer keyboard and mouse to check the vehicle programming and download updated programming as necessary.

Goodheart-Willcox Publisher

☐ 9. Download the updated programming into the scan tool.

Briefly describe the steps taken to begin the downloading process: _____

_____

_____

_____

Note

Several minutes may be needed to overwrite the existing programming. The computer and/or scan tool will indicate the finish of the downloading process.

☐ 10. When the new programming has been installed in the scan tool, unplug the tool and take it to the vehicle.

☐ 11. Plug the scan tool into the diagnostic connector and, if necessary, turn the ignition switch to the *On* position.

☐ 12. Operate the scan tool as necessary to install the new programming into the vehicle ECM.

Briefly describe the steps taken to install the new programming, including scan tool menus selected:_____

_____

_____

_____

13. After reprogramming is complete, start the engine and test drive the vehicle to ensure that the new programming has been properly entered.

Does operation of the ECM and vehicle indicate that the new programming has been properly installed? Yes ___ No ___

If No, describe the problem(s):_____

_____

What could be the reason for the problem(s)? _____

_____

_____

> **Note**
>
> After reprogramming, many ECMs must go through a relearn procedure to properly control idle speed and other vehicle functions. This may take several minutes of driving. Some manufacturers require the technician to perform a specific series of relearning steps. Consult the manufacturer's service information for these procedures.

14. Park the vehicle and turn the ignition switch to the *Off* position.
15. Unplug the scan tool from the diagnostic connector.

Pass-Through Method

> **Note**
>
> This method is sometimes referred to as direct programming, flash reprogramming, or J2534 programming.

1. Park the vehicle at a place in the shop where it can be attached to the Internet connection using the available connecting cables.
2. If not done previously, ensure that the ignition switch is in the *Off* position.
3. Connect the scan tool or reprogramming tool to the vehicle diagnostic connector.
4. Attach the scan tool or reprogramming tool to the Internet connection using correct cables. This connection is usually made through an Internet-ready computer, **Figure 74-3**.
5. Turn the ignition switch to the *On* position if necessary.
6. Use the computer (and scan tool if required) to access the remote reprogramming website.

   Name of website:_____
7. Follow website instructions to reprogram the vehicle ECM.

   Briefly describe the steps taken to reprogram the ECM:_____

   _____

   _____

   _____

> **Note**
>
> Several minutes may be needed to overwrite the existing programming. The website will indicate when the program has finished downloading.

Job 74—Reprogram a Vehicle Computer (continued)

Figure 74-3. The reprogramming tool shown here is usually called a J2534 tool. Connection methods vary but usually consist of attaching one cable from the diagnostic connector to the tool, and another from the tool to the computer. The computer can be either a desktop model or a laptop model.

Goodheart-Willcox Publisher

☐ 8. After reprogramming is complete, exit the website and turn the ignition switch to the *Off* position.

☐ 9. Unplug the scan tool or reprogramming tool from the vehicle diagnostic connector and remove it from the vehicle.

☐ 10. Start the engine and test drive the vehicle to ensure that the new programming has been properly entered.

Does operation of the ECM and vehicle indicate that the new programming has been properly installed? Yes ___ No ___

If No, describe the problem(s):_____

_____

_____

What could be the reason for the problem(s)? _____

_____

_____

Note

 After reprogramming, many ECMs must go through a relearn procedure to properly control idle speed and other vehicle functions. This may take several minutes of driving. Some manufacturers require the technician to perform a specific series of relearning steps. Consult the manufacturer's service information for these procedures.

☐ 11. If necessary, disconnect the scan tool or reprogramming tool from the computer.

☐ 12. Turn off the computer and return any cables to storage.

Job Wrap Up

☐ 1. Return all tools and equipment to storage.

☐ 2. Clean the work area.

☐ 3. Did you encounter any problems during this procedure? Yes ___ No ___
   If Yes, describe the problems: _____
   _____
   _____

   What did you do to correct the problems?_____
   _____
   _____

☐ 4. Have your instructor check your work and sign this job sheet.

Performance Evaluation—Instructor Use Only

Did the student complete the job in the time allotted? Yes ___ No ___
If No, which steps were not completed?_____
How would you rate this student's overall performance on this job?_____
5–Excellent, 4–Good, 3–Satisfactory, 2–Unsatisfactory, 1–Poor
Comments: _____
_____
_____

INSTRUCTOR'S SIGNATURE _____

Job
Servicing Fuel Filter and Air Induction Components

75

After completing this job, you will be able to replace a fuel filter and inspect the air induction system, including the air filter and intake ducts.

Instructions

As you read the job instructions, answer the questions and perform the tasks. Print your answers neatly and use complete sentences. Consult the proper service literature and ask your instructor for help as needed.

Warning
⚠ Before performing this job, review all pertinent safety information in the text and discuss safety procedures with your instructor.

Procedures

Inspect Fuel Lines

Warning
⚠ Gasoline is extremely flammable, and can be ignited by the smallest spark. Even a spark caused by dropping a tool on the shop floor is sufficient to ignite gasoline. Be sure that a fire extinguisher is nearby and that you know how to use it before starting any procedure that requires removing fuel line connections.

 1. Obtain a vehicle to be used in this job. Your instructor may direct you to perform this job on a shop vehicle.

2. Gather the tools needed to perform this job.

 3. Verify that your fire extinguisher is handy and properly charged.

☐ 4. Visually inspect the fuel lines and hoses for the following defects:
- Leaks at connections.
- Kinked lines or hoses.
- Collapsed lines or hoses.
- Swollen hoses.
- Loose or missing clips or brackets.

Describe any fuel line and hose problems found: _____

_____

Describe what should be done to correct the problems: _____

_____

Remove, Replace, and Test Fuel Filters

☐ 1. Locate the fuel filter on the vehicle. **Figure 75-1** shows a typical location under the vehicle body.

☐ 2. Relieve fuel system pressure.

☐ 3. Remove the fuel filter bracket fasteners.

☐ 4. Place a drip pan under the filter.

☐ 5. Remove the fuel line fittings and allow excess fuel to drip into the pan.

> ### Warning
> ⚠ Some gasoline will spill as the fittings are removed. Be sure to clean up any spilled gasoline before proceeding.

Figure 75-1. This fuel filter is located at the rear of the vehicle under the body. Note that this filter has both push-on and threaded connectors.

Goodheart-Willcox Publisher

Job 75—Servicing Fuel Filter and Air Induction Components (continued)

☐ 6. Check the filter condition by one of the following methods:

Drain the fuel from the inlet side of the filter and observe the fuel's condition. If the fuel is contaminated, the filter must be replaced.

or

Attempt to blow through the filter. Restriction will make the filter difficult to blow through, indicating that the filter must be replaced.

> **Warning**
> ⚠️ Avoid breathing gasoline vapors.

☐ 7. Compare the old and new filters to ensure that the new filter is correct. Check for correct size, fittings, and number of outlets.

Do the filters match? Yes ___ No ___

If No, what could account for the difference?_____

_____

☐ 8. Install the new filter.

☐ 9. Tighten the fittings.

☐ 10. Install the bracket fasteners.

☐ 11. Start the engine and check for fuel leaks.

Inspect, Service, or Replace Air Filters, Filter Housings, and Intake Ducts

> **Note**
> 📄 Air filter housings are located at the top of the engine, or to one side of the engine compartment. Most filters are square and resemble the one shown in **Figure 75-2**.

☐ 1. Locate the air filter housing.

☐ 2. Remove any engine compartment parts covering the air filter.

Parts removed: _____

_____

☐ 3. Remove the fasteners holding the air cleaner cover in place.

Type of fasteners used?

☐ Wing nut.

☐ Clip(s).

☐ Screws.

☐ 4. Remove the cover to expose the air filter

☐ 5. Remove the air filter from the housing.

Figure 75-2. A typical modern air filter.

Goodheart-Willcox Publisher

☐ 6. Check the filter for excessive dirt.

   What method is used?

   ☐ Visual inspection.

   Were there obvious dirt accumulations? Yes ___ No ___

   ☐ Tapping on flat surface.

   Did excessive dirt fall from filter? Yes ___ No ___

   ☐ Observing light intensity with drop light behind filter.

   Was light obscured: Yes ___ No ___

   ☐ Other method.

   Describe:_____

   _____

☐ 7. Check the filter and housing for any signs of oil or water.

> **Note**
>
> If the filter and housing are coated with engine oil, determine the cause before proceeding.

☐ 8. Wipe out the housing to remove any loose dirt, or remove the housing from the vehicle and blow it clean with compressed air.

☐ 9. Compare the old and new air filter elements.

☐ 10. Install the new filter element in the air cleaner housing, ensuring that it is properly positioned.

☐ 11. Install the air cleaner cover, ensuring that it is properly positioned.

☐ 12. Install and tighten the air cleaner fasteners.

Job 75—Servicing Fuel Filter and Air Induction Components (continued)

☐ 13. Inspect the condition of the air intake system ductwork.
Are there tears or holes? Yes ___ No ___
Are there loose clamps or other fasteners? Yes ___ No ___
Are components missing? Yes ___ No ___
Are any vacuum lines disconnected? Yes ___ No ___
Are there any crushed components? Yes ___ No ___
Is there any other damage? Yes ___ No ___
If yes, describe:_____
_____

☐ 14. Consult with your instructor concerning needed repairs.
What repairs are needed?_____
_____
_____
_____

Job Wrap Up

☐ 1. Return all tools and equipment to storage.
☐ 2. Clean the work area.
☐ 3. Did you encounter any problems during this procedure? Yes ___ No ___
If Yes, describe the problems: _____
_____
_____
What did you do to correct the problems?_____
_____
_____

☐ 4. Have your instructor check your work and sign this job sheet.

Performance Evaluation—Instructor Use Only

Did the student complete the job in the time allotted? Yes ___ No ___
If No, which steps were not completed?_____
How would you rate this student's overall performance on this job?_____
5–Excellent, 4–Good, 3–Satisfactory, 2–Unsatisfactory, 1–Poor
Comments: _____
_____
_____

INSTRUCTOR'S SIGNATURE _____

Notes

After completing this job, you will be able to examine exhaust systems.

Instructions

As you read the job instructions, answer the questions and perform the tasks. Print your answers neatly and use complete sentences. Consult the proper service literature and ask your instructor for help as needed.

> **Warning**
> Before performing this job, review all pertinent safety information in the text and discuss safety procedures with your instructor.

Procedures

- [ ] 1. Obtain a vehicle to be used in this job. Your instructor may direct you to perform this job on a shop vehicle.
- [ ] 2. Gather the tools needed to perform this job.

Check and Refill Diesel Exhaust Fluid (Diesel Vehicles Only)

- [ ] 1. If a diesel vehicle is being serviced, check the diesel exhaust fluid (DEF) tank level. Some tanks have a gauge, while others require that the cap be removed and the level observed.

     Is the level adequate? Yes ___ No ___
- [ ] 2. If DEF is needed, remove the filler cap if not already removed, and pour DEF into the tank as needed.
- [ ] 3. Ensure that the instrument panel LOW DEF warning light goes off when the engine is started.

> **Note**
> DEF is not dangerous. Small amounts of DEF, if spilled, can be washed away.

Check for Exhaust Leaks and Other Exhaust System Damage

☐ 1.   Start the engine and set the speed to fast idle.

☐ 2.   Raise the vehicle on a lift and determine the exhaust system configuration.

What type of exhaust system does the vehicle have? Single ___ Dual ___

How many catalytic converters does the vehicle have? _____

Does the vehicle have one or more resonators? Yes ___ No ___

Warning
⚠ The vehicle must be raised and supported in a safe manner. Always use approved lifts or jacks and jack stands.

☐ 3.   Look and listen for leaks. Leaks can be heard, and rusted out components are usually visible.

Were any leaks found? Yes ___ No ___

If Yes, list: _____

Warning
⚠ Exhaust system parts become hot quickly. Do not touch any exhaust parts with your bare hands.

☐ 4.   Turn off the engine. If necessary, lower the vehicle to turn the engine off and then raise the vehicle again.

☐ 5.   Visually inspect the exhaust system.

Are there broken, missing, or corroded hangers? Yes ___ No ___

If Yes, describe:_____

_____

Are there bent or disconnected hangers? Yes ___ No ___

If Yes, describe:_____

_____

Is exhaust hanger or bracket attaching hardware loose or missing? Yes ___ No ___

If Yes, describe:_____

_____

Are there missing, loose, or badly corroded heat shields? (Some corrosion is acceptable, but there must be no missing sections or holes in the shields.) Yes ___ No ___

If Yes, describe:_____

_____

Are any heat shield–attaching fasteners loose or missing? Yes ___ No ___

If Yes, describe:_____

_____

☐ 6.   Lower the vehicle.

Job 76—Inspect Exhaust System (continued)

Job Wrap Up

☐ 1. Return all tools and equipment to storage.

☐ 2. Clean the work area.

☐ 3. Did you encounter any problems during this procedure? Yes ___ No ___

If Yes, describe the problems: _____

_____

_____

What did you do to correct the problems?_____

_____

_____

☐ 4. Have your instructor check your work and sign this job sheet.

Performance Evaluation—Instructor Use Only

Did the student complete the job in the time allotted? Yes ___ No ___

If No, which steps were not completed?_____

How would you rate this student's overall performance on this job?_____

5–Excellent, 4–Good, 3–Satisfactory, 2–Unsatisfactory, 1–Poor

Comments: _____

_____

_____

INSTRUCTOR'S SIGNATURE _____

Notes

Job

77

Replace Exhaust System Components

After completing this job, you will be able to replace exhaust system components, such as mufflers, exhaust pipes, and catalytic converters.

Instructions

As you read the job instructions, answer the questions and perform the tasks. Print your answers neatly and use complete sentences. Consult the proper service literature and ask your instructor for help as needed.

> **Warning**
>
> ⚠ Before performing this job, review all pertinent safety information in the text and discuss safety procedures with your instructor.

Procedures

☐ 1. Obtain a vehicle to be used in this job. Your instructor may direct you to perform this job on a shop vehicle.

☐ 2. Gather the tools needed to perform this job.

☐ 3. Raise the vehicle.

> **Warning**
>
> ⚠ The vehicle must be raised and supported in a safe manner. Always use approved lifts or jacks and jack stands.

☐ 4. Remove any heat shields or skid plates that prevent access to the exhaust system component to be replaced.

☐ 5. Apply penetrating oil to all pipe bracket fasteners and to joint clamps. If an exhaust manifold is being replaced, apply penetrating oil to the manifold-to-engine fasteners.

☐ 6. Remove any parts that are attached to the exhaust component, such as oxygen sensors or EGR tubes.

☐ 7. Remove the clamps and bracket fasteners.

☐ 8. Loosen the outlet joint and pull the pipe free with a chain wrench. If the parts are welded together, cut off the pipe where necessary, ensuring that the remaining pipe can engage the new parts.

> **Note**
>
> Carefully remove and handle any pipe or parts that will be reused, such as exhaust doughnuts.

☐ 9. If any parts are joined at flanges, remove the fasteners and separate the flanges.

☐ 10. Remove the components from the vehicle.

☐ 11. After removal, use a pipe-end straightening cone or a pipe expander to straighten the ends of all pipes that will be reused. See **Figure 77-1**.

☐ 12. Clean the inside or outside of the nipples that will be reused. If a nipple is distorted, use a pipe expander to restore it to a perfectly round state.

☐ 13. Inspect all bell-mouth connectors, **Figure 77-2**, and replace any that are damaged.

☐ 14. Determine what parts will be needed to finish the job.

List the parts: _____

_____

_____

☐ 15. Compare the old and new exhaust system parts.

Do the parts match? Yes ___ No ___

If No, explain why:_____

_____

_____

☐ 16. Scrape old gasket material off of any flanged connectors that will be reused, such as the one in **Figure 77-3**.

Figure 77-1. Carefully straighten the ends of exhaust components that will be reused.

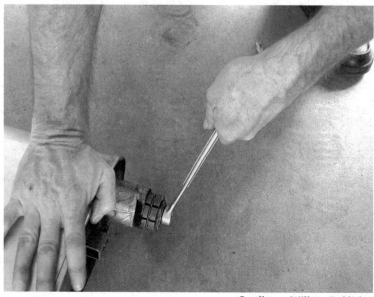

Goodheart-Willcox Publisher

Job 77—Replace Exhaust System Components (continued)

Figure 77-2. Check all bell-mouth connectors for distortion and replace as necessary.

Goodheart-Willcox Publisher

 17. Apply a coating of exhaust system sealant to any section of a component that will be installed inside of another pipe.

      18. Slide the pipes and nipples together.

> **Caution**
> ⚠ Make certain that the depth is correct.

Figure 77-3. A typical flanged connector is shown here.

Goodheart-Willcox Publisher

☐ 19. Slide the clamps into position and tighten them lightly.

☐ 20. Install and tighten any flanged connections, making sure that gaskets are used where necessary.

> **Caution**
>
> ⚠ Make sure that all parts are installed in the correct position and are facing in the proper direction. Make sure that the exhaust system parts are aligned with each other and do not contact any other part of the vehicle.

☐ 21. Tighten all clamps and brackets.

> **Caution**
>
> ⚠ Do not overtighten the clamps.

☐ 22. Install any related parts, such as oxygen sensors, EGR tubes, or heat shields.

☐ 23. Start the engine and check for exhaust leaks.

Job Wrap Up

☐ 1. Return all tools and equipment to storage.

☐ 2. Clean the work area.

☐ 3. Did you encounter any problems during this procedure? Yes ___ No ___

If Yes, describe the problems: _____

_____

_____

What did you do to correct the problems?_____

_____

_____

☐ 4. Have your instructor check your work and sign this job sheet.

Performance Evaluation—Instructor Use Only

Did the student complete the job in the time allotted? Yes ___ No ___
If No, which steps were not completed?_____
How would you rate this student's overall performance on this job?_____
5–Excellent, 4–Good, 3–Satisfactory, 2–Unsatisfactory, 1–Poor
Comments: _____

_____

INSTRUCTOR'S SIGNATURE _____

After completing this job, you will be able to test and service PCV systems.

Instructions

As you read the job instructions, answer the questions and perform the tasks. Print your answers neatly and use complete sentences. Consult the proper service literature and ask your instructor for help as needed.

> **Warning**
>
> ⚠ Before performing this job, review all pertinent safety information in the text and discuss safety procedures with your instructor.

Procedures

☐ 1. Obtain a vehicle to be used in this job. Your instructor may direct you to perform this job on a shop vehicle.

☐ 2. Gather the tools needed to perform this job.

☐ 3. Obtain the proper service information for the vehicle being serviced.

Test and Service a PCV System

> **Note**
>
> A few engines do not use a PCV valve. These engines have a calibrated orifice to control crankcase gas flow into the intake manifold. Check the appropriate service information to inspect and clean the orifice and related hoses.

☐ 1. Locate the PCV valve on the engine. Most are located on the valve cover, **Figure 78-1**, while a few are located on the valley cover under the intake manifold.

Describe the location of the PCV valve: _____

_____

Figure 78-1. A—Most PCV valves are installed on the valve cover. A few are mounted on the valley cover of V-type engines. Their removal may require that other components be removed. Note that the PCV shown here has been removed from its grommet. B—In-line PCV valve. Some valves are installed in the hose leading from the valve cover to the intake manifold.

PVC valve

Grommet

A

B

Goodheart-Willcox Publisher

2. Visually inspect the PCV system hoses. Look for hoses that are disconnected, leaking, or collapsed.

   Were any hose problems found? Yes ___ No ___

   If Yes, what was done to correct them? _____

   _____

3. Check PCV system condition by using one or more of the following procedures:

   • Use a tester to ensure that air is flowing into the crankcase when the engine is running.

   Did the PCV valve pass the test? Yes ___ No ___

   • Remove the PCV valve from its grommet with the engine idling.

   Does the engine speed up, even slightly? Yes ___ No ___

   Note

    Some late model PCV valves are attached to the valve cover with a cam lock. A special tool is needed to remove and install the cam lock.

   • Remove the PCV valve from its grommet. Place your finger over the PCV valve with the engine running.

   Is vacuum present? Yes ___ No ___

Job 78—Test and Service Positive Crankcase Ventilation (PCV) Systems (continued)

- Stop the engine with the PCV valve removed from its grommet. Shake the PCV valve.

  Does the PCV valve rattle when shaken? Yes ___ No ___

If the answers to any of the preceding questions is No, what could be the problem?

_____

_____

_____

What should be done to correct the problem? _____

_____

_____

Job Wrap Up

☐ 1. Return all tools and equipment to storage.

☐ 2. Clean the work area.

☐ 3. Did you encounter any problems during this procedure? Yes ___ No ___

    If Yes, describe the problems: _____

_____

_____

    What did you do to correct the problems?_____

_____

_____

☐ 4. Have your instructor check your work and sign this job sheet.

Performance Evaluation—Instructor Use Only

Did the student complete the job in the time allotted? Yes ___ No ___

If No, which steps were not completed?_____

How would you rate this student's overall performance on this job?_____

5–Excellent, 4–Good, 3–Satisfactory, 2–Unsatisfactory, 1–Poor

Comments: _____

_____

_____

INSTRUCTOR'S SIGNATURE _____

Notes

NATEF Correlation Chart
Maintenance and Light Repair (MLR)

The following chart correlates the jobs in this *Shop Manual* to the 2013 NATEF Maintenance and Light Repair (MLR) Task List.

ENGINE REPAIR

For every task in Engine Repair, the following safety requirement must be strictly enforced:
- Comply with personal and environmental safety practices associated with clothing; eye protection; hand tools; power equipment; proper ventilation; and the handling, storage, and disposal of chemicals/materials in accordance with local, state, and federal safety and environmental regulations.

I. ENGINE REPAIR
A. General

Task Number and Description	Priority	Job #s
1. Research applicable vehicle and service information, vehicle service history, service precautions, and technical service bulletins.	P-1	5
2. Verify operation of the instrument panel engine warning indicators.	P-1	6
3. Inspect engine assembly for fuel, oil, coolant, and other leaks; determine necessary action.	P-1	7
4. Install engine covers using gaskets, seals, and sealers as required.	P-1	8, 9
5. Remove and replace timing belt; verify correct camshaft timing.	P-1	10
6. Perform common fastener and thread repair, to include: remove broken bolt, restore internal and external threads, and repair internal threads with thread insert.	P-1	11
7. Identify hybrid vehicle internal combustion engine service precautions.	P-3	2

I. ENGINE REPAIR
B. Cylinder Head and Valve Train

Task Number and Description	Priority	Job #s
1. Adjust valves (mechanical or hydraulic lifters).	P-1	12

I. ENGINE REPAIR
C. Lubrication and Cooling Systems

Task Number and Description	Priority	Job #s
1. Perform cooling system pressure and dye tests to identify leaks; check coolant condition and level; inspect and test radiator, pressure cap, coolant recovery tank, and heater core and galley plugs; determine necessary action.	P-1	13

I. ENGINE REPAIR (continued)
C. Lubrication and Cooling Systems

Task Number and Description	Priority	Job #s
2. Inspect, replace, and adjust drive belts, tensioners, and pulleys; check pulley and belt alignment.	P-1	14
3. Remove, inspect, and replace thermostat and gasket/seal.	P-1	15
4. Inspect and test coolant; drain and recover coolant; flush and refill cooling system with recommended coolant; bleed air as required.	P-1	13, 16
5. Perform engine oil and filter change.	P-1	17

AUTOMATIC TRANSMISSION AND TRANSAXLE

For every task in Automatic Transmission and Transaxle, the following safety requirement must be strictly enforced:

- Comply with personal and environmental safety practices associated with clothing; eye protection; hand tools; power equipment; proper ventilation; and the handling, storage, and disposal of chemicals/materials in accordance with local, state, and federal safety and environmental regulations.

II. AUTOMATIC TRANSMISSION AND TRANSAXLE
A. General

Task Number and Description	Priority	Job #s
1. Research applicable vehicle and service information, fluid type, vehicle service history, service precautions, and technical service bulletins.	P-1	5, 18
2. Check fluid level in a transmission or a transaxle equipped with a dip-stick.	P-1	18
3. Check fluid level in a transmission or a transaxle not equipped with a dip-stick.	P-1	18
4. Check transmission fluid condition; check for leaks.	P-2	18

II. AUTOMATIC TRANSMISSION AND TRANSAXLE
B. In-Vehicle Transmission/Transaxle

Task Number and Description	Priority	Job #s
1. Inspect, adjust, and replace external manual valve shift linkage, transmission range sensor/switch, and park/neutral position switch.	P-2	19
2. Inspect for leakage at external seals, gaskets, and bushings.	P-2	18
3. Inspect replace and align power train mounts.	P-2	20, 21
4. Drain and replace fluid and filter(s).	P-1	22

II. AUTOMATIC TRANSMISSION AND TRANSAXLE
C. Off-Vehicle Transmission and Transaxle

Task Number and Description	Priority	Job #s
1. Describe the operational characteristics of a continuously variable transmission (CVT).	P-3	23
2. Describe the operational characteristics of a hybrid vehicle drive train.	P-3	23

MANUAL DRIVE TRAIN AND AXLES

For every task in Manual Drive Train and Axles, the following safety requirement must be strictly enforced:

- Comply with personal and environmental safety practices associated with clothing; eye protection; hand tools; power equipment; proper ventilation; and the handling, storage, and disposal of chemicals/materials in accordance with local, state, and federal safety and environmental regulations.

III. MANUAL DRIVE TRAIN AND AXLES
A. General

Task Number and Description	Priority	Job #s
1. Research applicable vehicle and service information, fluid type, vehicle service history, service precautions, and technical service bulletins.	P-1	5
2. Drain and refill manual transmission/transaxle and final drive unit.	P-1	24
3. Check fluid condition; check for leaks.	P-2	25

III. MANUAL DRIVE TRAIN AND AXLES
B. Clutch

Task Number and Description	Priority	Job #s
1. Check and adjust clutch master cylinder fluid level.	P-1	26
2. Check for system leaks.	P-1	26

III. MANUAL DRIVE TRAIN AND AXLES
C. Transmission/Transaxle

Task Number and Description	Priority	Job #s
1. Describe the operational characteristics of an electronically-controlled manual transmission/transaxle.	P-3	23

III. MANUAL DRIVE TRAIN AND AXLES
D. Drive Shaft, Half Shafts, Universal and Constant-Velocity (CV) Joints

Task Number and Description	Priority	Job #s
1. Inspect, remove, and replace front wheel drive (FWD) bearings, hubs, and seals.	P-2	27
2. Inspect, service, and replace shafts, yokes, boots, and universal/CV joints.	P-2	27, 28

III. MANUAL DRIVE TRAIN AND AXLES
E. Differential Case Assembly

Task Number and Description	Priority	Job #s
1. Clean and inspect differential housing; check for leaks; inspect housing vent.	P-2	24
2. Check and adjust differential housing fluid level.	P-1	24
3. Drain and refill differential housing.	P-1	24
E.1 Drive Axles		
1. Inspect and replace drive axle wheel studs.	P-2	29

III. MANUAL DRIVE TRAIN AND AXLES
F. Four-wheel Drive/All-wheel Drive

Task Number and Description	Priority	Job #s
1. Inspect front-wheel bearings and locking hubs.	P-3	30
2. Check for leaks at drive assembly seals; check vents; check lube level.	P-2	30

SUSPENSION AND STEERING

For every task in Suspension and Steering, the following safety requirement must be strictly enforced:

- Comply with personal and environmental safety practices associated with clothing; eye protection; hand tools; power equipment; proper ventilation; and the handling, storage, and disposal of chemicals/materials in accordance with local, state, and federal safety and environmental regulations.

IV. SUSPENSION AND STEERING SYSTEMS
A. General

Task Number and Description	Priority	Job #s
1. Research applicable vehicle and service information, vehicle service history, service precautions, and technical service bulletins.	P-1	5
2. Disable and enable supplemental restraint system (SRS).	P-1	31

IV. SUSPENSION AND STEERING
B. Related Suspension and Steering Service

Task Number and Description	Priority	Job #s
1. Inspect rack and pinion steering gear inner tie rod ends (sockets) and bellows boots.	P-1	32
2. Determine proper power steering fluid type; inspect fluid level and condition.	P-1	33
3. Flush, fill, and bleed power steering system.	P-2	35

IV. SUSPENSION AND STEERING (continued)
B. Related Suspension and Steering Service

Task Number and Description	Priority	Job #s
4. Inspect for power steering fluid leakage; determine necessary action.	P-1	33
5. Remove, inspect, replace, and adjust power steering pump drive belt.	P-1	14
6. Inspect and replace power steering hoses and fittings.	P-2	34
7. Inspect pitman arm, relay (center link/intermediate) rod, idler arm and mountings, and steering linkage damper.	P-1	32
8. Inspect tie rod ends (sockets), tie rod sleeves, and clamps.	P-1	32
9. Inspect upper and lower control arms, bushings, and shafts.	P-1	32
10. Inspect and replace rebound and jounce bumpers.	P-1	32
11. Inspect track bar, strut rods/radius arms, and related mounts and bushings.	P-1	32
12. Inspect upper and lower ball joints (with or without wear indicators).	P-1	32
13. Inspect suspension system coil springs and spring insulators (silencers).	P-1	32
14. Inspect suspension system torsion bars and mounts.	P-1	32
15. Inspect and replace front stabilizer bar (sway bar) bushings, brackets, and links.	P-1	32
16. Inspect strut cartridge or assembly.	P-1	32
17. Inspect front strut bearing and mount.	P-1	32
18. Inspect rear suspension system lateral links/arms (track bars), control (trailing) arms.	P-1	32
19. Inspect rear suspension system leaf spring(s), spring insulators (silencers), shackles, brackets, bushings, center pins/bolts, and mounts.	P-1	32
20. Inspect, remove, and replace shock absorbers; inspect mounts and bushings.	P-1	36
21. Inspect electric power-assisted steering.	P-3	37
22. Identify hybrid vehicle power steering system electrical circuits and safety precautions.	P-2	2, 37
23. Describe the function of the power steering pressure switch.	P-3	38

IV. SUSPENSION AND STEERING
C. Wheel Alignment

Task Number and Description	Priority	Job #s
1. Perform prealignment inspection and measure vehicle ride height; determine necessary action.	P-1	39

IV. SUSPENSION AND STEERING
D. Wheels and Tires

Task Number and Description	Priority	Job #s
1. Inspect tire condition; identify tire wear patterns; check for correct size and application (load and speed ratings) and adjust air pressure; determine necessary action.	P-1	40
2. Rotate tires according to manufacturer's recommendations.	P-1	41
3. Dismount, inspect, and remount tire on wheel; balance wheel and tire assembly (static and dynamic).	P-1	41
4. Dismount, inspect, and remount tire on wheel equipped with tire pressure monitoring system sensor.	P-2	42
5. Inspect tire and wheel assembly for air loss; perform necessary action.	P-1	40, 42
6. Repair tire using internal patch.	P-1	42
7. Identify and test tire pressure monitoring systems (indirect and direct) for operation; verify operation of instrument panel lamps.	P-2	42
8. Demonstrate knowledge of steps required to remove and replace sensors in a tire pressure monitoring system.	P-2	42

BRAKES

For every task in Brakes, the following safety requirement must be strictly enforced:

- Comply with personal and environmental safety practices associated with clothing; eye protection; hand tools; power equipment; proper ventilation; and the handling, storage, and disposal of chemicals/materials in accordance with local, state, and federal safety and environmental regulations.

V. BRAKES
A. General

Task Number and Description	Priority	Job #s
1. Research applicable vehicle and service information, vehicle service history, service precautions, and technical service bulletins.	P-1	5
2. Describe procedure for performing a road test to check brake system operation, including an anti-lock brake system (ABS).	P-1	43
3. Install wheel and torque lug nuts.	P-1	40

V. BRAKES
B. Hydraulic System

Task Number and Description	Priority	Job #s
1. Measure brake pedal height, travel, and free play (as applicable); determine necessary action.	P-1	43
2. Check master cylinder for external leaks and proper operation.	P-1	43

V. BRAKES (continued)
B. Hydraulic System

Task Number and Description	Priority	Job #s
3. Inspect brake lines, flexible hoses, and fittings for leaks, dents, kinks, rust, cracks, bulging, wear, loose fittings and supports; determine necessary action.	P-1	44
4. Select, handle, store, and fill brake fluids to proper level.	P-1	45
5. Identify components of brake warning light system.	P-3	46
6. Bleed and/or flush brake system.	P-1	45
7. Test brake fluid for contamination.	P-1	45

V. BRAKES
C. Drum Brakes

Task Number and Description	Priority	Job #s
1. Remove, clean, inspect, and measure brake drum diameter; determine necessary action.	P-1	47
2. Refinish brake drum and measure final drum diameter; compare with specifications.	P-1	48
3. Remove, clean, and inspect brake shoes, springs, pins, clips, levers, adjusters/self-adjusters, other related brake hardware, and backing support plates; lubricate and reassemble.	P-1	47
4. Inspect wheel cylinders for leaks and proper operation; remove and replace as needed.	P-2	47
5. Pre-adjust brake shoes and parking brake; install brake drums or drum/hub assemblies and wheel bearings; make final checks and adjustments.	P-2	47

V. BRAKES
D. Disc Brakes

Task Number and Description	Priority	Job #s
1. Remove and clean caliper assembly; inspect for leaks and damage/wear to caliper housing; determine necessary action.	P-1	49
2. Clean and inspect caliper mounting and slides/pins for proper operation, wear, and damage; determine necessary action.	P-1	49
3. Remove, inspect, and replace pads and retaining hardware; determine necessary action.	P-1	49
4. Lubricate and reinstall caliper, pads, and related hardware; seat pads and inspect for leaks.	P-1	49
5. Clean and inspect rotor, measure rotor thickness, thickness variation, and lateral runout; determine necessary action.	P-1	49
6. Remove and reinstall rotor.	P-1	49
7. Refinish rotor on vehicle; measure final rotor thickness and compare with specifications.	P-1	50

V. BRAKES (continued)
D. Disc Brakes

Task Number and Description	Priority	Job #s
8. Refinish rotor off vehicle; measure final rotor thickness and compare with specifications.	P-1	50
9. Retract and re-adjust caliper piston on an integral parking brake system.	P-3	49
10. Check brake pad wear indicator; determine necessary action.	P-2	49
11. Describe importance of operating vehicle to burnish/break-in replacement brake pads according to manufacturer's recommendations.	P-1	49

V. BRAKES
E. Power-Assist Units

Task Number and Description	Priority	Job #s
1. Check brake pedal travel with, and without, engine running to verify proper power booster operation.	P-2	51
2. Check vacuum supply (manifold or auxiliary pump) to vacuum-type power booster.	P-1	51

V. BRAKES
F. Miscellaneous (Wheel Bearings, Parking Brakes, Electrical, Etc.)

Task Number and Description	Priority	Job #s
1. Remove, clean, inspect, repack, and install wheel bearings; replace seals; install hub and adjust bearings.	P-1	52
2. Check parking brake cables and components for wear, binding, and corrosion; clean, lubricate, adjust or replace as needed.	P-2	53
3. Check parking brake operation and parking brake indicator light system operation; determine necessary action.	P-1	53
4. Check operation of brake stop light system.	P-1	64
5. Replace wheel bearing and race.	P-2	52
6. Inspect and replace wheel studs.	P-1	29

V. BRAKES
G. Electronic Brakes, and Traction and Stability Control Systems

Task Number and Description	Priority	Job #s
1. Identify traction control/vehicle stability control system components.	P-3	54
2. Describe the operation of a regenerative braking system.	P-3	54

For every task in Electrical/Electronic Systems, the following safety requirement must be strictly enforced:

- Comply with personal and environmental safety practices associated with clothing; eye protection; hand tools; power equipment; proper ventilation; and the handling, storage, and disposal of chemicals/materials in accordance with local, state, and federal safety and environmental regulations.

VI. ELECTRICAL/ELECTRONIC SYSTEMS
A. General

Task Number and Description	Priority	Job #s
1. Research applicable vehicle and service information, vehicle service history, service precautions, and technical service bulletins.	P-1	5
2. Demonstrate knowledge of electrical/electronic series, parallel, and series-parallel circuits using principles of electricity (Ohm's Law).	P-1	55
3. Use wiring diagrams to trace electrical/electronic circuits.	P-1	55
4. Demonstrate proper use of a digital multimeter (DMM) when measuring source voltage, voltage drop (including grounds), current flow, and resistance.	P-1	55
5. Demonstrate knowledge of the causes and effects from shorts, grounds, opens, and resistance problems in electrical/electronic circuits.	P-2	55
6. Check operation of electrical circuits with a test light.	P-2	55
7. Check operation of electrical circuits with fused jumper wires.	P-2	67
8. Measure key-off battery drain (parasitic draw).	P-1	55
9. Inspect and test fusible links, circuit breakers, and fuses; determine necessary action.	P-1	55
10. Perform solder repair of electrical wiring.	P-1	56
11. Replace electrical connectors and terminal ends.	P-1	56

VI. ELECTRICAL/ELECTRONIC SYSTEMS
B. Battery Service

Task Number and Description	Priority	Job #s
1. Perform battery state-of-charge test; determine necessary action.	P-1	57
2. Confirm proper battery capacity for vehicle application; perform battery capacity test; determine necessary action.	P-1	57
3. Maintain or restore electronic memory functions.	P-1	58
4. Inspect and clean battery; fill battery cells; check battery cables, connectors, clamps, and hold-downs.	P-1	58
5. Perform slow/fast battery charge according to manufacturer's recommendations.	P-1	58

VI. ELECTRICAL/ELECTRONIC SYSTEMS (continued)
B. Battery Service

Task Number and Description	Priority	Job #s
6. Jump-start vehicle using jumper cables and a booster battery or an auxiliary power supply.	P-1	59
7. Identify high-voltage circuits of electric or hybrid electric vehicle and related safety precautions.	P-3	56
8. Identify electronic modules, security systems, radios, and other accessories that require reinitialization or code entry after reconnecting vehicle battery.	P-1	58
9. Identify hybrid vehicle auxiliary (12v) battery service, repair, and test procedures.	P-3	57, 58

VI. ELECTRICAL/ELECTRONIC SYSTEMS
C. Starting System

Task Number and Description	Priority	Job #s
1. Perform starter current draw test; determine necessary action.	P-1	60
2. Perform starter circuit voltage drop tests; determine necessary action.	P-1	60
3. Inspect and test starter relays and solenoids; determine necessary action.	P-2	60
4. Remove and install starter in a vehicle.	P-1	61
5. Inspect and test switches, connectors, and wires of starter control circuits; determine necessary action.	P-2	60

VI. ELECTRICAL/ELECTRONIC SYSTEMS
D. Charging System

Task Number and Description	Priority	Job #s
1. Perform charging system output test; determine necessary action.	P-1	62
2. Inspect, adjust, or replace generator (alternator) drive belts; check pulleys and tensioners for wear; check pulley and belt alignment.	P-1	14, 62
3. Remove, inspect, and re-install generator (alternator).	P-2	63
4. Perform charging circuit voltage drop tests; determine necessary action.	P-1	62

VI. ELECTRICAL/ELECTRONIC SYSTEMS
E. Lighting Systems

Task Number and Description	Priority	Job #s
1. Inspect interior and exterior lamps and sockets including headlights and auxiliary lights (fog lights/driving lights); replace as needed.	P-1	64
2. Aim headlights.	P-2	65
3. Identify system voltage and safety precautions associated with high-intensity discharge headlights.	P-2	65

VI. ELECTRICAL/ELECTRONIC SYSTEMS
F. Accessories

Task Number and Description	Priority	Job #s
1. Disable and enable airbag system for vehicle service; verify indicator lamp operation.	P-1	31
2. Remove and reinstall door panel.	P-1	66
3. Describe the operation of keyless entry/remote-start systems.	P-3	66
4. Verify operation of instrument panel gauges and warning/indicator lights; reset maintenance indicators.	P-1	67
5. Verify windshield wiper and washer operation; replace wiper blades.	P-1	68

HEATING AND AIR CONDITIONING

For every task in Heating and Air Conditioning, the following safety requirement must be strictly enforced:

- Comply with personal and environmental safety practices associated with clothing; eye protection; hand tools; power equipment; proper ventilation; and the handling, storage, and disposal of chemicals/materials in accordance with local, state, and federal safety and environmental regulations.

VII. HEATING AND AIR CONDITIONING
A. General

Task Number and Description	Priority	Job #s
1. Research applicable vehicle and service information, vehicle service history, service precautions, and technical service bulletins.	P-1	5

VII. HEATING AND AIR CONDITIONING
B. Refrigeration System Components

Task Number and Description	Priority	Job #s
1. Inspect and replace A/C compressor drive belts, pulleys, and tensioners; determine necessary action.	P-1	14, 69
2. Identify hybrid vehicle A/C system electrical circuits and the service/safety precautions.	P-2	2
3. Inspect A/C condenser for airflow restrictions; determine necessary action.	P-1	69

VII. HEATING AND AIR CONDITIONING
C. Heating, Ventilation, and Engine Cooling Systems

Task Number and Description	Priority	Job #s
1. Inspect engine cooling and heater systems hoses; perform necessary action.	P-1	13

VII. HEATING AND AIR CONDITIONING
D. Operating Systems and Related Controls

Task Number and Description	Priority	Job #s
1. Inspect A/C-heater ducts, doors, hoses, cabin filters, and outlets; perform necessary action.	P-1	69
2. Identify the source of A/C system odors.	P-2	69

ENGINE PERFORMANCE

For every task in Engine Performance the following safety requirement must be strictly enforced:
- Comply with personal and environmental safety practices associated with clothing; eye protection; hand tools; power equipment; proper ventilation; and the handling, storage, and disposal of chemicals/materials in accordance with local, state, and federal safety and environmental regulations.

VIII. ENGINE PERFORMANCE
A. General

Task Number and Description	Priority	Job #s
1. Research applicable vehicle and service information, vehicle service history, service precautions, and technical service bulletins.	P-1	5
2. Perform engine absolute (vacuum/boost) manifold pressure tests; determine necessary action.	P-1	70
3. Perform cylinder power balance test; determine necessary action.	P-2	70
4. Perform cylinder cranking and running compression tests; determine necessary action.	P-1	71
5. Perform cylinder leakage test; determine necessary action.	P-1	71
6. Verify engine operating temperature.	P-1	73
7. Remove and replace spark plugs; inspect secondary ignition components for wear and damage.	P-1	72

VIII. ENGINE PERFORMANCE
B. Computerized Controls

Task Number and Description	Priority	Job #s
1. Retrieve and record diagnostic trouble codes, OBD monitor status, and freeze frame data; clear codes when applicable.	P-1	73
2. Describe the importance of operating all OBDII monitors for repair verification.	P-1	73

VIII. ENGINE PERFORMANCE
C. Fuel, Air Induction, and Exhaust Systems

Task Number and Description	Priority	Job #s
1. Replace fuel filter(s).	P-1	75
2. Inspect, service, or replace air filters, filter housings, and intake duct work.	P-1	75